VALUING LIFE

CASS R. SUNSTEIN

VALUING LIFE

Humanizing the Regulatory State

The University of Chicago Press

Chicago and London

CASS R. SUNSTEIN is the Robert Walmsley University Professor at Harvard Law School.

The University of Chicago Press, Chicago 60637
The University of Chicago Press, Ltd., London
© 2014 by The University of Chicago
All rights reserved. Published 2014.
Printed in the United States of America

23 22 21 20 19 18 17 16 15 14   1 2 3 4 5

ISBN-13: 978-0-226-78017-7 (cloth)
ISBN-13: 978-0-226-12942-6 (e-book)
DOI: 10.7208/chicago/9780226129426.001.0001

Library of Congress Cataloging-in-Publication Data

Sunstein, Cass R., author.
    Valuing life : humanizing the regulatory state / Cass R. Sunstein.
        pages cm
    Includes bibliographical references and index.
    ISBN 978-0-226-78017-7 (cloth : alk. paper) — ISBN 978-0-226-12942-6 (e-book)
1. Administrative procedure—Social aspects—United States.   2. Administrative
agencies—Social aspects—United States.   3. United States. Office of Management and
Budget. Office of Information and Regulatory Affairs.   I. Title.
    JK468.P64S958 2014
    306.20973—dc23

                                                                           2013035153

For Amartya Sen

The world of costs and benefits (which includes taking note of the badness of nasty actions and of violations of freedom and rights) is quite a different decisional universe from the sledgehammer reasoning of consequence-independent duties and obligations.

AMARTYA SEN[1]

The peculiar character of the problem of a rational economic order is determined precisely by the fact that the knowledge of the circumstances of which we must make use never exists in concentrated or integrated form but solely as the dispersed bits of incomplete and frequently contradictory knowledge which all the separate individuals possess. . . . Or, to put it briefly, it is a problem of the utilization of knowledge which is not given to anyone in its totality.

FRIEDRICH HAYEK[2]

CONTENTS

INTRODUCTION

Franklin's Algebra

Governments should focus on the human consequences of their actions. Whether the decision involves environmental protection, occupational safety, smoking, foreign aid, immigration, gun control, obesity, education, immigration, or military intervention into another nation, they should ask, What would be the effects of acting or of not acting? If lives would be saved, how many? If people would be burdened, by how much, and with what effects? And who, exactly, is being helped, and who is being hurt?

To answer these questions, governments should have a wide rather than narrow viewscreen. They should seek a method to allow them to make sensible comparisons and to facilitate choices among values that are difficult or impossible to quantify, or that seem incommensurable. And in doing this, they should draw not merely on the knowledge of public officials, but on that of citizens as well.

In 1772, Benjamin Franklin wrote an illuminating letter to an acquaintance who was faced with a hard decision:[1]

When these difficult Cases occur, they are difficult chiefly because while we have them under Consideration all the Reasons pro and con are not present to the Mind at the same time; but sometimes one Set present themselves, and at other times another, the first being out of sight. Hence the various Purposes of Inclinations that alternately prevail, and the Uncertainty that perplexes us. To get over this, my Way is, to divide half a Sheet of Paper by a Line into two Columns, writing over the one pro, and over the other Con. Then during three or four Days Consideration I put down under the different Heads short Hints of the different Motives that at different Times occur to me for or against the Measure.

When I have thus got them all together in one View, I endeavour to estimate their respective Weights; and where I find two, one on each side, that seem equal, I strike them both out: If I find a Reason pro equal to some two Reasons con, I strike out the three. If I judge some two Reasons con equal to some three Reasons pro, I strike out the five; and thus proceeding I find at length where the Balance lies; and if after a Day or two of farther Consideration nothing new that is of Importance occurs on either side, I come to a Determination accordingly. And tho' the Weight of Reasons cannot be taken with the Precision of Algebraic Quantities, yet when each is thus considered separately and compara-tively, and the whole lies before me, I think I can judge better, and am less likely to make a rash Step; and in fact I have found great Advantage from this kind of Equation, in what may be called Moral or Prudential Algebra.

With his moral or prudential algebra, Franklin tried to capture a wide range of variables and to ensure that none of them were neglected or ig-nored. In this respect, Franklin was an early practitioner of cost-benefit analysis—an approach that attempts to catalog the benefits and costs of various courses of action, to compare them with one another, and to see how to proceed so that the benefits justify the costs. Of course Franklin did not ignore qualitative differences. He did not think that it was pos-sible to make choices "with the precision of algebraic quantities." None-theless, he emphasized the necessity of seeking to identify all relevant considerations, and of seeing if competing variables might be offsetting and commensurable.

In government, as in personal life, difficult cases frequently arise. Should the government require cars and trucks to have greater fuel economy? How much greater? Should new regulations be issued to pro-tect food safety? What should they look like? Should the government require refrigerators and clothes washers to be more energy efficient? How much more? Public officials cannot answer such questions without trying to ensure that "all the reasons pro and con" are brought "pres-ent to the mind at the same time," and without trying "to estimate their respective weights." If officials do that, they will be far more likely to "judge better" and less likely "to take a rash step." Some kind of political algebra would help. To be sure, the effort might impose serious information-gathering demands on officials, and they need to find ways to respond to or minimize that problem.

From 2009 to 2012, I was privileged to serve in the Obama Administration as Administrator of the White House Office of Information and Regulatory Affairs (OIRA), sometimes described as the nation's "regulatory czar." The term "regulation" is a broad one, and it is not self-defining. As I use it here, it refers principally to legal controls (authorized by legislatures and implemented by executive officials) that *limit or authorize public or private conduct in order to promote some social goal.* That goal might be worker safety, cleaner air, increased homeland security, reduction of food-borne illness, nondiscrimination on the basis of disability or sexual orientation, greater privacy, better control of national borders, or a reduced risk of a financial crisis. Regulation includes some of the most important actions that a government can take—and those actions affect people's lives every day of every year.

Fortunately, the idea of a "regulatory czar" is a wild overstatement. The United States has no czars. But the term does provide a clue to the extraordinary range of the OIRA Administrator's responsibilities. The Administrator helps to oversee regulation in a dazzling variety of areas, including national security, immigration, energy, environmental protection, occupational safety, food safety, education, and much more. In 1981, President Ronald Reagan, emphasizing the need for some kind of political algebra, made cost-benefit analysis central to OIRA's mission, and both Republican and Democratic Administrations have affirmed the central approach.

In important respects, the Obama Administration actually increased the emphasis on costs and benefits, with a recognition that in an economically challenging time, high regulatory costs could prove particularly harmful or unwelcome. The point here was not to avoid costs on some abstraction called "business." It was to ensure that regulation would not have unfortunate human consequences, which can result when high burdens are imposed on real people (including those who run businesses).

Since President Reagan, the primary goal of the OIRA process has been to "maximize net benefits," meaning to ensure that the benefits exceed the costs by as much as possible. And indeed, the net benefits of regulations during the first term of the Obama Administration were about $150 billion.[2] Those benefits include significant savings for consumers (as from fuel economy and energy efficiency standards), large gains in terms of deaths, illnesses, and accidents avoided (as from highway safety and environmental regulations), and major gains from deregulation. The $150 billion figure is a stunning achievement, and well over double the net benefits in the first terms of the administrations of George W. Bush and Bill Clinton.

Insufficient regulation can be a serious problem, costing both lives and money. Indeed, the financial crisis of 2008 and succeeding years was, in part, a product of insufficient regulation, which could have provided safeguards against systemic risks. Or suppose that we decline to take steps to reduce air pollution that is producing thousands of premature deaths and tens of thousands of illnesses. But excessive regulation can also be a serious problem, potentially endangering economic growth and job creation—and thus hurting real people in the process, perhaps by raising prices, perhaps by decreasing wages, perhaps by throwing people out of work. If a nation takes expensive steps to reduce air pollution, it may protect public health, but it may also increase the price of energy. Significant increases in energy prices can create real hardship, especially for poor people.

A regulation that costs a great deal, but that has only a modest beneficial effect on public health, might well be a terrible idea. To know, we need to get into the specifics, with the help of something like Franklin's algebra. We need to go beyond the "more or less" debates about regulation—in which people argue abstractly over whether we have "too much" or "too little." We need to focus instead on how to trade off the costs of action and the costs of inaction. We need to focus directly on the human consequences of the alternatives. And we need to develop tools by which to obtain accurate information about those consequences.

Before joining the government, I had taught administrative law and regulatory policy for over two decades. Much of my focus was on low-cost, freedom-preserving, market-friendly tools (such as disclosure of information) and on cost-benefit analysis—its uses, its value, and its limitations. I emphasized the importance of maintaining freedom of choice, not least because the private sector has information that government lacks. I also emphasized that without an effort to catalog the consequences of rules, and without assessing the effects of alternative approaches, we cannot easily know whether and how to proceed. Should the fuel economy of cars be increased to 35 miles per gallon, or 45 miles per gallon, or 50 miles per gallon? In five years, or ten, or fifteen?

Despite the appeal of some kind of political algebra, a lot of reasonable people are acutely uncomfortable with cost-benefit analysis.[3] Their discomfort, which I saw both in the academic world and in government, raises serious and legitimate questions. Consider air pollution, privacy, distracted driving, unsafe mines, and discrimination on the basis of disability and sexual orientation. What do public officials know, exactly? How can they monetize the benefits of regulations that would respond to the problems? What is the economic value of allowing people in wheelchairs to have easy access to bathrooms? And what if the costs are imposed on people who really can bear those costs, and what if the benefits flow to people who really need them, perhaps to live?

While in government, I spoke a great deal about "humanizing cost-benefit analysis." With this phrase, I meant to refer to four related ideas. The first is the need to attend to the likely consequences—a point that accounts for my enthusiasm for cost-benefit analysis.[4] The second is to put a spotlight on what cost-benefit analysis struggles to capture, including human dignity. Humanized cost-benefit analysis does not ignore the nonquantifiable. The third idea involves the difference between real people and *Homo economicus*, the rational actor of standard economic analysis. For decades, psychologists and behavioral economists have emphasized that difference, suggesting that human beings are less selfish, and more error prone, than standard economists have acknowledged. Humanized cost-benefit analysis explores the effects of policies and regulations on real human beings. The fourth and final idea refers to the need to collect the dispersed information held by a nation's citizenry. Regulators usually know a lot, but often they know a lot less than citizens do. Before they finalize rules, they need to obtain public comments and thus learn from the people they are privileged to serve.

This book consists of seven chapters. The first three were written in the aftermath of my years in government, and they draw directly on what I learned. When I was there, and fortunate enough to work across the street from the White House, the question I was asked most often was, *What is it really like?* How does one work with other people in the

Executive Office of the President? With members of the Cabinet? With the President? When I left, many people asked whether I might give people a sense of the actual experience inside government, at least from the perspective of the OIRA Administrator.

Chapter 1 tries to provide that sense and in the process to correct some widespread misimpressions. It is unique in the book in its focus on the process of government—on how things actually work. At least in my experience (and some people will find this surprising), "politics," in the sense of interest-group pressures and electoral considerations, usually does not play a significant role in the regulatory process. Decisions were made on the merits, by reference to the information that officials were able to obtain—and where the law permitted, with close reference to something closely akin to Franklin's algebra. (Note that my role was to help implement the law through regulations and that I was usually not involved in the enactment of legislation by Congress.)

In the real world of regulation, good internal processes are immensely important, not least because they increase the likelihood that people will focus on what matters and get things right. Establishing that point is a major goal of the chapter. An additional point is simple: A well-functioning government obtains information from a wide array of people, both inside and outside the executive branch, who are likely to know things that the rulemaking agency does not. One of the central goals of the OIRA process is to obtain that widely dispersed information.

Chapter 2 also tries to give a sense of actual practice, but it focuses on what cost-benefit analysis entails and how that form of analysis is applied to real problems. Of course it is highly controversial to say that regulators should base their conclusions on cost-benefit analysis—or indeed on any kind of political arithmetic. Some people think that we cannot assign monetary values to mortality risks and that it is foolish, or worse, to try to use cost-benefit analysis to resolve disputes over workplace safety, environmental protection, and homeland security. Many of their concerns are reasonable. My hope is that some of the controversy will dissipate with a better appreciation of how cost-benefit analysis works in actual cases. At the same time, an understanding of the real world of cost-benefit analysis should lead to improvements in actual practice.

Chapter 3 turns directly to nonquantifiable values, including human dignity and personal privacy. Sometimes government cannot quantify benefits or costs for one simple reason: it lacks crucial information. It knows that a rule will reduce the risk of a terrorist attack, of prison rape, or of a financial crisis, but it cannot specify the benefits of that rule. In such circumstances, how does and how should government proceed (if at all)? Or suppose that a rule would enable people with disabilities to have access to the workplace. The benefits of that rule are not fully captured by the purely monetary benefits that it may generate; something important is missing. How should the government handle dignitary benefits? By explaining that economic analysis cannot provide a full answer (but is not entirely silent on that question), chapter 3 explores how nonquantifiable benefits might be handled.

Can government value human life? As a matter of actual practice, the short answer is yes (around $9 million in 2013 dollars). But what is the rationale for that number? Imagine that a regulation would mostly protect children, or old people, or those vulnerable to cancer, or those who are poor. Do demographic characteristics matter? In valuing life, the American government has not made distinctions among young and old or among different kinds of risks (such as the risk of cancer or of dying in a terrorist attack). And indeed, the Obama Administration did not make such distinctions throughout the President's first term.

Chapters 4 and 5 explore some of the hardest questions of valuation. Those questions remain at the theoretical and empirical frontiers. I explain that far from being preposterous, efforts to value human life (more accurately, statistical mortality risks) are rooted in exceedingly appealing ideas about welfare and autonomy—ideas that deserve a prominent place in a free society. In trying to value risks, we should begin by asking how people themselves value risks. But different statistical mortality risks are not the same, and individuals differ as well. We might well want to treat cancer risks differently from risks of a sudden unanticipated death. Risks associated with terrorism deserve special attention. Risks faced by poor people might also deserve such attention. Consider the idea of *prioritarianism*, insisting that public officials should give special priority to those who are least well-off.[5] These points bear on significant debates about how to value life—debates that are likely to become increasingly important in the next decades.

Behavioral economics has had a large impact on regulatory practice throughout the world, especially with the growing interest in the use of "nudges"[6]—low-cost, choice-preserving approaches that promise to have a large impact. Nudges might, for example, disclose the calorie content of food at chain restaurants, or the annual fuel cost of new vehicles. Psychologists and behavioral economists have focused in particular on the fact that people use heuristics, or mental shortcuts, in assessing risks. They have found that these heuristics generally work well, but they can also lead to large mistakes, potentially costing both money and lives. Consider the availability heuristic, which means that we assess probabilities by asking whether relevant events come readily to mind. The availability heuristic is not the worst way to approach probability questions, but it can get us in big trouble, making us overestimate some risks (when a fluke event happened in the recent past) and underestimate others (when the statistical risk is pretty high but nothing went wrong in the recent past).

Chapter 6 builds on these findings to suggest that in the domain of morality and ethics, we use heuristics too—and they can produce big blunders, especially when we are thinking about risk. Moral judgments that are mostly sensible can steer us in bad directions when we are investigating regulatory issues. An example: It is good not to lie, but if lying would save the lives of small children, it may be permissible, and even compulsory, to lie. Another example: Morality rightly condemns most actions that lead to the death of human beings, but regulation involves trade-offs, and we cannot possibly condemn every action that leads to the death of human beings (such as building roads and highways). Moral heuristics are pervasive, and they can get us into big trouble.

When regulators fail, it is often because they fall prey to one of two problems: hysteria or neglect. Chapter 7 attempts to illuminate the general phenomenon of *probability neglect*. In dealing with risks, we should focus not just on bad outcomes but also on the probability that they will occur—but when our emotions are strongly engaged, the human mind is sometimes reluctant to do that. Consider, for example, a risk that your child has fatal cancer. You might think about the worst-case scenario, not its likelihood.

To take just one example, terrorists try to exploit probability neglect. Regulators should not allow them to do so. They should consider both outcomes (what would be the consequences of an attack?) and probabilities (what is the likelihood of an attack?). At the same time, human fear is itself a cost, and it can impose further costs as well, by leading us to take expensive steps to avoid risks—a point that raises special problems for efforts to reduce risks that provoke strong emotions. The analysis bears on a wide range of problems that lead people to neglect the question of probability.

Too much of the time, hard questions about government policy are resolved by reference to anecdotes, recent history, intuitions, and dogmas—suggesting, for example, that we need "more protection" against risks from unsafe food, dirty air, or hazardous workplaces, or that we need "less intrusion" from government. Whether we need more protection or less intrusion depends not on anything abstract, but on the concrete effects of one or the other. As we will see, Franklin's algebra cannot tell us everything that we need to know, and one of my purposes here is to explore its limitations. But if we seek to value life, we cannot proceed without it.

ONE

Inside Government

The Office of Information and Regulatory Affairs (OIRA), a part of the Office of Management and Budget (OMB), has become a well-established, often praised, and occasionally controversial institution within the federal government. OIRA was initially created in 1980 by the Paperwork Reduction Act, with the particular responsibility of approving (or disapproving) information collection requests from federal agencies. In one of his early actions, taken less than a month after assuming office, President Ronald Reagan gave OMB an additional responsibility, which is to review and approve (or decline to approve) federal rules from executive agencies, after careful consideration of costs and benefits.[1]

Within OMB, that responsibility is exercised by OIRA. A primary goal of the OIRA process is to improve regulations by ensuring careful consideration of their likely effects before they are issued. The human consequences of federal rules are a central focus of OIRA review.

But what is the OIRA process actually like? How does that important part of government actually work? What is the purpose of the process? Even among close observers—in the media, in the business and public interest communities, and among academics, including professors of economics, political science, and law—the role of OIRA remains poorly understood. The misunderstandings are important, because they reflect a failure to appreciate the operations not only of the Executive Office of the President, but of the federal government as a whole.

My primary goal in this chapter is to dispel current misunderstandings. One of my central themes is that OIRA helps to collect widely dispersed information—information that is held throughout the executive branch and by the public in general. OIRA is largely in the business of helping to identify and aggregate views and perspectives of a wide range of sources both inside and outside the federal government. We shall see that while the President is ultimately in charge, the White House itself is a "they," not an "it." Outside of the White House, numerous agencies are also involved, and they may well be the driving forces in the process that is frequently misdescribed as "OIRA review." It would not be excessive to describe OIRA as, in large part, an information aggregator.

For example, the Department of Agriculture knows a great deal about how rules affect farmers, and the Department of Transportation knows a great deal about how rules affect the transportation sector, and the Department of Energy knows a great deal about implications for the energy sector. The OIRA process enables their perspectives to be brought to bear on rules issued by other agencies. Part of OIRA's defining mission is to ensure that rulemaking agencies are able to receive the specialized information held by diverse people (usually career officials) within the executive branch.

Another defining mission is to promote a well-functioning process of public comment, including state and local governments, businesses large and small, and public interest groups. OIRA and agencies work together to ensure that when rules are proposed, important issues and alternatives are clearly and explicitly identified for public comment. OIRA and agencies also work closely together to ensure that public comments are adequately addressed in final rules, often by modifying relevant provisions in proposed rules. Indeed, a central function of OIRA is to operate as a guardian of a well-functioning administrative process, to ensure not only respect for law but also compliance with procedural ideals, involving notice and an opportunity to be heard, that may not always be strictly compulsory but that might be loosely organized under the rubric of "regulatory due process." Indeed, OIRA helps to promote a system of deliberative democracy, which is a crucial safeguard against error.

In explaining these points, I emphasize four propositions that are not widely appreciated and that are central to an understanding of OIRA's role. These propositions will arise at various points in the discussion, and it will be useful to identify them at the outset.

1. *OIRA helps to oversee a genuinely interagency process, involving many specialists throughout the federal government.* OIRA's goal is often to iden-

tify and convey interagency views and to seek a reasonable consensus, not to press its own positions. While OIRA's own views sometimes matter, OIRA frequently operates as a conveyer and a convener. The heads of the various departments and agencies are fully committed to the process, and they play a crucial part in it. They understand, and agree, that significant concerns should be heard and addressed, whether or not they are inclined to agree with them.

2. *When a proposed or final rule is delayed, and when the OIRA review process proves time consuming, it is usually because significant interagency concerns have yet to be addressed.* Frequently there will be general agreement that a rule is a good idea, and the delay will be a product, not of any sense that it should not go forward, but of a judgment that important aspects require continuing substantive discussion. The relevant concerns may be highly technical; they may, for example, involve a complex question of law, or one or several provisions that are difficult to get right. One goal is to ensure that if a rule is formally proposed to the public, or finalized, it does not contain a serious problem or mistake. A final rule containing a problem or mistake creates obvious difficulties, perhaps above all if it is a mistake of law. But (and this is a more subtle point) even a proposed rule can itself significantly alter people's behavior, and thus create difficulties as well, if people believe that it is likely to be finalized in the same form.

3. *Costs and benefits are important, and OIRA (along with others in the Executive Office of the President, including the Council of Economic Advisers and the National Economic Council) does focus on them, but they are not usually the dominant issues in the OIRA process.* Especially for economically significant rules, the analysis of costs and benefits receives careful attention. To the extent permitted by law, the benefits must justify the costs, and agencies must attempt to maximize net benefits.[2] But most of OIRA's day-to-day work is usually spent, not on costs and benefits, but on working through interagency concerns, promoting the receipt of public comments (for proposed rules), ensuring discussion of alternatives, and promoting consideration of public comments (for final rules). OIRA also engages lawyers throughout the executive branch to help resolve questions of law, including questions of administrative procedure.

4. *Much of the OIRA process involves high-stakes issues with technical dimensions.* OIRA may seek, for example, to ensure careful consideration of the views of the Department of Justice on a legal issue, or of the views of the US Trade Representative on an issue that involves international trade, or of the views of the Department of Homeland Security and the National Security Council on an issue with national security implications, or of the views of the Department of Energy on the effects of a rule on the energy supply. In such cases, career officials, with technical expertise, are frequently the central actors. When rules are delayed, it is often because technical specialists are working through the technical questions. Much of the time, the problem is not that OIRA, or anyone else, has a fundamental objection to the rule and the agency's approach. It is that the technical questions need good answers.

In light of these points, my broadest themes here might loosely be described as Hayekian (after the great economist Friedrich Hayek), Frankfurterian (after the great American Supreme Court Justice Felix Frankfurter), and Millian (after the great social theorist John Stuart Mill). The Hayekian theme emphasizes the dispersed nature of human knowledge[3] and OIRA's role in attempting to acquire as much of that knowledge as possible, above all through careful attention to public comments. The Frankfurterian theme emphasizes the importance of fair process, in the particular form of "regulatory due process," requiring participation by a large number of people inside and outside the federal government.[4] The Millian theme, drawing on Mill's sympathetic but critical comments on Jeremy Bentham, emphasizes the importance of a form of utilitarian balancing (cost-benefit analysis, with commitments to ensuring that the benefits justify the costs and to maximizing net benefits), but also the need to acknowledge that some variables are qualitatively different from others, and are not easily quantified, but nonetheless deserve to count (see chapter 3 for more details).

There is also a fourth theme, associated with Amartya Sen (alas the term Senian does not quite work), which involves the ideal of "government by discussion," and the central importance of that ideal to the avoidance of bad outcomes.[5] Noting the importance of political accountability, and the information held by a nation's citizenry, Sen has urged that discussion and deliberation are critical safeguards against mistakes, including those that can produce widespread human suffering. As we shall see, the decision-making process within the executive branch—at least when it is working well—involves multiple forms of government by discussion.

Some necessary qualifications: This chapter is based on official documents and also on my own experiences as OIRA Administrator, and it is written with close reference to those experiences. To that extent, it has an impressionistic quality. Moreover, it is focused on practices and experiences from 2009 until August 2012. On the basis of discussions with OIRA staff and with former Administrators, I believe that the general account offered here is consistent with the practices in other Administrations. Insofar as I am stressing the role of OIRA as a convener and aggregator of information, and its attention to procedural requirements, the central claims cut across Administrations. But OIRA's practices are not identical over time, and the future may hold surprises. Other OIRA Administrators, past and future, may have somewhat different accounts and perspectives. While I do venture some evaluative comments, especially to correct misconceptions, I endeavor to make this account largely descriptive and free of evaluations, whether positive or negative. A full evaluation of OIRA's role, once it is accurately understood, is a matter for a separate occasion.

Importantly, my focus is not on OIRA in general, but narrowly on the process for the review of rules. Insofar as OIRA has other important functions, including helping to establish regulatory priorities and principles, I shall not discuss those functions here. Nor shall I be exploring (at least not in any detail) the role of other offices within the Executive Office of the President, which also help work closely with agencies, and which sometimes play an important part in the rulemaking process.

Reviewing Rules: The OIRA Process

I have suggested that OIRA helps to oversee an interagency process, and that when the review process is lengthy or complicated, it is often because of continuing discussions by participants in that process. I have also said that the process can be highly technical. To understand these claims, it will be useful to describe how the process works, with an emphasis on the actual mechanics.

To begin with some basics, OIRA consists of about forty-five people, almost all of them career staff. They work in a number of "branches," covering different agencies and areas. Each of the branches has a number of "desk officers," all with substantive expertise in one or more areas, and each with primary responsibility for particular agencies. For example, specified desk officers will generally handle regulatory actions from the Department of Homeland Security, the Department of Justice, or the Food and Drug Administration. Each branch is managed by a "branch chief," a member of OIRA staff with a great deal of experience and expertise. Desk officers are carefully supervised by branch chiefs, who give them detailed advice on how to review regulations. OIRA reviews several hundred regulatory actions every year.

OIRA is headed by an Administrator, who is confirmed by the Senate and who works under the Director of the Office of Management and Budget. OIRA's Deputy Administrator, who helps to manage the office and offers indispensable advice on a wide range of subjects, is nonpolitical. In the Obama Administration, OIRA has also had an Associate Administrator and a Chief of Staff, political appointees who are part of OIRA's leadership. OIRA may work closely with others in the Office of Management and Budget, including the five Resource Management Offices, which help to oversee the allocation of federal funds and which may have important perspectives on questions of policy. For example, OMB's Health Division has a great deal of expertise on health care questions, especially to the extent that they affect the budget. If those within OMB have serious concerns about a rule, those concerns will receive attention, and OIRA will work closely with the rulemaking agency to see whether and how they might be best addressed.

Insofar as it reviews rules, OIRA's central responsibilities are defined by Executive Order 13563, issued by President Obama in 2011, and by Executive Order 12866, issued by President Clinton in 1993. Executive Order 12866 establishes the central requirements for agencies and OIRA alike. Executive Order 13563—a document of signal importance in the

Obama Administration, indeed a kind of mini-constitution for the regulatory state, and one whose fundamental orientation has strong Millian features—reaffirms and incorporates Executive Order 12866. Significantly, it specifically quotes a number of provisions relating to cost-benefit balancing, with close reference to the human consequences. Perhaps most important, it states that each agency must, to the extent permitted by law

> propose or adopt a regulation only upon a reasoned determination that its benefits justify its costs (recognizing that some benefits and costs are difficult to quantify); (2) tailor its regulations to impose the least burden on society, consistent with obtaining regulatory objectives, taking into account, among other things, and to the extent practicable, the costs of cumulative regulations; (3) select, in choosing among alternative regulatory approaches, those approaches that maximize net benefits (including potential economic, environmental, public health and safety, and other advantages; distributive impacts; and equity).[6]

At the same time, Executive Order 13563 introduces several new principles and requirements, involving public participation; integration and coordination of regulatory requirements, designed to reduce overlap and inconsistency; consideration of flexible approaches, designed to promote freedom of choice; and scientific integrity, designed to separate purely scientific judgments from judgments of policy or politics. These principles and requirements play a significant role in agency thinking and in OIRA review.

After a rule is formally submitted, OIRA has ninety days to review it unless an extension is given.[7] Before or after the expiration of the ninety-day period, OIRA may (1) "conclude review," after which the rule is published in the Federal Register, either with or without change; (2) return the rule to the agency for reconsideration via a formal "return letter"; (3) encourage the agency to withdraw the rule in light of interagency concerns; (4) work with the Director of OMB to obtain an extension of up to thirty days; (5) work with the agency to obtain an extension of whatever length it deems appropriate. OIRA's authority to issue return letters is exceedingly important, because it means that OIRA can effectively prevent rules from being issued. But OIRA will not issue any such letter without agreement from a wide range of offices within the Executive Office of the President, and hence a return letter is hardly OIRA's alone.

The vast majority of rules proceed through the process within the ninety-day period, and they are generally changed (and improved) as a result. For example, OIRA reviewed 2,304 regulatory actions between January 21, 2009, and August 10, 2012. In that period, 1,758, or about 76 percent, were approved "consistent with change," whereas 320, or about 14 percent, were approved without change; 161, or 7 percent, were withdrawn.[8] In assessing the importance of review, it is important to be cautious about the percentage of rules that are approved "consistent with change." Those words reveal that the published rule is different from the submitted rule, but they do not specify the magnitude of the changes. In some cases, the changes are minor, perhaps even cosmetic; in others, they are substantial. The designation "consistent with change" is consistent with either possibility.

In the process of "government by discussion," agencies make changes in response to interagency comments (for example, from the Department of Justice or the Department of Energy), and the changes need not be suggested by OIRA itself. When changes result from the agency's acceptance of those suggestions, they might be substantive and significant, as the suggestions help to identify better approaches and lead the agency to make important corrections. Sometimes, of course, OIRA will have significant suggestions of its own, stemming in the first instance from OIRA staff. Some of the resulting changes are highly technical or procedural ones, and made without any involvement on the part of OIRA's political leadership. For example, the changes might be designed to promote compliance with the Paperwork Reduction Act (meant to prevent excessive paperwork burdens on the public), to ensure that the rule is consistent with the underlying law, or to raise certain issues and alternatives for public comment (so that the agency may consider the resulting comments before finalizing the rule). Agencies decline to accept suggested changes with which they disagree. When changes are made, the agency assents to them. Indeed there are countless instances in which the process of interagency comment during OIRA review, or the agency's own continuing consideration of the underlying issues, leads the agency to make changes quickly and with enthusiasm.

In some cases, however, there is no consensus on whether and how to proceed during the ninety-day period. Important agencies may remain. If so, agencies generally request extensions, which can be quite lengthy.

"UPLOADED INTO ROCIS"

Pre-OIRA. Agencies begin to draft rules long before OIRA is formally engaged—sometimes on their own, sometimes in consultation with other agencies, sometimes in consultation with one or more offices within the Executive Office of the President. OIRA may be aware of such rules, perhaps because of general discussion within the executive branch, perhaps because they are included in the Annual Regulatory Plan and Unified Agenda of Regulatory and Deregulatory Actions, whose components are submitted to OIRA every year before release to the public on regulations.gov. (Along with others in the Executive Office of the President, OIRA plays a role in finalizing the Plan and Agenda; the regulations listed there are at a very preliminary stage, and will be issued only if they survive both internal and public scrutiny.)

The OIRA Administrator is frequently engaged in informal discussions with leadership at the agencies (sometimes the Secretary or the Deputy Secretary). Coming rules may well be mentioned in those discussions. OIRA staff may discuss such rules with their colleagues at the agencies, which may lead to general awareness within OIRA and the Executive Office of the President. The OIRA Administrator is also frequently involved in informal conversations about policies and priorities with officials in the Executive Office of the President, and those conversations, which occur daily, may refer to coming rules. For example, the Domestic Policy Council (DPC), headed by an Assistant to the President (the highest rank within the White House), has responsibilities in the areas of health care, immigration, education, energy, civil rights, and labor, and discussions with DPC may alert OIRA to rules that are to come. In such discussions, OIRA may express a preliminary view. But at these stages, formal OIRA review is not involved.

For rules that are likely to attract interagency interest, or that would benefit from the expertise of other parts of the federal government, agencies may elect to consult with other offices or agencies well in advance of the OIRA process. In that way, rulemaking agencies will collect views on their own, largely to inform their own judgments about whether and how to proceed. For example, the Environmental Protection Agency might consult the Department of Energy before completing a draft of a rule that will affect the electricity sector. The Department of Agriculture might consult the Department of Labor before completing a draft of a rule that will affect working people.

For important and controversial rules, agencies may well engage closely with White House offices. For example, they may work with the National Economic Council (which advises the President on a wide range of economic issues) and the DPC. For such rules, especially those with effects on the budget, agencies may also engage with relevant officials in the Office of Management and Budget, specializing in budgetary questions.

In important but unusual cases, a White House policy office will itself initiate a process to consider or promote rulemaking and to help coordinate discussions, long before OIRA review begins. Such a process is especially likely to occur if an initiative is a presidential priority (perhaps because it might help stimulate economic growth) or otherwise of interest to the President himself or to his closest advisers. If so, the National Economic Council or the Domestic Policy Council might have an especially important role, perhaps in initiating agency activity, perhaps in helping to coordinate different parts of the federal government. The Office of Science and Technology Policy or the Council on Environmental Quality might play the same role for issues within their particular domains.

For rules with a national security component, the National Security Council or the National Security Staff will likely have the White House lead, perhaps promoting agency consideration of activities that may ultimately be subject to OIRA review. While OIRA has written formal "prompt letters," designed to promote agency action, such "prompting" is far more likely to occur informally and from other offices, which have a particular responsibility to explore and spur desirable policy initiatives.

This process of early interagency coordination can be extremely important and valuable in compiling pertinent information and in ensuring that from the very beginning, multiple and potentially diverse perspectives are taken into account. Draft regulations are often much better as a result. Such a process can simplify and ease the OIRA process, because much of the interagency thinking will have occurred in advance. It is also possible that interagency coordination will ultimately lead an agency to decide not to proceed with a rule, or not to do so at a certain time, and hence OIRA will never see it. For relatively less important rules, and those that do not implicate the interests or concerns of other parts of the government, agencies might engage in no interagency consultation in advance of the OIRA process.

Significance. Under Executive Order 12866, OIRA review is limited to "significant" regulatory actions,[9] and before OIRA becomes formally involved, a judgment has to be made (by OIRA itself) about whether a rule is "significant" within the meaning of that Executive Order. The basic goal is to ensure that all rules with real importance to the nation (or internationally) will be subject to the OIRA process. Agencies may of course have an interest in having their rules designated as nonsignificant, because such a designation means that OIRA review will not occur and thus expedites the rulemaking process.[10] Executive Order 12866 states, in relevant part, that

> "Significant regulatory action" means any regulatory action that is likely to result in a rule that may:
>
> (1) Have an annual effect on the economy of $100 million or more or adversely affect in a material way the economy, a sector of the economy, productivity, competition, jobs, the environment, public health or safety, or State, local, or tribal governments or communities;
>
> (2) Create a serious inconsistency or otherwise interfere with an action taken or planned by another agency;
>
> (3) Materially alter the budgetary impact of entitlements, grants, user fees, or loan programs or the rights and obligations of recipients thereof; or
>
> (4) Raise novel legal or policy issues arising out of legal mandates, the President's priorities, or the principles set forth in this Executive order.

Under this standard, many federal rules are not subject to OIRA review at all, because they do not impose high costs, are simple and routine, and are unlikely to attract interagency (or public) interest. And under the quoted standard, the significance question is usually easy. If a rule has an economic impact of $100 million or more in any single year, it is economically significant, and it automatically qualifies for OIRA review. (Note the important point, to which I will return, that a rule can have such an impact because its benefits exceed $100 million even if its costs do not—and that a budgetary transfer rule, required or authorized by Congress, might qualify because $100 million or more is changing hands.) Most of the time, fewer than 20 percent of rules reviewed by OIRA count as economically significant. One implication is that over 80 percent of such rules will not have a Regulatory Impact Analysis, which is a careful and detailed account of the costs and benefits of economically significant rules. The percentage of economically significant rules varies from year to year, and OIRA devotes special attention to such rules (the topic of chapter 2).

Under Executive Order 12866, rules that raise novel issues of law or policy must also be subject to OIRA review. This category is extremely important. Many rules are reviewed by OIRA because they raise such issues and thus have interest to a wide variety of people within the executive branch (as well as to the public). Such rules might, for example, establish new policies with respect to privacy or discrimination on the basis of race, sex, or sexual orientation, or they might contain disclosure requirements that (say, about environmental effects) would affect large numbers of consumers.[11] It is also worth emphasizing that rules count as significant if they would create "a serious inconsistency or otherwise interfere with an action taken or planned by another agency." These are of course the starkest cases of interagency concern.

On occasion, however, it is not clear whether a regulatory action is significant, and there will be discussions about that question. In that vast majority of cases, the issue is resolved at the staff level, without involving the OIRA Administrator. But the category of "novel" issues is hardly self-defining, and while disagreements are infrequent, they do occur between agencies and OIRA. An agency might contend that the rule is minor and routine, and not novel at all. OIRA staff might question this conclusion. In the rare cases in which the issue is difficult to resolve, high-level agency officials and the Associate Administrator or Administrator of OIRA might engage in further discussion. The Administrator will ultimately decide the significance question—sometimes following the recommendation of OIRA staff, sometimes accepting the view of the agency.

If a regulatory action is ultimately found to be significant, it is usually because it would have a major economic impact or raise serious policy questions (for example, if it would involve a novel question of civil rights or civil liberties). A rule might be projected to cost $50 million, well below the $100 million threshold, but its impact might be limited to a small sector, or the agency's cost estimate might seem optimistic, and thus deserve a degree of interagency scrutiny. Recall that a rule counts as economically significant if it will "adversely affect in a material way . . . a sector of the economy," and even if a $50 million price tag does not mean that a rule is economically significant, it might well be enough to trigger a judgment of significance.

Alternatively, a rule might be deemed significant because other offices and agencies are interested in it and would likely have views. In this respect, the significance determination itself has an interagency dimension. To say the least, it would be unusual for OIRA to conclude that a rule is not significant if two other Cabinet departments have substantial concerns, or if the DPC thinks that it needs an interagency process. Indeed, such a conclusion would be highly inappropriate. A chief goal of the OIRA process is to ensure that diverse voices are heard ("government by discussion"), and OIRA cannot legitimately refuse to engage in that process if diverse voices within the federal government seek some kind of hearing. And if a rule is closely connected with presidential priorities, it is highly likely to be deemed significant for that very reason. Serious congressional interest might also inform the significance determination. If members of Congress are concerned about a rule, there is some reason to think that it raises novel questions, and that the OIRA process would be a good idea.

Under Executive Order 12866, OIRA does not merely review regulations. It reviews regulatory actions, defined to include "any substantive action by an agency (normally published in the Federal Register) that promulgates or is expected to lead to the promulgation of a final rule or regulation, including notices of inquiry, advanced notices of proposed rulemaking, and notices of proposed rulemaking."[12] Under this provision, OIRA review unambiguously applies to "pre-regulatory" actions, by which agencies obtain information or public comments or provide guidance to the public. Such actions include (significant) requests for information, advanced notices of proposed rulemaking, guidance documents, or interpretive rules that initiate a process that will culminate in rulemaking. It is relevant here that OIRA staff has a great deal of experience with relevant forms and formalities, and thus can reduce the risk of technical mistakes, both large and small, with various documents. But what about a guidance document or an interpretive rule that is freestanding, in the sense that it is not expected to be followed by a final rule or regulation?

Across multiple administrations, OIRA has long reviewed such documents and rules so long as they count as "significant," and that understanding was reaffirmed in March 2009 in a short but significant memorandum from OMB Director Peter Orszag.[13] A central idea here is that important guidance documents and interpretive rules may well have large economic consequences, raise novel issues of law or policy, or trigger interagency interest, and a process of review and interagency comments may turn out to be helpful. Here as elsewhere, no Administration is likely to want to issue important regulatory documents that have not been seen by, or incorporated the perspectives of, senior officials inside the Administration.

A particular problem is that guidance documents and interpretive rules may turn out to be actually or nearly the equivalent of rulemaking, either as a matter of law or as a matter of practice. For example, an agency might issue a guidance document (involving, say, health care, traffic safety, or visa policy) and denominate it as such, even though it is actually a rule. There is a great deal of litigation on this topic, and the process of OIRA review can explore (with the engagement of relevant lawyers, including OMB General Counsel and the Department of Justice) the question whether guidance documents and interpretive rules are overstepping their legal bounds.[14]

Even if such a document or such a rule oversteps no such bounds, it may nonetheless have major effects on the private sector. A rule that declares an agency's views about what kinds of actions require permits under the Clean Air Act, or about how automobile manufacturers can reduce the risks of distracted driving, will affect what people do. OIRA review might be important to ensure interagency comments on that document; other departments may well have views. OIRA is also interested in promoting public comment on all significant regulatory actions, including guidance documents and interpretive rules—not because such comment is required as a matter of law,[15] and not because it is necessary or desirable in every instance, but because when the stakes are high and the issues novel, obtaining public comment is a good practice as a way of avoiding mistakes.

When draft regulatory actions are ready, they are "uploaded into ROCIS," which is to say submitted to OIRA via what is called "the RISC [Regulatory Information Service Center] and OIRA Consolidated Information System." Within a short period (usually less than twenty-four hours), the fact that a rule has been submitted is usually visible to the public on reginfo.gov, along with relevant information, often including a summary of the rule. The goal here is to promote transparency for the public (and indeed the Obama Administration took many steps to make reginfo.gov as transparent as possible[16]).

Submission to OIRA immediately triggers two sets of activities, both of which involve the aspiration to "government by discussion" and the acquisition of dispersed information. The first is internal. The second involves those outside the executive branch.

INTERNAL PROCESS

The basics. Very soon after submission, the relevant OIRA desk officer—as noted, a member of the career staff—will usually circulate the rule to a wide range of offices and departments, both within the Executive Office of the President and outside of it. Recall that while the President is ultimately in charge, the White House itself is emphatically a "they," not an "it."[17] Within the Executive Office of the President, frequent recipients of regulatory actions include

- The National Economic Council
- The Council of Economic Advisers
- The Office of Science and Technology Policy
- The US Trade Representative
- The Council on Environmental Quality
- The Domestic Policy Council

- The National Security Council
- The White House Counsel
- The Office of Management and Budget
- The Office of the Vice President
- The Office of Legislative Affairs

Within the executive branch as a whole, OIRA may well ask multiple departments and agencies for their views. The specific list of agencies consulted will depend on the subject matter and content of the rule. For example, a rule from the Environmental Protection Agency might be reviewed by the Department of Energy, the Department of Transportation, the National Oceanic and Atmospheric Administration (within the Department of Commerce), the Department of Agriculture, the Department of Justice, and the Department of Interior. On matters that particularly affect small business, the independent Office of Advocacy, within the Small Business Administration, will be consulted.[18]

The governing idea is that relevant agencies have information and expertise, and the rulemaking agency should benefit from their perspectives before they finalize or even propose rules. (Recall that even a proposed rule can have serious effects and create dislocations, especially if those in the private sector believe that the handwriting is on the wall, in such a way as to lead them to reorder their affairs.) A central goal of the OIRA process is to ensure that rulemaking agencies have access to the wide variety of perspectives that can be found throughout the executive branch.

For this reason, one of OIRA's most important jobs is to work with agencies to ensure that interagency comments are properly considered, and indeed, agencies give careful consideration to such comments without the slightest prodding from OIRA. The interagency comments may involve issues that are fundamental or narrow and quite technical. For example, the Department of Justice, the White House Counsel's Office, and OMB's General Counsel's Office might have views on a legal issue, and OIRA staff will ensure that they work with the agency's General Counsel to produce a mutually agreeable result. The General Counsel at the rulemaking agency is likely to listen carefully to these offices and departments, not least because the Department of Justice must ultimately defend agency rules. In most cases, the Administrator of OIRA is likely to be informed of that discussion, but not directly involved.

Alternatively, there might be a scientific question on which diverse scientists have questions and concerns. It is important, of course, for all participants to give careful consideration to the technical expertise of the rulemaking agency. The agency's own views are likely to provide the scientific foundation for what is proposed or finalized. But the federal government may well have multiple scientific experts (perhaps at the Office of Science and Technology Policy and perhaps in one or more agencies), and OIRA works to ensure that they are consulted. It is possible, for example, that technical experts at the rulemaking agency will decide to revise their analysis and even their conclusions in light of insights provided by other technical experts.

In such cases, the goal is to get the science right, because it provides the foundation for the assessment of the likely consequences of the rule. (Recall the commitment to scientific integrity.) It is essential to try to ensure that a lot of informed people agree that the assessment is right or at least reasonable. I have emphasized that the OIRA process is designed to promote clarity on the human consequences of rules; careful examination of the underlying science can be central to that process. And if the question is one of policy—of whether and how to proceed in view of a given understanding of the science—a number of people might have valuable contributions and perspectives.

Much of the time, the discussion thus far captures OIRA's entire role. In such cases, OIRA may act largely as a convener or a facilitator. Of course OIRA may also have its own views on both process and substance; it may believe that certain interagency comments are important and convincing, or instead that they are unimportant or mistaken. In the former cases, OIRA may be a central voice, working with the rulemaking agency to see how the comments might best be accommodated. In the latter cases, OIRA may work with the commenting agencies to explain why the rulemaking agency need not accommodate their concerns.

It is not unusual for OIRA to work either to accommodate the comments or to suggest that the comments ought not to be accommodated. In either case, however, it would not be appropriate for OIRA to be dismissive of those who have a point of view. Diverse agencies may well participate in such conversations—perhaps in writing, perhaps by telephone, perhaps in person. The resulting discussions typically produce rules that are stronger as a result.

In addition, members of OIRA's staff may well have independent views of their own, informed by their exposure to a large volume and variety of regulatory actions. They may believe, for example, that the draft rule imposes an excessive paperwork and reporting burden and that steps should be considered to reduce that burden. They may believe that the agency should consider discussing an alternative on which it has thus far remained silent. They may believe that the agency should ask for public comments on how to reduce costs. Often the agency will agree with such suggestions. The OIRA Administrator may well be informed of them. Whether or not he is, OIRA staff will respond both to his general direction, which emerges from repeated discussions within OIRA, and to OIRA's institutional culture, which favors reducing paperwork burdens and promoting public comments.

"Elevation." In some cases, it is not so easy for the relevant staff to work out the competing concerns. In that event, the issue may be "elevated," a bit of government-speak that means that it has to be resolved at a higher level. The career staff at the rulemaking agency may disagree with suggestions in the interagency process, and they may specifically ask that the issue be "elevated," perhaps to political officials. Or perhaps the commenters, in the agencies, do not agree with the rulemaking agency, and they may also ask for discussion at a higher level.

There are multiple levels of elevation, ultimately to the President himself. For example, the issue might rise to the level of an Assistant Secretary at one of the departments, who might discuss the question with counterparts at other offices or departments, with OIRA acting as convener. If there is a dispute about the assessment of costs and benefits, and if a member of the Council of Economic Advisers has a strong view, OIRA might arrange a call or a meeting with the relevant Assistant Secretary. In that discussion, OIRA's Associate Administrator or Deputy Administrator might be involved. OIRA's leadership will often work directly with someone at the relevant agency—say, the Assistant Secretary at the rulemaking department and the Assistant Secretary at the department that has concerns—to seek a resolution.

The focus of these discussions is intensely substantive. If a reviewing agency believes that it is important to ask for public comments on what it sees as a reasonable alternative to the main proposal, and if the rulemaking agency believes that such a request would be unhelpful and distracting, then a key question is whether the alternative is a reasonable one that might actually be chosen in the final rule. To answer that question, it is necessary to ask some questions about the content of the alternative—its legality and its potential effects. Similarly, there may be discussions about what should be chosen as the primary proposal and what should be discussed as an alternative. My own experience, by the way, is that alternatives that initially seem unpromising, and that are mentioned mostly as a way to ensure that the public sees them, sometimes turn out to be a lot better than originally believed—and hence are ultimately chosen in the final rule. This experience is a tribute to the system of government by discussion, and it suggests that it is quite important to err on the side of raising more rather than fewer alternatives for public comment.

OIRA may well serve as mediator in these discussions, with the principal goal of ensuring that there is a mutually agreeable outcome. Of course OIRA leadership may also have a view on the merits, perhaps even a clear view, and it may strongly encourage the rulemaking agency or the commenting agency to move in a certain direction. Typically, OIRA supports the inclusion of a wide range of alternatives for public comment. Recall that OIRA understands itself as a guardian of the rulemaking process and hence tends to promote public comment on a range of questions.

In relatively rare cases, discussion at the Assistant Secretary level does not resolve the issue, and it must be elevated still further. The Deputy Secretary (who serves directly under the Cabinet head) of a department (either the rulemaking agency or one with concerns) might believe that the issue is worth discussing. The OIRA Administrator would likely organize a call or convene a meeting, and other officials, at comparable levels, might be present as well. In very rare cases, the issue might go to "principals," meaning high-level White House officials and the heads of Cabinet departments. A call or a meeting might be arranged by OIRA, by the Director of OMB, or (in very rare cases) by the Chief of Staff's Office. These discussions are typically substantive as well; they might well be highly technical. Sometimes elevation, even at very high levels, will consist of a phone call, with a Deputy Secretary or Cabinet head calling the OIRA Administrator to talk through a complex issue.

In a well-known case, President Obama himself resolved a question about whether the EPA should finalize an ozone rule.[19] While that resolution was widely reported to be based on political grounds, the report was erroneous. As is typically the case for agency rulemaking, the decision was based on judgments about the merits, as reflected in the return letter that the President directed me to write.

OIRA as convener. In popular and academic discussions of the OIRA process, a great deal of attention is devoted to cost-benefit analysis and to OIRA's own views. Costs and benefits can matter a great deal, and OIRA's views can be important; OIRA and others involved in the process are interested in increasing net benefits (which may mean decreasing costs). Much of this book will focus on costs and benefits. But it should now be clear that OIRA is often operating as a convener—perhaps with a point of view, but perhaps not even that, and frequently OIRA is not the most important interlocutor on the rule. Recall that the White House itself is a "they," not an "it." OIRA is often in the position of transmitting comments with which it does not necessarily agree or on which it is neutral. Its goal is to find a reasonable and mutually agreeable resolution.

In the face of significant interagency concerns, the process of OIRA review typically continues until such a resolution is found. If, for example, a high-level presidential adviser does not believe that a proposed rule should go forward in its current form, or if a member of the President's Cabinet has severe reservations, OIRA cannot simply ignore their concerns. Its obligation is to work closely with others and with the relevant officials to address those concerns—by seeing if proponents of the rule can convince the skeptics that the concerns are unwarranted or by seeing if skeptics can convince the agency that the concerns need to be accommodated. As part of the Administration, agencies fully appreciate this process; the heads of Cabinet departments certainly do, even if they are not always enthusiastic about it. Of course OIRA might have some views of its own, perhaps even clear views. When it does, it is often because of OIRA's institutional commitment to fair procedure and to compliance with Executive Order 13563.

Why might an agency accept one or more of the comments made during the interagency process? In response to the Department of Justice, the agency might conclude that it has taken an approach that does indeed raise a serious legal problem, and that it might do better to proceed in a way that avoids the legal difficulty. In response to the Council of Economic Advisers, the agency might conclude that its assessment of costs is too optimistic, and that it would do better to offer other figures or a range. In response to the DPC, the agency might agree that it needs to take comment on a plausible alternative to the approach that it is proposing.

The role of OIRA itself is often to seek a sensible path forward—helping to identify an approach that meets the reasonable concerns while also enabling the agency to proceed. Of course it is also true that, in some cases, the concerns are sufficiently serious, and sufficiently appreciated by the rulemaking agency, that the rules will be unlikely to proceed.

EXTERNAL MEETINGS

Before formal submission of a rule to OIRA, members of the public may be able to meet with the rulemaking agency and with relevant offices within the Executive Office of the President. Such meetings are in fact common. Under Executive Order 13563, agencies are directed to obtain views from members of the public even before they issue a proposed rule. Until a regulatory action is formally submitted, OIRA itself is usually unavailable for meetings with members of the public; the standard practice is to wait until the time of submission, when a rule is under formal review. At that time, OIRA is immediately available for meetings, known as "12866 meetings," after Executive Order 12866.

Open doors. OIRA has an open-door policy. It accepts all comers. If affected companies want to come in person to make an argument for or against a draft rule, OIRA is unquestionably available. The same is true for public interest groups, state and local governments, and members of congressional staffs. In these meetings, OIRA's role is passive. It does not encourage or spur meetings. It does not affirm positions, volunteer information, or answer questions. The central goal is to hear what people have to say.

While OIRA holds a meeting, it always invites the agency whose rule is being discussed. Other offices may be present as well. For example, it would be usual for the Domestic Policy Council to attend a meeting relating to health care, because it plays a significant role on health care issues. If a scientific question is involved, the Office of Science and Technology Policy will be invited. On environmental questions, both the Council on Environmental Quality and the Domestic Policy Council will be invited. When a rule is under formal OIRA review (which is to say after the rule has been uploaded into ROCIS), it is usually OIRA that will convene any meeting with people in the Executive Office of the President. In general, it would not be appropriate for the Domestic Policy Council or the National Economic Council to convene such a meeting, though they are certainly entitled to be present. The reason for this practice is to avoid forum shopping and to ensure that the review process is orderly and well coordinated.

A skewed process and epistemic capture? In some circles, considerable attention has been devoted to the role of meetings in the OIRA process, with the suggestion that they compromise the process and lead to a form of interest-group "capture," or at least capitulation.[20] Ironically, one reason for the attention is that OIRA has a high degree of transparency. Meetings with those outside the federal government are docketed on the OIRA website, and OIRA also works to make available all documents received during meetings.

Nonetheless, the concerns remain. For those who express those concerns, the essential problem is that businesses and others subject to regulation arrange a strong majority of meetings, and public interest groups arrange far fewer. On many regulatory actions, those who oppose such actions, or seek to scale them back, meet with OIRA far more often do than those who support such actions, and seek to make them more protective.

Of course OIRA, with its open door policy, is not responsible for this asymmetry. OIRA cannot and does not pick and choose. There is no problem of differential access in any formal sense. But at least in theory, there is a possible risk of "epistemic capture,"[21] in the sense that a view might develop, at OIRA or within the Executive Office of the President, only because of the distinctive set of people who have provided relevant information. It has been speculated that the asymmetry, in terms of who requests meetings, has major consequences and that rules are affected and even compromised (or "weakened") as a result.[22] The issue is worth attention, because it bears on the role of meetings with public officials in general, and on the question whether such meetings reflect undue influence (perhaps in the form of epistemic capture) or instead some desirable form of information gathering.

At least in the abstract, the concern about epistemic capture cannot be dismissed. In some context, that concern is serious. Suppose that public officials are hearing mostly from people with a particular stake in the outcome—for example, people who would be burdened by rules protecting worker safety or the environment. Even if the officials want to be neutral and are seeking merely to obtain relevant information, their own perspectives might well be shaped by the limited class of people to whom they are listening. From a neutral starting point, and with all the good will in the world, they might be subject to epistemic capture in the sense that they will ultimately form a view that fits with what they learn from the particular people with whom they speak. The result could be a set of badly skewed judgments, as officials move toward the people with whom they engage—and ironically, not listening to anyone at all might, in principle, mean greater neutrality.

Compare the important idea of "crippled epistemology," applied by the political scientist Russell Hardin to extremists who think as they do because they are listening only to people with extreme views.[23] Hardin urges that many people become extremists simply because they suffer from a crippled epistemology, in which everything they hear is extreme. The broader point is that all of us have a crippled epistemology in the sense that we cannot know everything, and we learn from the people with whom we speak. In principle, regulators could well have a crippled epistemology simply because of the particular people from whom they hear.

Though the speculation is not implausible on its face (and though it might be more than plausible at some times and places), I believe that it should be viewed with considerable skepticism in this context, because it is based on an inaccurate understanding of the role of meetings in the OIRA process. In fact it is largely a product of a "focusing illusion," in which people err because they focus unduly on a single aspect of a complex situation and give it undue prominence.[24] In discussions of the OIRA process (and government in general), the role of meetings tends to be greatly exaggerated. The first point is that, in general, the review process relies above all on interagency comments and written comments from the public. When rules change as a result of review, it is usually because of interagency or public comments, not because of meetings.

The second point is that the sheer number of meetings is quite uninformative. Some meetings have no effect at all, because the presentations supply no new information. Sometimes presenters speak in vague and general terms and for that reason offer nothing new. Sometimes presenters offer arguments that are significant but that are already well known within the federal government, because officials have raised the arguments on their own. If presenters offer arguments that are significant, it is overwhelmingly likely that they are already in public comments (or were previously outlined, by essentially the same presenters, to staff at the rulemaking agency during the formulation of the rule)— and are already well known for that reason.

Sometimes presenters offer the equivalent of enthusiastic support or extreme skepticism, not so different from loud applause or sustained hissing. Because support and skepticism are rarely informative, and almost never surprising, such meetings do not have any impact on actual decisions. Other unhelpful meetings treat OIRA as if its central concerns are political, which they emphatically are not. It is not helpful for those in meetings to refer to opinion polls or to suggest that the Administration will in some vague sense be helped or hurt by proceeding with a rule.

It follows that OIRA could hold two hundred meetings with affected industry, and no meetings with anyone else, and there might be no effect on the rule under review—even if the rule in fact changes during the review, and indeed even if it changes in exactly the direction sought by affected industry. It also follows that if, with respect to certain rules in the future, public interest groups meet with OIRA even more often than affected industry does, there might well be no effect on what happens as a result of the review. For all of these reasons, the sheer number of meetings, and the identity of those who ask for meetings, says very little about the nature of the OIRA process.

Nothing I have said means that meetings never matter or cannot affect the content of a rule. On some occasions, they are indeed helpful—

when they provide relevant information and, in particular, when they offer concrete suggestions about how best to proceed. The most useful meetings are specific. For example, presenters might emphasize potential unintended consequences, legal difficulties, unexpectedly high costs, or international trade implications—and suggest a concrete way of handling the relevant problems, perhaps by changing one or two provisions, while nonetheless achieving the agency's basic goals. Suggestions of this kind can be valuable and informative. They are part and parcel of government by discussion.

I have noted that meetings will rarely include information that is not available through public comments, and in fact, I cannot recall a single case in which a meeting offered entirely novel information. Nonetheless, a meeting can focus the government's attention on certain questions and problems, and those who request meetings will sometimes single out one or a few concerns for special consideration, thus highlighting them in ways that public comments may not have. Even if the public comments include all of the substance, the focus on those concerns, especially when accompanied with a proposed way of addressing them, can be informative for those who are seeking to put the rule in the best possible form. But it is important to emphasize that the rulemaking agency, and those involved in the review, often believe that, however well presented, the arguments made by those at meetings are unconvincing and should be rejected.

It remains true that the helpful meetings can matter, especially when people outside of the federal government have information that public officials lack. A key value of the public comment period is that agencies frequently learn something that bears on the ultimate content of a rule—even after a thorough process of interagency review. On some occasions, OIRA's meetings are a useful supplement to the period of public comment. But in practice, the supplement does not present a problem of epistemic capture. On the contrary, it adds usefully to the stock of information that is held by government.

Even when the provisions of published rules are consistent with the ideas and goals of those at meetings, however, it is hazardous to infer causation. Most of the time, the published version of the rule has not been affected by meetings, even if it is consistent with what some presenters sought. This conclusion should not be surprising. If presenters are seeking a particular resolution, there is a good chance that people inside the government were (independently) doing so as well.

Costs, Benefits, and Politics

I have said that costs and benefits matter a great deal, but that they are usually not the dominant issue in the process of OIRA review. My goals in this section are to elaborate these points, to explore OIRA's role (of course with many others) as guardian of administrative procedure, and also to discuss the place of "politics" in the OIRA process.

THE IMPORTANT BUT LIMITED ROLE OF COSTS AND BENEFITS

Costs and benefits, in actual practice. Much of the academic and public discussion of the OIRA process focuses on the analysis of costs and benefits.[25] Cost-benefit analysis is exceedingly important, and in the Obama Administration, several steps were taken to strengthen it, contributing to a situation in which the net benefits of economically significant rules were extraordinarily high. In the first three fiscal years of the Obama Administration the net benefits of economically significant regulation exceeded $91 billion—more than twenty-five times the corresponding figure for the Bush Administration, and more than six times the corresponding figure for the Clinton Administration.[26] Recall too that through the first four fiscal years the net benefits figure climbed to $150 billion. I have noted that by Executive Order, OIRA is charged with ensuring (to the extent permitted by law) that the benefits of rules justify the costs and that the agency has selected the approach that maximizes net benefits. These two principles are exceedingly important, and they matter both to rulemaking agencies and in OIRA review.

To carry out their responsibilities under Executive Order 13563, OIRA and other interagency reviewers (including the Council of Economic Advisers and the National Economic Council) must carefully assess the agency's estimates of both costs and benefits, and they must also ensure that relevant alternatives are considered, including assessment of their costs and benefits. Without consideration of alternatives, it is not possible to know that the agency has chosen the approach that maximizes net benefits.

In actual practice, this role is important for a variety of reasons. If the quantifiable benefits are lower than the quantifiable costs, agencies must explain why they seek to proceed. Perhaps they should not proceed as planned, or perhaps they should adopt a different approach, one that has net benefits. Within the federal government, agencies are acutely aware of the cost-benefit requirements of Executive Order 13563 and Executive Order 12866. These requirements undoubtedly affect the design of rules presubmission, and they certainly are an important part of interagency review and an enduring feature of OIRA's own role. OIRA itself may offer views about how costs and benefits are most accurately assessed, and also about how best to proceed in light of the economic impacts. If the benefits of the agency's chosen approach do not appear to justify the costs, OIRA (along with others in the Executive Office of the President) will, under Executive Order 13563, raise questions about whether the agency should proceed with that approach.

But even if the rule does not have net benefits, and even if the benefits do not appear to justify the costs, agencies may have plausible explanations.[27] Perhaps the law requires them to proceed even if the monetized benefits are lower than the monetized costs. Perhaps the relevant rule has nonmonetizable benefits that are hard to quantify but nonetheless important to consider (see chapter 3 for details). Under the governing Executive Orders, agencies must show that the benefits "justify" the costs, not that they "exceed" the costs, in a clear recognition that even if the monetized benefits are lower than the monetized costs, the costs might nonetheless be justified—as, for example, when there are significant benefits that cannot be quantified. Executive Order 13563 explicitly states that "each agency may consider (and discuss qualitatively) values that are difficult or impossible to quantify, including equity, human dignity, fairness, and distributive impacts."[28]

In the Obama Administration, it has been very rare for a rule to have monetized costs in excess of monetized benefits, but nonquantifiable benefits may turn out to be important, and in some cases, they have mattered. A disclosure requirement, for example, may have benefits that cannot be quantified, but an agency is nonetheless entitled to conclude that, all things considered, they are likely to justify the costs.[29] Or consider a rule from the Department of Justice, designed to reduce the incidence of prison rape.[30] In explaining the effects of the rule, the Department described the costs, which involved hundreds of millions of dollars that state and local governments would have to spend on monitoring and training. The Department also described the benefits, which involved a significant reduction in the incidence of rape in prison.

The Department did its best to specify that reduction and even to say how reductions in rape could be turned into monetary equivalents. But it frankly acknowledged the limits of this effort, emphasizing that human dignity was involved and had to be taken into account: "this analysis inevitably excludes benefits that are not monetizable, but still must be included in a cost-benefit analysis. These include the values of equity, human dignity, and fairness. Such non-quantifiable benefits will be received by victims who receive proper treatment after an assault. . . . [N]on-quantifiable benefits will accrue to society at large, by ensuring that inmates re-entering the community are less traumatized and better equipped to support their community."[31]

In many cases, then, protection of human dignity and other non-quantifiable benefits have helped to inform the ultimate decision. I shall have much more to say about these questions in chapters 2 and 3. Nonetheless, it is true that monetized benefits and costs are central considerations in the process of OIRA review, especially for economically significant rules.

Because of the requirements of Executive Order 13563, the agency's assessment of costs and benefits is likely to be subject to considerable internal scrutiny. I have stressed that if the benefits do not justify the costs, there will be a significant question about whether a proposed or final rule should move forward, and the numbers themselves are carefully reviewed. Here as well, OIRA's own views are highly relevant, but OIRA is far from the only actor. Economists and other analysts at OIRA will scrutinize the agency's numbers and reasoning, and if the benefits or costs seem to be overestimated or underestimated, OIRA and the agency will discuss how to produce the most accurate assessments.

In such cases, the Council of Economics Advisers and the National Economic Council may well be involved. Indeed, CEA may turn out to be the agency's most important interlocutor, because of its expertise and central role in economic analysis. If CEA believes that the agency estimates are correct, or that they include serious errors, its view will receive considerable attention. Questions about costs and benefits will typically involve a number of agencies and offices.

It is not at all unusual for the agency to adjust its initial estimates as a result of the process. Beyond adjusting the numbers, the agency may elect to shift one or another aspect of its approach as a result of OIRA review. For example, the agency might end up selecting an approach that has higher net benefits. Nor is it at all unusual for the agency's initial estimates to turn out to be fundamentally right, and for the agency to have sufficient answers to the various questions raised during the review. The outcome depends on discussions that are substantive and often highly technical.

It has been suggested that in its Annual Report to Congress on the Benefits and Costs of Federal Regulations,[32] OIRA should reassess, and not simply use, the agency's estimates.[33] It should now be clear why OIRA does not do this. Because of the intense level of interagency engagement, and because the internal process has reached agreement on a set of figures, it would be awkward, to say the least, for OIRA (or any other office that is part of the internal process) to provide its own independent assessment of costs and benefits. When a rule is published, OIRA (along with other offices and agencies) has already given the assessment considerable scrutiny. This is not to say that OIRA would always, in the first instance, have landed exactly where the agency has. But it is to say that OIRA has decided that the agency's assessment is sufficiently reasonable to justify concluding its review, and that the interagency process has agreed.

Why costs and benefits, while frequently important, are not usually the central issue. Many people think that cost-benefit analysis is always or generally the central issue in the OIRA process. Not so. As noted, more than 80 percent of rules reviewed by OIRA are not economically significant, in the sense that they do not have an annual economic impact of at least $100 million. Recall that rules that are not economically significant need not have a Regulatory Impact Analysis, which consists of a careful treatment of costs and benefits.

In a sense, moreover, the numbers given thus far overstate the number of rules that require cost-benefit analysis. I have noted that a significant percentage of economically significant rules—in some years a majority—count as such because they involve high transfer payments, not high regulatory costs. Such rules do not require the kinds of cost-benefit analysis, and the kinds of justification, that are standardly mandatory for rules that impose high regulatory costs on the private sector. For example, Congress may require or authorize certain expenditures, and because of the sums involved, the relevant rules are subject to OIRA review even if they do not impose significant regulatory costs. If Congress requires $200 million to be given to a certain group, a transfer payment is involved, making it difficult to use the standard tools to test the question whether the benefits justify the costs.

To be sure, agencies do provide a Regulatory Impact Analysis for budgetary transfer rules, but they typically outline the budgetary costs and do not discuss social costs and benefits (which are difficult to measure). When OIRA reviews budgetary transfer rules, it works closely with budgetary specialists in OMB and elsewhere to ensure that the numbers are right and to avoid excessive or unjustified expenditures.

It is true that even when rules are not economically significant, agencies must give some account of costs and benefits and must show (to the extent permitted by law) that the benefits justify the costs—and hence they must attempt to be accurate. A rule that is projected to impose $50 million in annual costs, and $80 million in annual benefits, is likely not to be economically significant within the meaning of the governing Executive Orders. But those are hardly trivial numbers, and it is possible that the numbers are not correct. The interagency process is concerned with both accuracy and avoidance of unjustified costs, and hence OIRA and others might well devote considerable attention to such numbers.

In the majority of cases, however, costs and benefits are not the key issue. For a rule that is not economically significant, the question of costs and benefits will not usually be the main one. Of course the review process will ask how and if the rule fits with the law and with presidential commitments, goals, and priorities. Several specific issues are typical of the review process and closely connected with the ideal of government by discussion, because they involve efforts to promote public participation on the regulatory process. They include the following:

1. *Alternatives.* In the context of a proposed rule, it might be asked whether the agency would consider listing several alternatives in addi-

tion to its preferred option, on the ground that it would be valuable to receive public input on those alternatives. As noted, the agency might not want to identify alternatives to which it does not intend to give serious attention. Interagency reviewers might believe that those alternatives are reasonable and deserve some kind of public hearing.

2. *Explicitly seeking public comments on relevant issues.* Sometimes OIRA asks the agency explicitly whether it would consider seeking public comments on a range of specific issues, perhaps including (for example) the reasonableness of exempting small businesses and the analysis of costs and benefits. Sometimes the agency may not be initially inclined to seek comments on such questions, on the ground that explicit requests for comments might suggest more tentativeness than is real or warranted.

3. *Logical outgrowth.* Under the Administrative Procedure Act, agencies are not permitted to finalize provisions of a rule that are not a "logical outgrowth" of the proposal.[34] This somewhat technical idea is a tribute to a larger ideal, which is that binding rules should not be issued unless the public has had an opportunity to comment on them. In the context of a final rule, interagency reviewers might question whether a particular approach is a logical outgrowth of the proposed rule, so that it is a lawful candidate for finalizing. A great deal of the OIRA process can be devoted to the issue of logical outgrowth. Some apparently reasonable approaches might be forbidden because they do not count as logical outgrowths. Some attractive approaches do so qualify, on reflection, and considerable attention might have to be devoted to that question.

4. *Interim final rule.* An agency might submit a draft in the form of an interim final rule. OIRA and others might ask the agency whether it might be best to proceed with a proposal—so as to ensure that a final rule, even if interim, does not impose mistakes on the public. There may be good justifications for proceeding with an interim final rule—for example, because of some kind of legal deadline—but bypassing the public comment period can produce interagency concerns.[35] In addition, Executive Order 13563 places a large emphasis on public participation and on ensuring a period of public comment on rules.

5. *Statutory process requirements.* OIRA spends a great deal of time helping to promote compliance with various statutory requirements, including those associated with the Regulatory Flexibility Act[36] (designed

to protect small business from excessive regulation) and the Paperwork Reduction Act,[37] which is relevant to rulemaking that includes an information collection request.

6. *Science.* Sometimes the underlying issue involves science. OIRA may consult a range of scientists within the federal government, perhaps including the Office of Science and Technology Policy and the Centers for Disease Control and Prevention. In the process, there might be discussion of whether the agency considered relevant scientific studies and responded to comments and concerns raised during peer review. (Recall the commitment to scientific integrity.) OIRA will not reach a scientific conclusion on its own (though in recent years it has generally had two scientists on its staff), but it will promote discussion of the underlying issues. There might also be discussion of whether policy choices are compelled by, or being conflated with, the scientific evidence.

TECHNICAL ISSUES, POLICY ISSUES, AND POLITICS

To the extent that the OIRA process produces controversy, it is often because of a concern that "politics," in some pejorative sense, plays a role in that process.[38] The idea of "politics" is of course not self-defining, but in this context, the concern is that interest groups, public reactions, and perhaps electoral concerns end up influencing judgments about whether and how to proceed with rules.

To sharpen the concern, let us describe that concern in the starkest fashion. Agencies consist of specialists. Their concerns are the facts and the law. They attempt to implement statutes faithfully, applying their technical (and sometimes scientific) expertise. By contrast, OIRA consists largely of unelected bureaucrats, who may have agendas of their own. OIRA is also part of the White House, and for that reason, it is necessarily part of a politicized process. OIRA lacks the specialized competence of the agencies. Insofar as other White House offices, with their own agendas, are involved in the OIRA process, the problem of comparative ignorance may be compounded.

The result—on the view that I am describing—is that agencies are sometimes unable to achieve their goals, and to implement their understanding of the law, simply because of the interference from either unelected bureaucrats at OIRA or political actors at the White House. Note that, so summarized, the concerns involve two different points. The first has to do with the role of OIRA itself and in particular its career staff. The second has to do with the role of the White House as such.

What this account ignores is that most of the OIRA process is technical, not political, and it is technical in an appropriate sense, involving an extraordinarily wide range of officials, many of them outside of the White House. I have emphasized that, not infrequently, the underlying issues involve the law, and the rulemaking agency's lawyers work closely with the Department of Justice, White House Counsel, the OMB General Counsel's Office, and other offices to produce the best judgments about what the law requires. Here OIRA's role will involve convening, not deciding. If the issue is one of economics, OIRA is likely to play a substantive role, but as I have emphasized, a number of other economists will be involved.

When scientific issues are engaged, there is no "political interference with science" (in my experience). Scientific issues are explored as such, by people who are competent to explore them. Some questions can be seen as those of "science policy," in the sense that they involve not strictly scientific questions, but questions about how to proceed in the face of scientific uncertainty. Those questions will also be engaged as such.

Sometimes, of course, the issues include significant issues of policy, including the kind that might be "elevated." Suppose that interagency reviewers, including OIRA, CEA, and the Office of Advocacy at the Small Business Administration, are arguing in favor of flexibility for small businesses, in the form of a lower level of stringency or a delayed compliance date. Their shared argument might be that it would be costly or difficult for small businesses to comply and that little would be lost, from the standpoint of the agency's own goals, with greater flexibility. The agency might respond that such flexibility would create legal problems or that it would compromise important goals, such as public health or safety.

At that point, the legal issue would be engaged directly. If the law does not give the agency discretion, the issue is at an end. If the law does turns out to grant discretion, reasonable questions would be to what extent flexibility would be important or beneficial to small business, and to what extent public health or safety goals would actually be compromised by greater flexibility. At that stage, additional work, above all involving the facts, would be necessary to answer these questions. Most of the time, clarification of the underlying questions, along with that work, produces a solution that is both sensible and agreeable to those involved.

It is true, of course, that OIRA has a good deal of formal authority under Executive Orders 12866 and 13563; it can refuse to allow rules to go forward (ultimately subject to the direction of the President). That authority matters. But in important cases, the agency convinces OIRA and others, on the merits, that its position is indisputably correct, or that it is reasonable enough even if not indisputably correct. And in important cases, the agency concludes that the views suggested by OIRA, and pressed by interagency reviewers, are clearly correct, or that they are reasonable enough even if not clearly correct. In a well-functioning process, the substance is what matters.

Of course any OIRA Administrator will pay a great deal of respectful attention to the views of others. The Administrator is not likely to feel so confident about his personal judgment, and that of his staff, if it differs from the considered judgments of the agency and lacks substantive support within other offices and agencies involved in the interagency process.

What about "politics"? If the term refers to interest groups, public reactions, and electoral factors, consideration of "politics" is not a significant part of OIRA's own role. To be sure, political issues might be taken into account by other offices. The White House Office of Legislative Affairs and OMB's Office of Legislative Affairs work closely with Congress, and those offices have the lead in coordinating discussions between the Administration and Congress, including discussions about regulations. For example, a member of Congress may send letters to the OIRA Administrator, and members and their staffs may seek a 12866 meeting. OMB's Office of Legislative Affairs or the White House Office of Legislative Affairs might help coordinate that meeting. Members of Congress may have valuable information about the likely effects of rules. The White House Office of Intergovernmental Affairs is in charge of relations with state and local governments, and it might help to ensure that the views of state and local officials are communicated to OIRA, usually through public comments, but sometimes through meetings. State and local officials may also have important information to convey. White House Communications and OMB Communications are in charge of relationships with the media, and when proposed and final rules need to be explained to the public, they help develop press releases and other relevant documents.

In addition, others in the White House—including the Chief of Staff's Office—will be alert to a wide range of considerations, including the relationship between potential rulemakings and the President's overall priorities, goals, agenda, and schedule. Any Administration has specific priorities and limited "bandwidth," in the sense that it has time and resources to devote attention to, and to focus on, only a subset of proposals and reforms. It is important to emphasize that with respect to the Administration as a whole, the Office of the Chief of Staff has an exceedingly important role insofar as it works to advise on and help coordinate executive branch activity with close reference to the President's own commitments. All executive offices, including OIRA, work under the President and are subject to his supervision, to the extent permitted by law.[39] Insofar as the President and his closest advisers are clear on their priorities, OIRA will of course be made aware of their views and act accordingly. Those involved in the OIRA process are alert to the concerns and priorities of the President himself, and they take direction from him.

OF DISPERSED INFORMATION

The executive branch of the federal government is exceedingly large and diverse, and it is important to ensure that before significant rules are proposed or finalized, rulemaking agencies have an opportunity to consider the diverse perspectives and information of those who work there. I have emphasized that while the President is ultimately in charge, the White House itself is a "they," not an "it," and the same is even more true of the executive branch as a whole. While OIRA's own views may be significant and will be conveyed, OIRA is the convener of an interagency process that draws on the specialized competence of experts throughout the federal government. To be sure, costs and benefits are an important and sometimes critical part of the review process, especially for economically significant rules, and I shall have much more to say about cost-benefit analysis in subsequent chapters. But most rules do not qualify as economically significant, and in most cases, costs and benefits are not the central issue.

One of OIRA's most important missions is to increase the likelihood that rulemaking agencies will benefit from dispersed information inside and outside the federal government. OIRA sees itself as a guardian of a well-functioning administrative process, involving government by discussion. Federal officials, most of them nonpolitical, know a great deal, and OIRA helps to ensure that what they know is incorporated in agency rulemakings. Those outside of the federal government often have indispensable information, and OIRA understands one of its crucial tasks as encouraging receipt and careful consideration of that information.

In these respects, OIRA does not so much promote centralized direction of regulatory policy as incorporation of decentralized knowledge. Of course OIRA plays an important role in the process of White House oversight of executive branch rulemaking. What I have emphasized here is that a key part of that role is the function of information aggregator.

TWO

Human Consequences, or The Real World of Cost-Benefit Analysis

When I was in government, a colleague had an unusual and construc-
tive phrase. After lengthy and intense discussions of options, and of the
difficulties associated with each, he would respond, "OK, we have now
admired the problem. What are we going to do about it?" The response
was important, because it shifted the group's attention from people's
concerns, worries, and objections, and toward exactly what was needed,
which was a sense of the best, or the least bad, solutions.

The world of regulation is full of admirable problems. For example,
there is an elaborate literature on the problems of risk and uncertainty,
and also on how regulators should deal with them.[1] Situations of risk
exist when we can identify outcomes and assign probabilities to each
of them.[2] Situations of uncertainty exist when it is possible to identify
outcomes but not to assign probabilities.[3] Both situations create serious
challenges for regulators. We can imagine, for example, a regulation for
which estimates of both benefits and costs span a wide range. Perhaps
regulators cannot identify the probabilities that ought to be assigned to
various points along the continuum. Even if they can do so, it may not be
self-evident what ought to be done when benefits exceed costs at some
points within the respective ranges, but fail to do so at others.

We can easily imagine cases in which there is a risk of catastrophe—
involving, say, climate change, financial meltdowns, and terrorist attacks—but in which regulators cannot specify the relevant probabilities,
or identify the contribution of the particular regulation to reducing the
central risks. We can imagine cases in which the discount rate greatly
matters, so that a regulation is justified with a low rate, but not with a
high one.[4] We can imagine cases with "fat tails" (distributions with a

large number of extreme events), perhaps confounding cost-benefit analysis, perhaps suggesting that the quantified benefits of risk reduction are far higher than we initially anticipated.[5] We can imagine cases in which certain benefits, such as protections of privacy and prohibitions on the denial of health insurance to those with preexisting conditions, are hard to quantify and monetize.

All of these are admirable problems, and it is admirable, and sometimes highly illuminating, to admire them. Indeed, the admiration may well be a necessary precondition for deciding how to handle them. But the act of admiring problems has its own benefits and costs. One benefit, of course, is improved understanding, which is a good in itself. Another benefit is improved practice and policies. A cost is associated with the very effort to resolve difficult and potentially intractable problems—a cost that may loom especially large if those problems do not arise often. With respect to both practice and policies, it is important to understand the extent to which answers to the hardest and most interesting questions will actually matter, and how, and when.

During my period in government, essentially all of the most admirable problems came to my attention. To take just one example, I participated in an interagency working group that settled on values for the social cost of carbon.[6] In 2010 dollars, the central value was $21.40 per ton, with a range from $4.70 to $64.90. (In 2013, the number was increased by about 40 percent;[7] see appendix B.) These values are used to establish the benefits of regulatory efforts to reduce greenhouse gas emissions, and they have played a role in many rulemakings.

It is also true, however, that the most difficult problems appeared quite rarely, and when they did, there were generally standardized methods of handling them. OMB Circular A-4, issued in 2003, outlines many of those methods,[8] and I shall be relying on that document for some of the discussion here. One of my central points is that the analysis of the social cost of carbon, Circular A-4, and related or similar documents are binding until they are changed, and for that reason, some of the hardest questions cannot be revisited during the process of rule review. To be sure, authoritative documents can be altered. But their alteration requires some kind of formal process, requiring significant time, effort, and commitment from a large number of public officials, and perhaps a period of public comment as well. Any such process will need a substantial investment of resources. For this reason, it is no light thing to attempt a revision of authoritative documents.

The remainder of this chapter has a simple structure. I divide the thirty-six scenarios into eight categories, starting with the basics, and turning respectively to valuations of mortality risks; cobenefits and risk-risk trade-offs; wide ranges; benefits that are hard or impossible to quantify; net benefits; climate change; and discount rates. Each of the scenarios is brisk and highly stylized. A full picture would of course include not only a description of the various dollar figures, but also an understanding of what, concretely, those figures mean.

The Basics

1. The annual costs of a regulation are $200 million. The annual benefits are $400 million. There are only two alternatives: issuing or not issuing the regulation.[9] In the process of OIRA review, the numbers will be carefully scrutinized, and many questions will be asked about their accuracy and meaning, but if those questions have good answers, this is an easy one in favor of proceeding. The regulation also has the standard characteristic of most economically significant regulations that agencies submit to OIRA: If both benefits and costs are monetized, the monetized benefits are usually significantly higher than the monetized costs. For regulations that are submitted to OIRA or published in the Federal Register, and for which benefits and costs are monetized, agencies usually find substantial net benefits. (See appendix C for numerous examples.)

This is hardly an accident.[10] We have seen that under Executive Order 13563, the benefits must "justify" the costs, and while I shall spend some time with that idea, the easiest way to show justification is to establish that the monetized benefits are simply higher than the monetized costs. If the monetized benefits are lower than the monetized costs, agencies may choose not to submit the draft rule at all, unless there are special considerations (such as a legal obligation or important nonquantifiable benefits). If the costs exceed the benefits, agencies might devote their resources to other rules, or work to identify an approach for which benefits exceed costs. The monetized benefits exceeded the monetized costs for the vast majority of recent economically significant rules for which agencies monetized both benefits and costs.

2. Same as (1), but the agency provides a benefits range of $400 million to $700 million. There are only two alternatives: issuing or not issuing the regulation. This is also likely to be an easy one in favor of proceeding. To be sure, the process of OIRA review will devote considerable attention to the sheer width of the benefits range. Why is the agency unable to narrow the range? Do the uncertainties involve economics? Do they involve science? A great deal of time might be spent on these questions, in an effort to promote a better understanding, within the federal government and within the public at large, of the likely effects of the regulation. One goal will be to narrow the range, to the extent that doing so reflects the best available evidence. But on the facts as stated, it seems clear that the agency ought to proceed.

3. The annual costs of a regulation are $200 million. The annual benefits range from $50 million to $75 million. Unless the law requires the agency to proceed, or unless the regulation has some special feature, the agency is unlikely to attempt to go forward with this regulation. If it submits the rule to OIRA, many questions will be asked, for one simple reason: Executive Order 13563 requires the benefits to justify the costs. If the monetized benefits are much lower than the monetized costs, it may nonetheless be possible to show that the benefits "justify" the costs; perhaps nonquantifiable benefits are anticipated to be large and to provide that justification. But this will not be easy to establish.

4. The annual costs of a regulation are $200 million. The benefits range from $50 million to $205 million. The agency invokes the Precautionary Principle, a popular idea in Europe and in various international documents.[11] It contends that because the benefits justify the costs at the highest end of the range, it should be entitled to go forward. The Precautionary Principle has many different forms, but the agency emphasizes, very simply, that health and safety should be given the benefit of the doubt, and that because the benefits exceed the costs at the high end of the range, it should be entitled to proceed.

This claim will be met with many questions and considerable skepticism. It is noteworthy that the Precautionary Principle does not appear in the governing Executive Orders; as we have seen, cost-benefit balancing is endorsed instead. The agency will therefore be required to show that the benefits justify the costs. Because the costs exceed the benefits for most of the range, it will not be easy for it to do so.

There are, however, several possibilities. If the statute requires the agency to proceed, or if it forbids consideration of costs, the question may well be at an end; agencies must follow the law. And if the agency can show that the high-end estimate is by far the most probable, so that the expected value of the rule exceeds $200 million, the benefits would appear to justify the costs. If the agency can show that the rule would produce significant nonquantifiable benefits, it may be able to proceed even if, taking account solely of quantified benefits, the expected value of the rule is negative. But on the facts as stated, there will be many questions in the review process.

Valuation of Mortality Risks

5. The annual costs of a regulation are $300 million. The regulation is expected to prevent forty premature deaths. The agency uses $9 million as the value of a statistical life (VSL), and therefore estimates the benefits as $360 million. In the absence of various imaginable problems, the regulation will likely go forward, because $9 million is within the range recommended by OMB for the VSL,[12] and also within the range suggested by the current technical literature.[13]

An important clarification: With these values, the government is not actually "valuing life." It is valuing the reduction of mortality risks— typically by eliminating low-level risks, for example, risks of 1 in 100,000. When it is said that a life is "worth" $9 million in such cases, what is really meant is that people are willing to pay, or ask to be paid,[14] $90, on average, to eliminate a risk of 1 in 100,000. I will explore this question in detail in chapters 4 and 5.

6. The annual costs of a regulation are $200 million. The regulation is expected to prevent ten premature deaths. The agency contends that the VSL is $21 million, and that the regulation is therefore justified. The

regulation is not likely to proceed (unless some statute says that it must). The $21 million figure is inconsistent with OMB guidance, which has a recommended ceiling of $10 million,[15] and is in any case well outside of the range of the technical literature, which shows little support for values as high as $21 million. The agency will have to produce a special justification to go forward, and it will not be easy for it to do so. And indeed, this example is wildly hypothetical, because no agency now uses a VSL in the vicinity of $21 million.[16]

7. Under Approach A, the annual costs of a regulation are $200 million. Under that approach, the regulation will save fifty-one lives annually. Under Approach B, the annual costs of the regulation are $300 million, and the regulation will save sixty lives annually. If a statistical life is valued at $4 million, Approach A is justified by the monetized figures, and Approach B is not. If a statistical life is valued at $7 million, both approaches are justified, and Approach B is better, because it has significantly higher net benefits. Because the technical literature supports a VSL of $7 million or higher, there is likely to be a great deal of interagency interest in Approach B. The agency would be entitled to use a VSL of $7 million (or higher) and to proceed on the ground that it has chosen the approach that maximizes net benefits. If it favors Approach A, it will likely face a number of questions about why it has done so.

8. The annual cost of a potential regulation, offering a new approach to safety in some area, is $200 million. The regulation is expected to save thirty lives. The agency uses a VSL of $4 million, and for that reason, it is reluctant to proceed, and it submits a draft rule that explains why it is maintaining the status quo. In the interagency process, there will be considerable interest in going forward with the new approach, because (as noted) the technical literature supports a VSL of $7 million or higher.

9. The annual costs of a regulation are $200 million. The agency uses a VSL of $8 million. The regulation is expected to prevent twenty-four premature deaths. The relevant deaths involve cancer. The agency argues that it should be able to use a "cancer premium,"[17] which would increase the VSL by 10 percent, thus ensuring that the benefits exceed the costs. This is an open question in the technical literature and in the federal government, and it is a legitimate subject for discussion. At the very least, it will be acceptable for the agency to do a sensitivity analysis in which it increases the VSL because cancer is involved.[18] It is possible

that with reference to the sensitivity analysis, the agency will be able to conclude that the benefits "justify" the costs.

10. The annual costs of a regulation are $1 billion. The annual benefits are $650 million. The majority of those benefits come from preventing seventy deaths, with each statistical life being valued at $8 million. The agency notes that of the seventy deaths, forty involve children under the age of five. It contends for reasons of equity, and because children and many "life years" are at stake, it is reasonable to proceed, notwithstanding the fact that the monetized benefits fall far short of the monetized costs.[19] This is a legitimate topic for discussion; the questions that it raises are open ones.[20]

11. The annual costs of a regulation are $300 million. It would prevent forty premature deaths annually. The agency uses a VSL of $8 million, and it concludes that the benefits justify the costs. The agency acknowledges that all of those deaths would involve elderly people—typically extending their lives by merely a few months. In the public comment process, some people object that it is not reasonable to use the standard VSL for very brief extensions of life. These objections will not go unnoticed in interagency discussions, but OMB guidance does not call for reducing the VSL in such cases.[21] The relevant question might well be discussed in the review process. Within the government, some people may agree with the objection expressed in the comment period.

12. The annual costs of a regulation are $300 million. It is anticipated to prevent thirty premature deaths each year. The agency uses a VSL of $8 million. The agency adds that the regulation will prevent a specified number of accidents or illnesses and also a specified amount of property damage, and it asserts that the value of these benefits exceeds $75 million. If the numbers survive interagency scrutiny, and if there is no other problem (such as an alternative approach that would have higher net benefits), the regulation will go forward, because the benefits justify the costs.

Wide Ranges

13. The annual costs of a regulation are $200 million. Approach A has annual benefits of $400 million to $900 million, and Approach B has

annual benefits of $500 million to $1 billion. Within the OIRA process, there will be considerable discussion of what accounts for the width of the ranges, and of whether an understanding of the underlying materials suggests that the ranges can be narrowed. If, for example, the agency is using several scientific studies, the question will be whether one of them is better, and whether it can be used to narrow the range or to produce a point estimate. And if the range is as wide as it is because the agency is using a VSL range of $1 million to $10 million (and this would be highly surprising, indeed so far as I know unprecedented), the interagency process will work toward using the technical literature to see if a single number can be used as the primary estimate. In principle, the estimates should be subject to probability weighting, to come up with some kind of expected value. In practice, probability weighting may not be possible. A great deal of work would be done to try to achieve greater precision and confidence in the numbers. We would need to know much more about Approach A and Approach B to be confident, but it is not impossible that Approach B dominates Approach A along every dimension.

14. The annual costs of a regulation are $200 million. The annual benefits range from $150 million to $400 million. Here as well, a great deal of work would be done to explore the benefits range. In principle, and as in (13), the estimates should be subject to probability weighting, to come up with some kind of expected value. Perhaps regulators can conclude that there is a 75 percent chance that the benefits are $150 million, a 10 percent chance that the benefits are $150 million to $200 million, a 10 percent chance that the benefits are $200 million to $300 million, and a 5 percent chance that the benefits are $200 million to $300 million. In the absence of some kind of probability weighting, many questions would be asked about whether the low ends of the range are the most highly probable, so that there is a realistic chance that the costs will exceed the benefits. Suppose—as is not unimaginable—that it is not possible to do more than to state the existence of a range. It would be tempting to consider using the midpoint for purposes of analysis, but without evidence establishing that the midpoint is accurate, this approach runs into obvious objections and concerns.[22]

15. The annual costs of a regulation are $1.5 billion. The annual benefits range from $800 million to $2 billion. As in previous cases, a great

deal of work would be done to explore the benefits range, and in fact, the agency will be asked in this case to do a formal uncertainty analysis, because the costs exceed $1 billion.[23] The various points within the range must, to the extent feasible, be subject to probability weighting, to come up with some kind of expected value. It is possible, of course, that existing information does not make such weighting feasible, but a great deal of technical work is likely to be done to obtain a better understanding of the range and of what might be done to narrow it. Especially because the economic stakes are so high, there will be considerable attention to the question whether the benefits actually exceed (or outweigh) the costs.

16. The annual costs of a regulation are $200 million. Under Approach A, the annual benefits are between $100 million and $400 million. Under Approach B, the benefits are between $50 million and $700 million. This example is also exceedingly unusual; in fact I cannot recall any like it. As in previous scenarios, there would be a great deal of interest in understanding what accounts for these ranges and whether they might be narrowed. There would be interest in exploring the possibility that Approach B has a higher expected value and should therefore be chosen.

17. The annual costs of a regulation are $200 million. The annual benefits range from $25 million to $225 million. It will be noticed that most of the benefits range is significantly lower than the cost. Reviewers will ask whether the agency can show that the higher ends of the range are more likely than the lower, or whether special circumstances (such as a legal requirement or nonquantifiable benefits, see chapter 3) are involved.

Cobenefits and Risk-Risk Trade-Offs

18. A regulation designed to reduce mercury emissions would simultaneously serve to reduce emissions of other air pollutants, including particulate matter.[24] While the benefits of mercury reductions cannot be monetized (because of the limitations of the existing science), the benefits of reducing particulate matter can be, and they clearly exceed the costs of the regulation. The agency invokes the cobenefits as part of its assessment of costs and benefits, and as a central factor in its explana-

tion of why the benefits justify the costs. Commenters on the proposed rule object that cobenefits should not be considered, because the rule is designed to reduce mercury emissions. Under OMB Circular A-4, the agency is entitled to consider the cobenefits. What the agency is required to do is to offer a full accounting,[25] and so long as they are real, and no double counting is involved, cobenefits are unquestionably part of that full accounting.

19. A regulation designed to increase fuel economy also has real effects on safety. The best analysis (we are speaking hypothetically[26]) suggests that those effects will be negative, in the sense that there will be a modest increase in deaths and accidents. The agency is required to discuss those negative effects and to include them in its full accounting.

20. The principal benefits of an energy efficiency requirement (applicable to refrigerators) will consist of economic savings for consumers. The rule would also provide significant benefits in terms of air pollution reductions, including greenhouse gas reductions, and energy security. Nonetheless, the costs would greatly exceed the benefits if the agency did not include consumer savings.

In the public comment period, some commentators contend that there is no market failure, that consumers should be able to make such choices as they like, and that the government cannot legitimately treat savings to consumers as "benefits." In the view of these commentators, the economic savings to consumers are purely "private" and do not deserve to count in the analysis. The commentators agree that air pollution reductions and energy savings do count—but as noted, they are significantly lower than the costs.

The agency is entitled to reject this contention. Agencies have long counted such private savings as benefits, and they are not prohibited from doing so. At the same time, the agency will have to meet two challenges. First, it will have to identify the relevant market failure. Drawing on behavioral economics, it may well be able to rely on behavioral market failures associated with the Energy Paradox[27]—suggesting that with respect to energy efficiency, consumers do not always make decisions that serve their long-term interests.[28] If the energy savings are not salient at the time of purchase, or if consumers are myopic (in the sense that they disregard or downplay the long term), consumers may make such decisions. In explaining the fuel economy rules issued in 2012, for example, the Department of Transportation referred to

> phenomena observed in the field of behavioral economics, including loss aversion, inadequate consumer attention to long-term savings, or a lack of salience of relevant benefits (such as fuel savings, or time savings associated with refueling) to consumers at the time they make purchasing decisions. Both theoretical and empirical research suggests that many consumers are unwilling to make energy-efficient investments even when those investments appear to pay off in the relatively short-term. This research is in line with related findings that consumers may undervalue benefits or costs that are less salient, or that they will realize only in the future.[29]

Second, the agency will have to investigate whether energy efficiency requirements might result in less desirable refrigerators. If so, there will be a consumer welfare loss. That loss must be treated as a cost, and possibly a high one. If, for example, refrigerators will cool less well, or if they will be less pleasing aesthetically, there will be an offsetting loss, potentially sufficiently high as to raise questions about the agency's basic analysis. The process of OIRA review will devote considerable attention to that possibility. Reviewers will want assurance that no significant consumer welfare loss will occur.

21. Same as (20), but the rule is designed to increase the fuel economy of vehicles. The agency invokes not only private fuel savings but also time savings as benefits. It notes that consumers will save a great deal of money at the pump, and also that they will have to go to the gas station far less often, thus saving time (and it monetizes that benefit). The agency finds that because these (private) benefits are high, the costs of the proposed regulation are justified. But without these benefits, the regulation could not easily be justified in that way.

As in (20), commentators object that the private fuel savings should not be counted, and also that time savings should not be counted, because consumers are perfectly able to take account of those savings in deciding which vehicles to buy. The agency is entitled to reject the objection. Again as in (20), it should identify the market failure[30] and explore the possibility of consumer welfare losses, which would unquestionably count as costs.[31]

Benefits, Hard or Impossible to Quantify

22. The annual costs of a regulation are $200 million. The regulation would increase water quality, but it would have no beneficial effects on human health, and the agency is unable to use market measures to quantify and monetize other benefits (for example, aesthetic or recreational benefits). The agency relies on contingent valuation studies (sometimes called "stated preference" studies), which suggest that people would be willing to pay a significant amount to improve water quality in the relevant respects. Reliance on such studies is not forbidden by OMB Circular A-4.[32] The interagency process will devote careful scrutiny to the relevant studies, to ensure that they are credible and meet appropriate standards; but they are not out of bounds.[33]

23. The annual costs of a regulation are $200 million. The monetized annual benefits are $175 million. The regulation is designed to promote building access for people in wheelchairs, and the agency believes that the $25 million shortfall is not fatal, because nonquantifiable values are involved. Those values may or may not be sufficient to justify the regulation. (See chapter 3 for details.)

24. Same as (23), but the cost of the regulation is $1 billion, not $200 million, and so the shortfall is $825 million. The question is whether that shortfall, which is (obviously) significant, can be justified by reference to nonquantifiable values. Authoritative documents do not give specific answers. To resolve the question, many agencies have found it useful to engage in what is called *breakeven analysis*, explored at length in chapter 3.

25. Same as (24), but we are dealing with a regulation designed to protect clean water, not disabled people. Suppose that the agency does not rely on contingent valuation studies but suggests that the nonquantifiable benefits are substantial and justify the costs. Relevant questions would be, How many water bodies? What kinds of improvements? What would those improvements actually achieve? Would they help hu-

man beings, and if so, how? An expenditure of $1 billion would not be easy to defend, assuming that the quantifiable benefits are in the range of $175 million, and unless the law required the agency to proceed, the rule would encounter serious questions.

Suppose, however, that once we investigate the details, we find that the rule would achieve a great deal—for example, because it would protect a very large number of water bodies, and do a great deal for them, with a wide range of aesthetic and ecological benefits (including the protection of fish and wildlife). Once these questions are explored, we may have enough to justify a serious discussion. If, by contrast, the number of water bodies is relatively small, and the benefits for them would not be great, a significant expenditure would not be easy to justify.

26. The annual cost of a regulation would be $100 million. It would have no easily monetized benefits. Its principal benefits would accrue to animals, in the form of longer and healthier lives (and let us stipulate far less suffering as well). One possibility would be to use stated preference studies to obtain monetary equivalents, though it would be challenging to make such studies credible and reliable. Another possibility would be to engage in breakeven analysis here as well. As before, a degree of quantification may be helpful short of monetization. Would there be benefits for human beings? Of what kind? How many animals would be helped? A very large number? How much would they be helped? A great deal? Answers to those questions might well prove to be clarifying.

27. A regulation is designed to reduce the risk of a financial crisis by stabilizing the financial system. Its annual costs are projected to be $400 million. The agency states that the regulation will make a crisis less likely, but it cannot quantify the extent of the effect. In its Regulatory Impact Analysis, the agency describes the cost of a crisis, if it should occur, and states that if the rule reduces the risk even by a very small percentage (which is specified), its benefits will justify its costs. These claims will receive considerable scrutiny in the review process. Under the circumstances, a form of breakeven analysis may be the best that can be done (again see chapter 3 for more details).

28. The annual cost of a regulation is $200 million. The annual benefits are $180 million. The benefits would be enjoyed by low-income workers, who would be protected from serious safety risks. The costs

would be imposed on companies that produce a good enjoyed mostly by wealthy people; let us stipulate that the costs would fall on consumers. The agency contends that while the benefits do not "exceed" the costs, the distributional impact matters, and supports its conclusion that the benefits "justify" the costs. The agency urges that the costs will be widely distributed throughout society and that the benefits will be enjoyed by an especially vulnerable group. In principle, this argument is fully available under Executive Order 13563, which explicitly refers to "distributive impacts." (Recall the idea of prioritarianism, which emphasizes the importance of protecting the least well-off, even if the result would be to sacrifice overall welfare.[34])

Net Benefits

29. The costs of a regulation, under Approach A, are $250 million. The benefits range from $350 million to $400 million. Under Approach B, the costs of the regulation are $1 million, and the benefits are $250 million. The strong presumption would be in favor of Approach B. Although the benefits of Approach B are significantly smaller, the net benefits are higher. Net benefits are what matter. Unless the law requires Approach A, or unless special considerations can be identified (such as nonquantifiable benefits to Approach A), there will be considerable interest in Approach B.

30. The costs of a regulation, under Approach A, are $1 billion. The benefits are $200 million. Under Approach B, the costs are $20 million, but the benefits are merely $1 million. Approach A has a cost-benefit ratio of 5 to 1, whereas Approach B has a cost-benefit ratio of 20 to 1. While Approach B seems unlikely to meet the requirements of the applicable Executive Orders, because its costs exceed its benefits, it is far preferable to Approach A, because (and this is a fundamental point) *what matters is the net benefits figure, not the cost-benefit ratio.*[35] To see the point, consider a rule with costs of $1 and benefits of $10, and compare that rule with one having costs of $300,000 and benefits of $400,000. The first has a benefit-cost ratio of 10 to 1, and the second has a far inferior 4 to 3 ratio—but in terms of social welfare, net benefits of $100,000 are much

better than net benefits of $9, and the whole point of cost-benefit analysis is to provide some insight into how to increase social welfare.

Climate Change

31. The annual costs of a regulation are $200 million. As a result of air pollution reductions, the regulation will produce monetized health benefits of $50 million. It will also eliminate ten million tons of carbon dioxide emissions. The central value for the social cost of carbon is around $36,[36] and hence the ten-million-ton reduction is valued at $360 million. The benefits of the regulation appear to justify the costs. If the numbers are reliable, and if there is no legal or other problem, it can go forward.

32. The annual costs of a regulation are $450 million. The regulation will produce annual health benefits, as a result of air pollution reductions, of $30 million. It will also eliminate ten million tons of carbon dioxide emissions annually. The central value for the social cost of carbon is $36, and hence the ten-million-ton reduction is valued at $360 million. In light of standard requirements, the benefits of the regulation do not appear to justify the costs, and serious questions will be raised in the process of interagency review.

Invoking the latest work by economists and scientists, however, the agency contends that the social cost of carbon figure is too low and that it should be at least $60 per ton, in which case the benefits would justify the costs. This argument would be unsuccessful. The social cost of carbon was a product of an interagency process, and it reflects the official position of the U.S. government. Until it is changed through an appropriate process, it is binding.

33. Same as (32), except that the agency notes that the social cost of carbon is a range, not a point estimate,[37] and that at the higher end of the range, the relevant figures are $58 and $109, and that with these values, the benefits justify the costs. The agency contends that the central value should not be decisive and that it should be able to exercise its discretion so as to proceed. This contention would be an appropriate matter for discussion.

Discount Rates

34. Same as (32), but the agency notes that many people believe that a low discount rate is justified for the climate change problem, and that with an appropriately low rate—say, 2 percent—the regulation is justified. This argument would be unsuccessful. The official discussion of the social cost of carbon includes a discussion of the discount rate problem and settles on a particular approach. It was a product of an interagency process, and it reflects the position of the U.S. government. Until it is changed through an appropriate process, it is binding.

35. The cost of a regulation is $200 million. At a 7 percent discount rate, the benefits are $120 million. At a 3 percent discount rate, the benefits are $170 million. At a 2 percent discount rate, the benefits are $205 million. The agency contends that the appropriate discount rate is 2 percent. There are no issues of intergenerational equity; the principal benefits will occur in the next fifteen years. The regulation will run into serious questions. OMB Circular A-4 calls for discount rates of 7 percent and 3 percent, and it does not allow agencies to depart from those figures (with a qualification for very long time horizons[38]). Until OMB Circular A-4 is changed, it is binding, because it reflects the official position of the U.S. government. (Note that a low discount rate, sometimes thought to be in the interest of future generations, may actually harm them, because it may lead to precautions that lead to lower economic growth, thus damaging them.[39])

36. The cost of a regulation is $200 million. At a 7 percent discount rate, the benefits are $150 million. At a 3 percent discount rate, the benefits are $210 million. The agency proposes to use a 3 percent discount rate. It is possible that the agency may proceed. Circular A-4 offers relevant guidance:[40]

> As a default position, OMB Circular A-94 states that a real discount rate of 7 percent should be used as a base-case for regulatory analysis. The 7 percent rate is an estimate of the average before-tax rate of return to private capital in the U.S. economy. . . . It approximates the opportunity cost of capital, and it is the appropriate discount rate whenever the main effect of a regulation is to displace or alter the use of capital in the private sector. . . .

The effects of regulation do not always fall exclusively or primarily on the allocation of capital. When regulation primarily and directly affects private consumption (e.g., through higher consumer prices for goods and services), a lower discount rate is appropriate. The alternative most often used is sometimes called the "social rate of time preference." . . . If we take the rate that the average saver uses to discount future consumption as our measure of the social rate of time preference, then the real rate of return on long-term government debt may provide a fair approximation. Over the last thirty years, this rate has averaged around 3 percent in real terms on a pre-tax basis.

It follows that the choice between 7 percent and 3 percent depends on whether the costs of regulation fall on the allocation of capital or on private consumption. In practice, agencies have often used both measures, and as a general rule, the choice between 7 percent and 3 percent has not mattered to the ultimate decision about whether and how to proceed.

Admirable Problems and Institutional Constraints

My goal in this chapter has been to explore how certain highly stylized problems are likely to be handled, in an effort to cast light on the real world of cost-benefit analysis. Inside the federal government, the central decisions are made by reference to authoritative documents and to standard operating procedures under the shadow of those documents—a kind of common law for cost-benefit analysis.

Needless to say, legitimate and even serious objections might be mounted against some existing practices. The problem of climate change raises especially vexing questions. Some people have questioned the analysis that underlies the current social cost of carbon.[41] One of my central points here is an institutional one. Substantive judgments are embodied in binding documents and settled practices. If they are to be changed, it is typically a result of an extended process, which will involve many officials and sometimes a public comment period, and which is likely to bear fruit only if and when a consensus emerges. As we saw in chapter 1, that process embodies a form of "government by discussion."

To be sure, this constraint can cause real problems, because it might ensure that decisions that are imperfect, or worse, remain entrenched for significant periods. A form of status quo bias—well known within behavioral economics[42]—is unquestionably part and parcel of government practice. But the constraint is also an important safeguard. By ensuring both internal and external scrutiny of new initiatives, it increases the likelihood that they will become binding only if their foundations are genuinely secure.

THREE

Dignity, Financial Meltdown, and Other Nonquantifiable Things

A Problem, a Practice, and a Puzzle

This chapter explores a problem, a practice, and a puzzle. The problem is that the benefits of regulations are sometimes nonquantifiable (in the sense that agencies lack information that would make quantification possible). The practice, which is widespread within the U.S. government, is *breakeven analysis*.[1] The puzzle is whether breakeven analysis is or can be made adequate, or at least good enough for government work. My principal goal is to resolve that puzzle by exploring what breakeven analysis should entail and how agencies should use it in deciding whether and how to proceed.

It will be useful to clarify the practice before we begin. Suppose that you are deciding whether to take a vacation in Florida, to drive to an adjacent state in order to purchase a desirable product, or to join a sports club. In all of these cases, you might have a clear sense of the costs but only a vague sense of the benefits, which may not be quantifiable. You might think, *What would the benefits have to be, in order to justify the costs?* Breakeven analysis, thus understood, plays a significant role in ordinary life.

It plays a role in business as well. Suppose that a real estate investment company does not know for how much certain apartments will rent, but it does know that other, less desirable apartments in the area rent for $900 per month. Suppose too that the company knows that the investment will be worthwhile if it can rent its apartments for more than $800 per month. If so, it makes sense to proceed. Or consider the decision whether to purchase insurance in circumstances in which potential purchasers cannot quantify the probability of a bad outcome. In deciding whether to proceed, potential purchasers might well engage in a kind of informal breakeven analysis.

When benefits cannot be quantified, breakeven analysis is also a significant part of federal agency practice. Agencies typically engage in a kind of *conditional cost-benefit analysis*, stating that the benefits would justify the costs if certain assumptions hold and certain conditions are met. At the same time, the practice has thus far remained unanalyzed, and its uses and limitations remain unclear—hence the puzzle.

In response to that puzzle, my first and principal suggestion is that breakeven analysis *is most helpful when agencies are able to identify either a lower or upper bound for regulatory benefits, with point estimates or with estimates of expected value.* In such cases, agencies might say that a regulation with an annual cost of $200 million, but with nonquantifiable benefits, is justified if and because the lower bound for such benefits is at least $200 million. It should be clear that when lower bounds can be specified, agencies are faced with only partial nonquantifiability. Uses of breakeven analysis frequently depend on an implicit understanding to this effect. Agencies have generally not made that understanding explicit. I suggest that they should do so.

When lower or upper bounds cannot be specified in any way, it might be objected that breakeven analysis is not much more than a description or a hunch—or (when an agency decides to proceed) a shorthand way of announcing that the agency is in favor of precautions. But even without lower or upper bounds (and this is my second suggestion), breakeven analysis can be made more tractable if agencies draw comparisons with cases in which monetary values have previously been assigned.

As we have seen, the value of a statistical life is now around $9 million. When dealing with nonquantifiable benefits, that value can help to orient judgment about whether to proceed. In fact the value of a statistical life might provide an upper bound for an assortment of regulatory benefits (including harms that fall short of death), and in this way, the comparison can make breakeven analysis more useful. Agencies have assigned monetary values to a number of other benefits, and those assignments might provide helpful orientation when they deal with nonquantifiable benefits.

These points suggest a simple framework for use in dealing with non-quantifiable benefits. When quantified benefits justify quantified costs, of course, agencies should proceed (to the extent permitted by law). When quantified benefits do not justify quantified costs, but when non-quantifiable benefits are involved, agencies should identify those benefits and, to the extent possible, identify lower and upper bounds. They might be able to do so because of existing information about the problem at hand or because of relevant information from comparison cases. After lower and upper bounds have been identified, agencies should add that information to the benefits estimate, and, to the extent permitted by law, proceed if the benefits justify the costs (and not if otherwise).

In some cases, however, agencies will not be able to identify lower and upper bounds in any way, and breakeven analysis will be helpful largely insofar as it explains what information is missing and why some cases are especially difficult. In such cases, a distinctive feature of breakeven analysis is the specification of the conditions under which benefits would, in fact, justify costs. If the absence of information makes the specification less than conclusive for purposes of decision, at least it will be useful in identifying the assumptions under which the benefits would justify the costs, and thus in promoting transparency and accountability, and perhaps in spurring acquisition of information in the future. As we will see, this kind of conditional justification plays a significant role in current practice.

My focus throughout is on regulatory policy, but it should be clear that the implications are far broader. In many areas of law and policy, it is important and perhaps even necessary to catalog both costs and benefits and to explore whether the benefits justify the costs. In the law of tort, of course, judgments of negligence may depend on some such inquiry.[2] Budgetary decisions may also depend on an accounting of costs and benefits.[3] In numerous domains, that accounting matters, and non-quantifiable variables turn out to be relevant. What is said here may well be relevant to those domains as well.

Three Challenges for Quantifiers

The task of quantifying regulatory benefits raises many puzzles.[4] Agencies have long produced a monetary value for the loss of a life,[5] but skeptics doubt both the sense and morality of such efforts.[6] As noted in chapter 2 (and explored in detail in chapters 4 and 5), agencies do not "value life" or assign monetary values to a human life. Instead they are concerned with statistical mortality risks—finding, for example, that people are willing to pay $90, and no more, to eliminate a risk of 1 in 100,000.[7] If this is true as an empirical matter, then agencies might build on that evidence to value risks of 1 in 100,000 at $90 as well. A practice of this sort has become pervasive. Those influenced by behavioral economics might note that willingness to pay need not equal willingness to accept,[8] and perhaps we should be asking how much people are willing to accept to face mortality risks. But the answers to such questions do not appear to be different from those that are given to willingness to pay questions.[9]

When it is objected that some regulatory benefits are not quantifiable, the central claim might be that public officials cannot specify important numbers (for example, the number of premature deaths prevented by an air pollution regulation or by a measure designed to reduce the risk of terrorist attacks), or that even if they can do so, such officials cannot, and perhaps should not, turn those numbers into monetary equivalents. Consider, for example, the dignitary benefits produced by protecting personal privacy or by allowing people in wheelchairs to use public bathrooms without the assistance of others. The objection to monetization might take three different forms. *First*, regulators might lack reliable tools for converting the relevant benefits into money. They might not know how much people are willing to pay to obtain (or how much they would be willing to accept to give up) such benefits. (Do regulators actually know how much people would be willing to pay to protect their privacy online?) *Second*, regulators might think that even if they did know, the resulting numbers would not be the appropriate basis for policy. Is willingness to pay the appropriate measure of provision of access to people in wheelchairs?[10] *Third*, regulators might want to emphasize that human goods are diverse, not unitary, and they might conclude that human dignity is not the "equivalent" of a stated monetary sum. The three objections might apply to many different problems, and they require independent treatment.

It is true that the lack of reliable tools can be a serious challenge, and in fact it is my central topic here. I shall be exploring a large number of benefits that cannot be monetized easily or at all, simply because we lack relevant information. The second objection raises quite different issues. Suppose that we learn that people in wheelchairs would pay $200 each year to have independent access to public bathrooms. Does that mean that government should value that benefit at $200 per person? The answer is hardly clear. Perhaps the willingness to pay figures are not entirely informative;[11] perhaps they do not answer the right question.[12] Perhaps independent access would give people in wheelchairs a great deal in terms of welfare (even if they are not willing to pay a lot), and perhaps those who paid the relevant amounts would not lose much in welfare terms. Or perhaps an access requirement would promote a distributive goal—promotion of equality of opportunity for disabled people—and the willingness to pay numbers should not be decisive when we are deciding whether and how to promote that goal.

These are points about the possible limitations of the willingness to pay criterion (see chapters 4 and 5). Note that even if we insist on those limitations, we will have to assign *some* value to the protection of dignity. It is not possible to escape some such assignment. Perhaps the willingness to pay number is a lower bound or the place to start.[13]

It is also both true and important that human goods are plural rather than unitary. In his great essay on Bentham, John Stuart Mill made the point in a passage that is worth quoting at length:[14]

> Nor is it only the moral part of man's nature, in the strict sense of the term—the desire of perfection, or the feeling of an approving or of an accusing conscience—that he overlooks; he but faintly recognises, as a fact in human nature, the pursuit of any other ideal end for its own sake. The sense of honour, and personal dignity—that feeling of personal exaltation and degradation which acts independently of other people's opinion, or even in defiance of it; the love of beauty, the passion of the artist; the love of order, of congruity, of consistency in all things, and conformity to their end; the love of power, not in the limited form of power over other human beings, but abstract power, the power of making our volitions effectual; the love of action, the thirst for movement and activity, a principle scarcely of less influence in human life than its opposite, the love of ease:—. . . . Man, that most complex being, is a very simple one in his eyes.

Because human beings are complex rather than simple, they value the goods at stake in regulation in qualitatively distinct ways.[15] They do make trade-offs among diverse goods,[16] but without valuing them in the same way. Any effort to quantify and monetize the wide range of variables involved in regulation might be seen as erasing qualitative differences among human goods. Suppose that a rule would protect human health, improve visibility, reduce risks to animals, decrease employment, and increase the costs of energy. If so, does it really make sense to align those effects along a monetary scale?

If we seek to obtain a full understanding of the various values at stake, the answer may well be negative. But that answer is not a decisive objection to quantification and monetization, if these are understood as an effort, not to provide that full understanding, but to ensure that we are in a good position to make trade-offs among the relevant values. The argument for quantification is intensely pragmatic (recall Franklin's algebra). It is important to know whether it is worthwhile to spend $100,000, $1 million, $5 million, or $20 million to achieve certain goals. Whether we are explicit about the trade-offs or not, we will be spending a specific amount, and neither more nor less, to achieve those goals.

Quantification helps to promote accountability, transparency, and consistency, and it can also counteract both excessive and insufficient stringency. When regulators quantify and monetize relevant goods, the goal is to promote sensible choices, not to erase differences among qualitatively distinct goods. Nor should this point be unfamiliar from daily life. People decide how much to spend to educate their children, on health insurance, to reduce risks on the highway (as, for example, by purchasing especially safe cars), on food, on housing, and on vacations. When they make trade-offs among these and countless other diverse goods, they do not pretend that they are qualitatively identical.

Lack of Information

We have seen that under Executive Order 13563, agencies are required to produce detailed regulatory impact analyses for economically significant rules,[17] and indeed, that Executive Order requires agencies "to quantify anticipated benefits and costs as accurately as possible."[18] We have also seen that this requirement, alongside a commitment to scientific integrity, attests to the importance of both quantification and monetization. A primary goal is to ensure that regulations are based on a fair assessment of the likely consequences—on evidence and data rather than intuition, dogma, and anecdote.[19] But the same Executive Order recognizes that, because of conceptual and empirical obstacles, quantification may present serious challenges. Thus the Order states that "each agency may consider (and discuss qualitatively) values that are difficult or impossible to quantify, including equity, human dignity, fairness, and distributive impacts."

Both outsiders and insiders are aware that in some important cases, an absence of information makes it difficult or even impossible to quantify the benefits of federal regulations.[20] This point can be understood as a Hayekian one, pointing to the limited information of even the most expert and well-motivated officials.[21] In areas that include terrorism, financial reform, environmental protection, and civil rights, numbers or monetary values may not be easy to generate.

In the most extreme (and admittedly rare) cases, agencies may be operating under circumstances of *ignorance*, in which they cannot specify either outcomes or probabilities.[22] Alternatively, agencies may be operating under uncertainty rather than risk,[23] in the sense that they may be able to identify the range of possible outcomes, but without being able to specify the probability that any of them will occur. They may know, for example, that a certain regulation will reduce the likelihood of terrorist attack, but they may not be able to quantify the probability that such an attack will occur, or even the likely result if it does. They might know the direction of an effect, but they might be unable to say much about the magnitude. They may know that a regulation will reduce the risk of financial catastrophe, but they may not know the extent of its contribution.[24] They may know that a rule will reduce the number of rapes in prison, but they may not know by what amount.

In some cases, agencies might be able to specify either ranges or lower and upper bounds, without being able to offer probability estimates. They might know that a rule would save between 2,000 and 4,000 lives, without having a clear sense of the probability that it will save 2,000, 2,500, 3,000, 3,500, or 4,000.[25] And in other cases, individuals may have, or believe that they have, specific knowledge about probabilities and outcomes, but government as a whole might not, in the sense that officials might not be able to achieve consensus on the relevant judgments. For example, some individuals in government might credit the studies that a rule will save 2,000 lives and no more, but others might believe that those studies are not reliable—and the government, as an institution, might lack an agreement on anything other than a range.

In the area of climate change, the government has identified a social cost of carbon, but the "central value" in 2013 (about $36) is part of a range (from about $11 to about $107).[26] No one thinks that these numbers represent the last word on the underlying questions of science and economics (or ethics). It is exceptionally challenging to attempt to identify an "expected value" with respect to the harms of climate change.

Even when agencies are able in some sense to *quantify* the benefits of regulation, they may not be able to *monetize* those benefits. An agency may know that a rule will help to protect an endangered species by saving a specified number of its members (or at least a specified range), but it may not have confidence in any effort to turn that benefit into monetary equivalents. An agency may know that a rule will reduce water pollution, thus producing ecological benefits, but it may not know how to monetize those benefits. Perhaps an agency is able to project the number of prison rapes that will be prevented by a regulation, but it may not be confident about any effort to turn those benefits into dollars. An agency may know that a rule will reduce the risk of a terrorist attack, but it might have great difficulty monetizing the costs of such an attack, even if it can produce nonmonetary estimates for a range of potential consequences. The indirect costs of a terrorist attack (including both economic and emotional effects) make monetization exceptionally difficult.

An agency might believe that a rule would have dignitary as well as economic benefits—for example, because it will require employers to provide reasonable accommodation to people with mental illness. Even if it has a sense of the number of people who will be benefited, it may not be able to monetize those benefits. To be sure, some tools are available for monetizing some of these benefits (including willingness to pay and contingent valuation studies), but it may not be feasible to use those tools in particular cases, and they may not be reliable even if their use is feasible.[27]

An agency might also be motivated by considerations of equity or fairness, or by distributional considerations. For example, the Affordable Care Act forbids insurance companies from denying people coverage because of preexisting conditions and disallows lifetime limits on coverage. How should agencies decide whether the benefits of implementing regulations justify the costs? As noted, Executive Order 13563 expressly authorizes agencies to consider equity, fairness, and distributive impacts. Perhaps the Affordable Care Act, and other statutes that make such considerations relevant, are sufficiently prescriptive that agencies must go forward whatever the costs and benefits. In such cases, any analysis is essentially irrelevant to the ultimate decision—but it must nonetheless accompany economically significant rules (see chapter 1). How shall agencies proceed?

Or suppose that the agency has a measure of discretion. It might be inclined to say that the benefits of its preferred approach, understood in terms of (say) equity, justify the costs. On ground of equity, the agency might be drawn to prioritarianism, which, as I have noted, places special emphasis on helping those at the bottom of the social ladder. But how does it know if the equity benefits are sufficient to provide the necessary justification? The agency might seek to answer by quantifying the number of people who are helped and also by specifying the extent to which they are helped. If large numbers of people are being helped, and if they are being helped in important ways (perhaps because their longevity is increased), the agency might start to get traction, if only because it knows some of the most important numbers. But if it is unable to turn them into monetary benefits, how can the agency compare such numbers against (say) a cost of $500 million?[28]

Of course all of these points might hold for costs as well. For example, a rule that improves scanning technology at airports might be thought to impose privacy "costs" insofar as it makes bodily images available to those who see them. Some people vigorously object to the imposition of those costs, but the agency might not be able to turn them into monetary equivalents. But because the problem of nonquantifiability is far more common for benefits than for costs, and because the underlying analysis is the same in the two contexts, I focus on benefits here.

The Practice

As noted, the central goal of breakeven analysis is straightforward. It is to pose this question: How high would the benefits have to be, in order for the costs to be justified? Those who engage in such analysis hope that, however simple, that question will help agencies to answer otherwise intractable questions. To orient the discussion, here are seven applications. The examples are highly stylized, but each of them draws very closely on actual uses of breakeven analysis (see appendix D).

1. A regulation is designed to protect clean water. It costs $200 million. The benefits, which are ecological and do not involve human health, cannot be quantified. The agency does not know exactly what the benefits will be (except at a certain level of generality); on the basis of current knowledge, it cannot specify them. It certainly is unable to monetize those benefits. Nonetheless, the agency is inclined to believe that the nonquantifiable benefits are likely to be substantial and may well justify the costs. Under breakeven analysis, relevant questions would be, How many water bodies would be affected? What kinds of improvements can be expected? What would those improvements actually achieve? Would they help human beings, and if so, how?

Suppose that there are only twenty relevant water bodies, that they are relatively small, that they lack a great deal of aesthetic or recreational importance, that human health is not involved in any way, and that for each of those water bodies, the improvement in water quality, while real, would be modest. Under breakeven analysis, an expenditure of $200 million would not be easy to defend. The question would be, On what assumptions is it worthwhile to spend $10 million per water body for such apparently modest improvements? Unless there is a reasonable answer to this question, the agency is likely to elect not to proceed.

Now suppose that there are two hundred thousand such water bodies, that some of them are very large, and that the improvement in water quality would be substantial, with attendant ecological benefits (including significant recreational benefits). Under those assumptions, much more would have to be said to obtain a full picture. But the argument for proceeding would be plausible under breakeven analysis as it is ordinarily used, and the agency might well go forward.

2. The agency is imposing a new disclosure requirement on the automobile industry, designed to ensure that consumers can learn about the economic and environmental benefits of increased fuel economy.[29] The cost of the requirement is $15 million. The agency knows (on the basis of evidence) that, with the new requirement, the public will have a significantly better understanding of those benefits and thus be able to make more informed decisions and to save money. The agency believes that the social gains will be substantial, especially in light of the fact that it anticipates annual sales of over twelve million cars. At the same time, it is not able to specify those social gains. The agency does not know how to monetize more informed decision making as such, and it does not know how much consumers will save as a result of the new requirement. But the agency is inclined to conclude that under breakeven analysis, the requirement is justified, because millions of people are likely to incorporate the information and to save money.

3. An agency is issuing a regulation designed to reduce the incidence of prison rape.[30] The annual cost of the regulation is $470 million. The agency cannot specify the number of prison rapes that the regulation will prevent. In addition, it believes that its efforts to monetize the costs of prison rapes—suggesting a value of between $300,000 and $600,000 per rape prevented—are speculative and tentative. Under breakeven analysis, it nonetheless decides to go forward. It finds that at least 160,000 prison rapes occur every year, and it concludes that if a single rape is valued at $500,000, the rule would be easily justified if it prevented only 1,600 rapes, about 1 percent of the total. It believes that the rule is highly likely to achieve that goal.

4. The annual cost of an animal welfare regulation, issued under the Animal Welfare Act, would be $200 million. The regulation would have no easily monetized benefits. Its principal benefits would accrue to animals, in the form of longer and healthier lives (and let us stipulate far less suffering as well). One possibility would be to use stated preference studies to obtain monetary equivalents, though it would be challenging to make such studies credible and reliable, and though the agency does

not believe that the results of any such study would fully capture the benefits of its regulation (which would accrue principally to animals, not people). Another possibility would be to engage in breakeven analysis here as well. As before, a degree of quantification may be helpful short of monetization. Would there be benefits for human beings? Of what kind? How many animals would be helped? A very large number? How much would they be helped? A great deal? The agency believes that answers to those questions would prove to be clarifying.

5. A regulation is designed to reduce the risk of a financial crisis by stabilizing the financial system. Its annual costs are projected to be $200 million. The agency states that the regulation will make a crisis less likely, but it cannot quantify the extent of the effect. In its analysis, the agency describes the cost of a crisis, if it should occur, and adds that if the rule reduces the risk by even a very small percentage (which is specified), its benefits will justify its costs. The agency also explains why its regulation would contribute to that reduction. Under the circumstances, the agency thinks that a form of breakeven analysis is the best that can be done. Having offered that analysis, with an account of the costs of a crisis and the potential contribution of the rule to reducing the underlying risk, it is inclined to proceed.

6. A regulation is designed to reduce the risk of a successful terrorist attack by requiring improved scanning technology at airports. The cost of the technology is $900 million. The Transportation Security Administration is unable to quantify the benefits. It notes, however, that the cost of even a single terrorist attack can be far in excess of $900 million. Applying breakeven analysis, the agency concludes that the requirement is justified. It states that even if the probability of an averted terrorist attack is very small, the benefits justify the costs in light of the extraordinary cost of such an attack. It offers some rough numbers to support that conclusion.

7. A regulation costs $500 million. Its goal is to make buildings more accessible to people who use wheelchairs.[31] The monetized benefits of the regulation are $450 million. The agency contends that the regulation will promote human dignity—for example, by allowing wheelchair-bound workers to have access to bathrooms. It cannot monetize the dignitary value of the regulation. It does not have willingness to pay studies in this domain, and it is skeptical about the idea that the results of those

studies would be sufficiently informative. But applying breakeven analysis, it concludes that the regulation is justified, because the dignitary value is at least $50 million.[32]

The Puzzle

To be sure, the cases just given are different from one another. In all of them, quantification is difficult or impossible, but the underlying reasons are divergent. Whatever the source of the problem, the appeal of breakeven analysis is not obscure. By hypothesis, standard cost-benefit analysis is not possible. In the absence of such analysis, the agency calculates the costs and offers a judgment about the conditions under which the benefits would justify them, along with an explanation of that judgment. Recall the standard uses of a rough form of breakeven analysis in ordinary life, and also its uses in business. The challenge is to understand the underlying structure of that analysis and to see how it might be made both useful and disciplined.

Easy Cases, Hard Cases

Before exploring that structure, let us simply observe that under the basic approach, some cases do seem genuinely easy. Suppose that a rule would cost $1 billion and that the nonquantifiable benefits would seem modest in individual cases and accrue to a very small set of beneficiaries—for example, by improving disclosure to them about potential economic savings from a particular energy-efficient appliance. Unless there are special circumstances, it is probably sensible to conclude that the expenditure is not worthwhile. To be sure, the number of beneficiaries may not be decisive (perhaps each is being helped a great deal), but if the value of a statistical life is $9 million, it will be hard to justify an expenditure of $1 billion to benefit a very small group. And if a rule would cost merely $10,000 and if the nonquantifiable benefits are real and would accrue to a very large group, it might well make sense to move forward.

When cases are difficult, a virtue of breakeven analysis is that it helps to explain why, exactly, that is the case. If a rule would reduce the risk of a financial crisis by some unquantifiable amount and cost $500 million, the reason for the difficulty is clear. And if a rule would cost $500 million but produce $450 million in monetizable benefits by enabling people in wheelchairs to have easier access to bathrooms, the $50 million shortfall might turn out to raise hard questions. The question would be, What are the nonquantifiable benefits that might make up the difference? As we shall see, it might be feasible to provide an answer.

Floors and Ceilings

It would be possible to insist that when breakeven analysis turns out to be helpful, there must be at least a degree of quantification. An agency may not be able to specify benefits, but it might have a sense (perhaps intuitive, perhaps more formal than that) of a lower or upper bound—and that sense may be doing the real work in breakeven analysis.

Point estimates. Suppose that a rule would cost $1 million and prevent, as a lower bound, twenty incidents of prison rape. We might be able to say that the lower (monetary) bound, in terms of prevention of a single prison rape, is certainly over $300,000, and hence the rule is justified. When an agency says that a rule survives breakeven analysis, it is often saying that the rule's benefits have a floor, in the form of a sufficiently high lower bound. In individual lives and in business decisions, breakeven analysis often works in precisely that way; the same is true in government.

Suppose, by contrast, that a rule would cost $500 million and prevent only a few cases of relatively harmless water pollution. In that case, the higher bound would not justify the rule. Or suppose that the cost of a financial crisis is $1 trillion and that the cost of a regulation, designed to reduce the risk of such a crisis, is $5 billion. With these numbers, the agency might decide that the probability that the regulation will avoid a crisis is at least or at most $1/n$, and if n can be specified, the agency will have a better sense of whether to proceed.

When an agency says that a rule does not survive breakeven analysis, it might well be saying that the benefits have a ceiling. The upper bound of the benefits of the rule is insufficiently high to justify the rule. It follows that breakeven analysis is most useful when the agency is able to quantify and monetize the floors or ceilings of the relevant benefits. If so, it might nonetheless have a great deal of difficulty in deciding which approach maximizes net benefits, but at least it should be in a good position to say whether benefits justify costs.

Within this framework, we could imagine different degrees of knowledge, precision, and candor. In the most straightforward cases, the agency is actually able to identify a point estimate for the lower or upper bound. In such cases, its conclusion—that the regulation is or is not justified—is reliable and not speculative (so long as the numbers can be trusted). The uncertainty exists in producing a point estimate or possibly even a range beyond the relevant bound.

Expected value. In other cases, the agency cannot make a point estimate, but it can describe the range of benefits at the lower and upper ranges, and perhaps specify an expected value at the low and high ends. Suppose, for example, that the cost of a rule is $100 million, and that at the low end, the benefits range from $80 million to $300 million. (This example might be realistic if the agency can quantify but not monetize the benefits.) If the agency can produce a probability distribution,[33] the ultimate judgment might be tractable even if, at the middle and higher ends, the agency is at sea.

To be sure, assessment of expected values might present serious empirical challenges, especially in cases of the kind I have outlined. In most cases, agencies are unlikely to have anything like a probability distribution. It may well be important to examine the question of density and to explore how often the benefits may fall below the breakeven point. Even when agencies do not have a full probability distribution, however, they may have a sufficient if rough sense of expected value, one that enables them to decide whether to proceed.

Nonquantifiable versus Nonmonetizable

Quantification without monetization. Suppose that the agency is able to quantify the benefits but not to monetize them. For example, it might know a great deal about the effects of regulations designed to protect water quality, to reduce prison rape, and to protect privacy or wheelchair access, but even if it can specify those effects, it may not know how to turn them into monetary equivalents. Is breakeven analysis helpful in such cases?

As before, the easiest problems arise when monetary equivalents have a lower bound. Suppose that we have reason to believe that the lowest value for prevention of a rape is $300,000. If so, perhaps that is all we need to know to find that the benefits justify the costs. The same is true in cases of upper bounds. If a statistical life is worth $9 million, then that amount, or something below it, might serve as an upper bound for a wide variety of injuries and diseases. When quantification is possible but monetization is not, lower bounds and upper bounds might nonetheless be feasible. And even if they are not, perhaps it is possible to generate expected values or lower and upper bounds.

Monetization without quantification. More subtly, breakeven analysis might be helpful when agencies can monetize benefits but cannot quantify them. Suppose that an agency knows that in each case, a "benefit unit" is worth $5,000, but that it cannot specify the number of units that a regulation will produce. Even when this is so, perhaps the agency can specify lower or upper bounds with respect to the number of units. An agency might know that the regulation will produce at least 10,000 benefits units, or that it will produce at most 5,000 of them. Or perhaps the agency cannot make point estimates but can produce expected values with respect to benefits units. If so, it might be able to use breakeven analysis when monetization is possible and when quantification is not.

Comparisons

Is breakeven analysis at sea in the absence of lower and upper bounds? At first, it might seem so—but perhaps not. Agencies might engage in a series of comparisons that help to discipline the analysis. Generalizing from the example of the value of a statistical life, they might examine monetary equivalents that are well established, and compare those to the nonquantifiable benefits at hand.

For example, it would be hard to defend an approach that would value a modest improvement in water quality at the same level as a human life.

It would also be hard to defend an approach that would value the life of a sea otter at the same level as a human life. An agency might not know the monetary value of protection of human dignity through wheelchair accessibility, but it would seem extravagant to assign a value in excess of the value of human life. By comparing nonmonetizable benefits to those benefits that have been monetized, agencies might be able to use breakeven analysis to gain traction in difficult cases.

In fact agencies have a significant comparison set on which to draw, certainly in the domain of health. For example, EPA values a nonfatal heart attack between $100,000 and $200,000; cardiovascular problems at $42,000; chronic lung disease at $21,000; and an emergency visit for asthma at $430.[34] For purposes of breakeven analysis, it would be possible to draw on such figures to make more informed choices. (See appendix E for a number of valuations.)

Sparse Knowledge and Conditional Justifications

It is evident that the hardest cases will arise when agencies cannot produce floors, ceilings, or expected values, when neither quantification nor monetization is possible, and when comparisons are not helpful. In such cases, agencies use breakeven analysis to produce *conditional justifications*, which may not resolve the question whether they should go forward, but which have the virtue of providing information about what is missing, and about what kinds of assumptions would be necessary to provide a basis for proceeding. (Of course it remains true that agencies must proceed if the law requires them to do so, whatever the outcome of cost-benefit analysis.)

Consider a water pollution regulation that would cost $200 million while producing ecological benefits that cannot be either quantified or turned into monetary equivalents. The case would be more tractable if the agency knows (1) that the number of benefited water bodies is either small or large, (2) that the benefited water bodies are important (in some relevant sense) or not, and (3) that the improvements in water quality are either de minimis or very large. But if the answers to all of these questions are unclear (fortunately, an unrealistic assumption), how shall it proceed? Or return to the case of financial regulation and suppose that a rule would cost $500 million and that it would contribute, in a way that cannot be specified, to reduction of the risk of a financial crisis (unfortunately, not an unrealistic assumption). If the agency decides to go forward with the rule on the ground that the benefits justify the costs, it is essentially opting for precaution, relying on a hunch, or stating the conclusion. The same is true if the case involves protection against the risk of terrorist attack.

Critics might object that in cases of this kind, breakeven analysis is not useful, because it cannot do relevant work and is giving the agencies no traction in deciding whether to go forward. On the most extreme version of this objection, agencies might as well flip a coin, at least until they acquire additional information. Perhaps breakeven analysis draws attention to the need to acquire that information, and in that sense might eventually spur its acquisition; but in its absence, the analysis cannot offer much help.

The objection has considerable force. But defenders of breakeven analysis might respond in the following way. Some cases are genuinely hard.[35] On the basis of what the agency knows, neither action nor inaction is readily justified. The reason is that crucial information is absent. To be sure, agencies should work to acquire that information, but if it is lacking, they must be candid about that fact. When they exhaust the limits of what they know and are uncertain whether to proceed, at least breakeven analysis helps them to specify the source of uncertainty, and what they would need to know in order to reduce it.[36] Moreover, and importantly, conditional justifications have the advantage of transparency, because they specify the factual assumptions that would have to be made for the benefits to justify the costs. That specification is exceedingly important, because it can promote accountability, because it can promote consideration of the plausibility of those assumptions, and because it can also promote testing and revisiting over time as new information becomes available.[37]

What Breakeven Analysis Can and Cannot Do

In ordinary life, breakeven analysis is a common practice. In government, it is a reasonable way to handle the problem of nonquantifiability, above all when agencies can produce lower or upper bounds, which may show that on any plausible assumptions, a certain approach is or is not justified. Sometimes lower or upper bounds take the form of a point estimate; sometimes they represent expected values. Agencies should clarify their use of breakeven analysis by explicitly referring to the use of such bounds. It should be clear that if they are able to do so, the problem of nonquantifiability is only partial.

When lower or upper bounds are unavailable, it is far more challenging to use breakeven analysis. I have suggested that agencies can enlist comparisons, above all by reference to cases in which monetary values have previously been assigned. If, for example, the value of a statistical life is $9 million, then injuries and illnesses that fall short of death cannot plausibly be valued in excess of $9 million, and a wide variety of other harms must be assigned a lower value as well. When useful comparisons are not available, breakeven analysis is not much more than a conclusion or a hunch, but at least it can help to identify what information is missing and why some cases are genuinely hard. Breakeven analyses sometimes amount to conditional justifications. Such justifications are far from useless, because they promote transparency and allow scrutiny of the assumptions on which they are based.

FOUR

Valuing Life, 1: Problems

The Question and an Extended Preview

We have seen that in order to conduct cost-benefit analysis, agencies must assign monetary values to the human lives that would be saved by a proposed regulation. How do they come up with the numbers that they use? Do some deaths count for more than others?

No agency treats cancer risks, or other mortality risks that produce unusual fear or involve special suffering, as worthy of more concern (and a higher monetary valuation) than other risks. No agency contends that distinctive values should be assigned to the risks associated with airplane deaths, motor vehicle deaths, or deaths from defective children's toys. No agency treats young people as worth more than old people. No agency values the lives of poor people less (or more) than the lives of rich people. No agency distinguishes between whites and African Americans or between men and women. For statistical lives, the governing idea is that each life is worth exactly the same. With respect to cost-benefit analysis, much is disputed. But on the idea of a uniform value per life saved, there is a solid consensus, at least in terms of regulatory practice.

The stakes are not low. If cost-benefit analysis is the basis for the ultimate decision to approve or reject a proposed regulation, a lot may turn on the selected VSL. If an agency uses a VSL of $15 million, many more regulations will be justified than if it uses a VSL of $2 million. And if a uniform number is rejected, the pattern of justified regulations will shift dramatically. Some existing regulations will be revealed as too weak, and more stringency will be required; others will seem too aggressive and will have to be weakened or even eliminated. If agencies shifted to using VSLs that varied along one or more dimensions, the regulatory system would look very different from how it does today.

In this chapter and the next, I intend to question the consensus in favor of a uniform VSL, and to do so in a way that raises foundational issues about the economic valuation of human lives. In brief, I suggest that the governing theory involves both welfare and autonomy. On that theory, regulators value risks not by consulting their own intuitions or asking abstract questions, but by seeing how actual people value risks. This approach can claim to promote people's welfare, because it does not force them to buy more risk protection than they want. It can also claim to respect people's autonomy, because it follows their own judgments about risk protection. By building on actual choices, government can counteract some of its own informational deficits, and rely on some of the advantages of free markets. But this theory does run into serious questions and objections,[1] and I will turn to them in chapter 5.

For present purposes, one implication is clear: Under the governing theory, a uniform value is obtuse. In light of the very approach that agencies use to produce the current numbers, VSL should vary along two dimensions. VSL is calculated based on people's willingness to pay (WTP) to avoid particular risks, and if WTP is particularly high, VSL will be high as well. For two reasons, VSL should be expected to be variable, in a way that makes a uniform number senseless.

First, VSL should vary across risks. For example, some evidence suggests that people are willing to pay high amounts to avoid cancer risks, and hence there is reason to think that people's VSL is higher for cancer deaths than for sudden, unanticipated deaths.[2] Cancer risks are involved in the work of many regulatory agencies, and while the evidence is not yet decisive, people do seem to be particularly concerned about such risks, in a way that might well produce a high VSL—very possibly higher than the values that agencies now use. More generally, deaths that produce unusual fear,[3] or that are accompanied by high levels of pain and suffering, should be expected to produce a higher VSL. Human beings face countless mortality risks. It would be truly bizarre to maintain that people value avoiding each of those risks identically.

Second, VSL should vary across individuals, simply because different people are willing to pay different amounts to avoid risks.[4] People who are risk averse will be willing to pay more, and will therefore show a higher VSL, than people who are risk seeking. Those who are rich will show a higher VSL than those who are poor. People who are thirty might well show a higher VSL than people who are seventy.[5] It follows that different demographic groups will show diversity in their VSLs as well.[6] To be sure, some and perhaps all of these points run afoul of widespread moral intuitions, and I will engage them in due course.

If these two forms of variability—across risks and across persons—are put together, it will be clear that a unitary number is far too crude. Each person in society is willing to pay a distinctive amount to avoid each risk. It follows that, in theory, each person should have a particular VSL for each and every risk, resulting in a fully individuated VSL. Such a fully individuated VSL would mean, for example, that agencies would likely value avoidance of cancer risks more highly than many other mortality risks—and that the VSL of some racial groups would likely be lower than that of others.[7] But the latter differences would not be the result of a governmental decision to take racial characteristics into account; in fact it would not be a product of any kind of group-level discrimination on the government's part.[8] The differences would be the result of disaggregating VSLs for individuals.

Such differences can be found today in ordinary consumer markets, which establish prices for the reduction of the statistical risks associated with smoke alarms, unusually safe cars, and much more. It is highly likely that people in different demographic groups—men, women, the elderly, the young, Hispanics, African Americans—pay different amounts to reduce statistical risks. This is not invidious discrimination. It is a product of different values, tastes, and situations (including economic situations).

In practice, of course, a fully individuated VSL is not feasible, for two different reasons. First, government lacks the information that would permit the calculation. Regulators do not know how much each person would be willing to pay to reduce each statistical risks. Generalizations through the use of categories are therefore inevitable. Second, many regulatory programs involve collective goods and protect many people at once. A clean air regulation, for example, cannot easily ensure that some people in a geographical region are exposed to no more than 10 parts per billion (ppb) of some pollutant, while others in the same region are subjected to 50 ppb. Because collective goods are typically involved in regulation, the problem is pervasive. When government is providing a regulatory good to many people at once, feasibility requires that it use a single VSL, not a range of VSLs.

Notwithstanding issues of feasibility, an understanding of the reasons for individuating VSL is important for two reasons. The first involves conceptual clarity. When a particular VSL is used (say, $9 million), it is because the agency estimates that people are willing to pay a certain amount to reduce statistical risks of a specified magnitude. If the real question is the identification of values for the reduction of risks, a unitary VSL will be hard to defend, simply because there is no such thing. An appreciation of the case for individuation will clarify the theory— both its rationale and its limitations, empirical and ethical. I emphasize that the theory is undergirded by considerations of both autonomy and welfare—and that those considerations also show when the use of WTP to calculate VSL is misguided.

The second reason involves the possibility of moving some distance toward greater individuation, even if full individuation is not feasible. With respect to the reduction of cancer risks, for example, there is reason to believe that people are willing to pay an extra amount. For this reason, the government's current valuation of cancer risks is probably too low, resulting in underprotection of the public. Similarly, there is reason to think that VSL should be higher for mortality risks from airplanes than for statistically identical risks on the highways.[9]

A far more troublesome problem, to which I will devote considerable attention, involves disparities along demographic lines. For now, notice a simple factual point: WTP is dependent on ability to pay, and those with little income and wealth will show lower WTP.[10] It follows that the VSL of poor people, when calculated on the basis of WTP, will be lower than the VSL of rich people, simply because poor people are poorer. Suppose that a $9 million figure is used by the EPA and that it represents the average WTP of a population-wide sample. When risks are faced disproportionately by wealthy people, VSL, based on actual WTP, should be higher than $9 million. On the same view, VSL should be lower when the regulated risks are faced disproportionately by poor people.

Some people believe that cost-benefit analysis should be conducted with "distributive weights" (sometimes called "distributional weights"), which would respond to the fact that poor people, by virtue of their poverty, have less willingness to pay.[11] A poor person might be willing to pay a small amount to reduce a risk, not because reducing that risk would not give that person a lot of welfare, but because of poverty. A distributive weight would seem to supply a correction. The irony is that an individuated VSL might go in the opposite direction by giving a higher figure for rich people than for poor people. But if we are really tracking WTP, that is the correct conclusion.

It is inevitable that people in poor nations will have a lower VSL than people in rich nations, a point with strong implications for international variations in VSL and for valuation of the harms from climate change. Similarly, people in poor areas will have a lower VSL than those in wealthy areas, a point with implications for valuation of a variety of risks in the domestic setting. If variations across risks and persons are significant, the question of individuation should be a central part of the next generation of cost-benefit analysis—a step beyond the first-generation debate about whether to do such analysis at all, and a step toward doing such analysis in a way that is more refined and more closely attuned to the consequences of regulations in terms of choice, welfare, and distributional equity.[12]

Of course it is offensive and wrong to suggest that, in principle, poor people are "worth less" than rich people. If poor people are subject to a risk of 1/10,000, they do not have less of a claim to public attention than wealthy people who are subject to exactly the same risk. In fact they may have a greater claim, if only because they lack the resources to reduce that risk on their own. Those who believe in "prioritarianism" insist that government should give special attention to those who are least well-off, even if the result would be to decrease overall welfare. Consider, for example, the choice between two options. (a) Give $200 million in benefits to the entire population. (b) Give $190 million in benefits to those at the bottom of the economic ladder. It is quite possible that (b) is preferable strictly on welfare grounds, because those at the bottom of the economic ladder may get more, in terms of welfare, from that option than the entire population would from (a). But if (b) is preferable on welfare grounds, it would be better on prioritarian grounds, and prioritarianism has powerful defenses.[13]

But the topic here is regulation rather than subsidy, and the two ought not to be confused. In principle, government should not force people to buy protection against statistical risks at a price that seems excessive to them. At least as a general rule, people should not be required to pay $70 to reduce a risk of 1/100,000 if they are willing to pay no more than $50.

If a uniform VSL would actually benefit the poor, there is a strong argument for a uniform VSL. But (and this is the key point) regulation based on a uniform VSL may or may not produce a more equitable distribution of income. In fact any redistribution may be perverse, and a single VSL might not promote equality at all. (If wealthy people are the principal beneficiaries of a particular regulation chosen on the basis of a uniform VSL, and if the public as a whole pays for it, then any redistribution will benefit the wealthy, not the poor.) And if poor people are forced to pay an amount for risk reduction that exceeds their WTP, desirable redistribution will hardly result. Forced exchanges, on terms that people would voluntarily reject, are not a good way of redistributing wealth to the disadvantaged. (Requiring poor people to buy Volvos is not the most sensible means of assisting them.) On the other hand, it is possible that some regulatory programs, based on a uniform VSL, will help those in need, if their beneficiaries receive risk reduction for which they pay little or nothing—an issue to which I will devote considerable attention.

A larger lesson follows from this discussion. For purposes of law and politics, there is no sensible answer to the abstract question about the correct monetary value of human life (or more accurately, about statistical mortality risks). Whether government should use a higher or lower VSL across demographic lines cannot be answered simply. Any judgment about the appropriate VSL, and about individuation, must be heavily pragmatic. It must rest on the human consequences of one or another choice.

An important implication involves the assessment of VSL across nations. A poor nation would do well to adopt a lower VSL than a wealthy nation; for China or India, it would be disastrous to use a VSL equivalent to that of the United States or Canada. But this point should not be taken to support the ludicrous proposition that donor institutions, both public and private, should value risk reduction in a wealthy nation more than equivalent risk reduction in a poor nation. Here again is a pragmatic point. Donors may well want to give more to poor nations than to wealthy ones, because the former are poor. But that conclusion does not mean that regulators in poor nations should use a VSL equal to that of regulators in rich nations. If they did, they would make their nations poorer.

Now for the details.

WTP: Theory and Practice

To produce monetary amounts for statistical risks, agencies rely on two kinds of evidence. The first and most important involves real-world markets, producing evidence of compensation levels for actual risks. In the workplace and in the market for consumer goods, additional safety has a price; market evidence is investigated to identify that price. The second kind of evidence comes from contingent valuation studies, which ask people how much they are willing to pay to reduce statistical risks. The relevant risks usually are in the general range of 1/10,000 to 1/100,000. The calculation of VSL is a product of simple arithmetic. Suppose that workers must be paid $900, on average, to assume a risk of 1/10,000. If so, the VSL would be said to be $9 million.

For a few of the foundational labor market studies on which agencies have long relied, consider table 4.1.[14]

A large advantage of labor market studies of this kind is that they

TABLE 4.1: Labor Market Studies on the Value of Life

Study	VSL (in US$)
Kniesner and Leith (1991)	.7 million
Smith and Gilbert (1984)	.8 million
Dillingham (1985)	1.1 million
Marin and Psacharopoulos (1982)	3.4 million
V. K. Smith (1976)	5.7 million
Viscusi (1981)	7.9 million
Leigh and Folsom (1984)	11.7 million
Leigh (1987)	12.6 million
Garen (1988)	16.3 million

avoid the lively disputes over the use of "willingness to pay" or "willingness to accept" (WTA) in regulatory policy.[15] In both experiments and the real world, people tend to demand more to give up a good than they are willing to pay to obtain it in the first instance—a disparity that seems to complicate efforts to assign monetary values to regulatory benefits, including mortality and morbidity.[16] If people are willing to pay $25 to eliminate an existing risk of 1/100,000, but demand $100 to incur a new risk of 1/100,000, then it is difficult to know how to proceed for purposes of monetary valuation of risks. Should agencies use $25, $100, or some intermediate figure?

Fortunately, this problem dissipates in the context of labor market studies. If workers who face a risk of 1/10,000 are paid $600 more for doing so, and if workers who refuse to face such a risk are paid $600 less, then it is irrelevant whether agencies speak in terms of WTP or WTA. And as I have noted, there appears to be no difference between the two in this context.[17]

Of Welfare and Autonomy

Why do regulators care about market valuations of statistical risks? There are two answers. The first and more conventional involves welfare. The second and perhaps more interesting involves autonomy.

In economic terms, market valuations provide a strong clue to the welfare consequences, for individuals, of one or another outcome. Suppose that people are willing to pay $60, but no more, to eliminate a risk of 1/100,000. If so, then it might be assumed that their welfare is increased by asking them to pay that amount—and that their welfare is decreased by asking them to pay more. There are many demands on people's budgets. If they prefer not to spend more than $60 to eliminate a risk of 1/100,000, it may be because they would like to use their money for food, shelter, recreation, education, or any number of other goods. It is true that with respect to mortality risks, people may be inadequately informed or suffer from some form of bounded rationality (emphasized by behavioral economists), and if so, there might be reason to question their judgments. I will return to this point. But so long as such problems are not involved,[18] the welfare argument is straightforward.

Perhaps regulatory policy should not be based on welfare. Perhaps it is unclear what "welfare" really means; perhaps welfare is not what matters. Even if so, WTP might be defended on the ground of personal autonomy. On this view, people should be sovereign over their own lives. Government should respect people's choices about how to use limited resources (again so long as those choices are informed). When people decline to devote more than $90 to the elimination of a 1/100,000 risk, it is because they would prefer to spend the money in a way that seems to them more desirable. If regulators do not use people's actual judgments, then they are insulting their dignity.

Consider in this regard Amartya Sen's instructive words on Friedrich Hayek's great work, *The Road to Serfdom*.[19] Sen points to "Hayek's insistence that any institution, including the market, be judged by the extent to which it promotes human liberty and freedom. This is different from the more common praise of the market as a promoter of economic prosperity."[20] Sen urges that it "is the perspective of seeing markets and other institutions in terms of their role in advancing freedoms and liberties of individuals that Hayek brought into singular prominence." WTP is based, of course, on market ordering, and it can claim a strong foundation in respect for individual freedom. The use of WTP therefore can claim a simultaneous defense from both utilitarian and deontological accounts.

Questions and Doubts

Nonetheless, serious questions might be raised about the use of the labor market and other studies by federal agencies. Most obviously, table 4.1 shows significant variety in the crucial numbers. In fact a more general look at the VSL data produces further puzzles, wider ranges, and some stunning paradoxes.

Some studies find no compensating differentials at all, indicating a VSL of zero[21]—implausibly low, to say the least, for purposes of policy. Others find that nonunionized workers receive *negative* compensating differentials for risk—that is, they appear to be paid less because they face mortality risks.[22] Another study finds that African Americans receive no significant compensating wage differential and hence that their particular VSL is zero.[23] On the other hand, some studies find VSLs actually above those presented in table 4.1; consider one finding that for people who choose jobs with low-level risks, the VSL is as much as $22 million.[24]

The most detailed meta-study, far more comprehensive than the EPA's own analysis, identifies a central value in the general vicinity of $8 million and finds that most studies produce VSLs ranging from $3.8 million to $9 million.[25] That range is fairly compressed, in a way that suggests that the range is not alarmingly wide. For many regulations, the "bottom line" of the cost-benefit assessment will not be affected by a choice of $3.8 million or $9 million. But that range still leaves significant room for discretion, in a way that could have implications for policy and law. Consider the fact that the monetized value of a program that saves two hundred lives would range from $760 million to $1.8 billion; note also that the EPA's highly publicized arsenic regulation, issued by the Bush Administration after considerable controversy, would easily fail cost-benefit analysis with a $3.8 million VSL but easily pass with a $9 million VSL. The simple point is that the variety of the outcomes raises some questions about the reliability of any particular figure. (Note that on the basis of their reading of the technical literature, agencies actually use a narrow range of $6 million to $9 million, with increasing consensus in the vicinity of $9 million.)

I have noted that the relevant numbers deserve respect only if they do not result from an absence of information or bounded rationality on the part of the people whose choices generate them. Suppose, for example, that workers do not know the risks that they face or that their decisions are products of the availability heuristic (see chapter 6) or unrealistic optimism.[26] In either case, regulators should not use, for purposes of policy, a finding that workers are paid $60 to run a risk of 1/100,000; by hypothesis, that number does not reflect a rational trade-off by informed workers. Current practice is based on an assumption, not that all or even most workers make informed choices, but that market processes ensure the right "price" for various degrees of safety. Compare pricing for soap, cereals, and telephones: most consumers do not have full information and use heuristics that lead them astray, but market competition produces a sensible structure of prices, at least most of the time. Perhaps the same is true of statistical risks. I will explore this question in detail in chapter 5.

The Value of Statistical Risks

Suppose that the relevant problems can be solved and that regulators can identify a number, call it $9 million, that really represents people's valuations. Recall that even if this were so, it would be grossly misleading to offer the following suggestion: *The value of a statistical life is $9 million*. It would be much more accurate to say that for risks of 1/10,000, the median WTP in the relevant population is $900—or that for risks of 1/100,000, the median WTP is $90. If true, these statements would, on assumptions later explored, be extremely helpful for purposes of policy. But even at first glance, it is clear that these numbers need not be taken to support a VSL that is independent of probability.

Suppose that people would be willing to pay $90 to reduce a risk of 1/100,000. From this it need not follow that people would be willing to pay $9 to eliminate a risk of 1/1 million, or $9,000 to reduce a risk of 1/1,000, or $90,000 to reduce a risk of 1/100. It is plausible to think that people's WTP to reduce statistical risks is nonlinear. As the probability approaches 100 percent, people become willing to pay an amount for risk reduction that rises nonlinearly to 100 percent of their wealth; as the risk approaches zero, WTP nonlinearly approaches nothing. For a risk of 1/1 million, for example, some reasonable people would be unwilling to pay anything, treating that risk as inconsequential.

Hence the claim that VSL is $9 million is merely a shorthand way of saying that people are willing to pay from $900 to $90 to eliminate risks of 1/10,000 to 1/100,000. Because this is the range for risks with which most agencies deal, the relevant data are at least informative. For current purposes, this point is the crucial one.

Individuation

One of my basic claims is that VSL will inevitably vary across both risks and persons. If people's WTP is higher to avoid cancer risks than risks of unanticipated, sudden deaths, then the use of a VSL, drawn from studies of the latter risks, will provide insufficient protection of the exposed population. If people in different occupations are paid different amounts to incur a risk, then use of a uniform VSL will not track actual behavior, which is what it is supposed to do. If wealthy people show a higher WTP than poor people, then a uniform WTP, based on a population-wide median, will ensure insufficient protection of wealthy people and excessive protection of poor people—in a way that might well prove harmful to both groups. And if the use of WTP is justified on grounds of welfare and autonomy, then a more individuated approach is justified on those same grounds.

I begin this section by considering differences among risks and then exploring differences among persons. I then explain and endorse the claim that in theory, full individuation, giving all people the risk reduction for which they are willing to pay, is required by the prevailing theory. From this point, I emphasize the problem with full individuation, which is that it is not feasible. But an intermediate approach, moving in that direction, would make a great deal of sense.

RISKS

I have emphasized that the data that underlie the current unitary VSL come largely from risks of accidents in the workplace—and that even if these data could be generalized, they would not justify a probability-independent VSL. But there is a point of greater practical importance. A 1/100,000 risk of dying in a workplace accident might well produce a different WTP from a 1/100,000 risk of dying of cancer from air pollution, which might in turn be different from a 1/100,000 risk of dying in an airplane as a result of a terrorist attack or a 1/100,000 risk of dying as a result of a defective snowmobile. The very theory that lies behind the government's current use of VSL justifies a simple conclusion: *VSL should be risk specific; it should not be the same across statistically equivalent risks.* The use of a single number almost certainly produces significant blunders and incorrect decisions about the appropriate amount of regulatory protection.

1. Data. To test these issues in an informal and preliminary way, I conducted a small contingent valuation study. Eighty-four University of Chicago law students were asked about their WTP to eliminate each of five risks of 1/100,000. The simplest of these risks involved dying from an automobile accident as a result of a defective brake. The four other risks might be expected to occasion greater concern; they involved deaths from lung cancer, AIDS, Alzheimer's disease, and airplane crashes resulting from terrorist attacks. The 1/100,000 risk of dying in an automobile accident produced a mean WTP of $156, whereas the four other accidents produced higher values (ranging from $184 for the AIDS risk to $193 for Alzheimer's disease).

In addition, there was substantial heterogeneity across individuals. For each of the questions, about ten respondents were willing to pay nothing to eliminate the 1/100,000 risk, producing a VSL of zero. At the opposite end of the spectrum, about fifteen people were willing to pay at least $500 to eliminate each of the 1/100,000 risks, producing a VSL of $50 million. This small, informal study suggests that even within a relatively homogenous group (law students), people do not treat statistically identical risks in the same way, and indeed there are differences across persons as well as across risks.

With respect to the data on which agencies generally rely, notice initially that the very category of "workplace risks" conceals relevant differences. The American economy contains a wide range of occupations and industries, and a uniform VSL should not be expected to emerge from each of them. Indeed, one study finds significant differences across both occupations and industries,[27] with blue-collar workers showing a higher VSL than others.[28] It is inevitable that a wide range of values would emerge from studies looking separately at machine operators, executives, sales associates, dental technicians, equipment cleaners, security guards, and secretaries[29]—and diverse values undoubtedly could be found within each category.

If we turn to environmental protection in particular, we might note that many risks controlled by the EPA are qualitatively different from the workplace risks that the EPA has used to generate its VSL. Two differences are particularly important. First, the workplace studies do not involve cancer, and cancer risks are often involved in environmental decisions. As noted, there is evidence that the risks associated with cancer produce a higher WTP than other kinds of risk.[30] For example, Professors Hammitt and Liu find that in Taiwan, WTP to eliminate a cancer risk is about one-third higher than WTP to avoid a risk of a similar, chronic degenerative disease.[31] Some contingent valuation studies suggest that people are willing to pay twice as much to prevent a cancer death as an instantaneous death.[32] Because people seem to have a special fear of cancer, they appear willing to pay more to prevent a cancer death than a sudden, unanticipated death, or a death from heart disease.[33] The "cancer premium" might be produced by the "dread" nature of cancer; it seems well established that dreaded risks produce special social concern, holding the statistical risk constant.[34]

I have noted that existing evidence on this count is not unambiguous. One study of occupational exposures does not find a significantly higher VSL for cancer risks.[35] But that study assumes that occupational cancers account for 10 to 20 percent of all cancer deaths—an amount that is almost certainly too high. If occupational exposures account for 5 percent of all cancers—a far more realistic number—then the VSL for cancer risks may be as high as $12 million, about double the amount that the EPA now uses. The current findings do conflict.[36] But in principle, the VSL figures should be risk specific, and some evidence supports the view that cancer risks produce an unusually high VSL.

The second difference between workplace risks and the risks that concern the EPA is that the latter risks seem peculiarly involuntary and uncontrollable.[37] Unlike the risks of workplace accidents, (most) pollution risks are not assumed voluntarily in return for compensation.[38] Some research suggests that involuntary, dread, uncontrollable, and potentially catastrophic risks produce unusually high levels of public concern.[39] The research is far from conclusive, but if so, the numbers that derive from workplace accidents might understate WTP for regulatory benefits provided by the EPA and many other agencies.[40] (I will return to some of the complexities here.)

The implications of risk-specific VSL go well beyond the distinction between workplace accidents and environmental risks. For example, people appear to be willing to pay far more to produce safety in the air than on the highways.[41] If this evidence is reliable, that VSL should be higher for the Federal Aviation Administration than for the National Highway Traffic Safety Administration. Some diseases would produce a higher VSL than others. A 1/100,000 risk of death from Alzheimer's disease, for example, might well produce a higher VSL than a 1/100,000 risk of death from a heart attack. A 1/50,000 risk of an AIDS death might not produce the same VSL as a 1/50,000 risk of death from a defective brake system on an automobile. Perhaps most people would pay more to reduce a risk of dying from slow-acting strokes than from strokes that kill outright. There might be a distinctive, population-wide median VSL for mortality risks of airplane accidents, of cancer from air pollution, of motor vehicle accidents, of defective toys, of cancer from water pollution.

In fact studies that have been done for seatbelt use, automobile safety, home fire detectors, and more find a wide variety of numbers, producing a VSL ranging from $770,000 (smoke detectors, based on data from the 1970s) to $9.9 million (fatality risks associated with safety belts and motorcycle helmets).[42] And within each of these categories of risk, further distinctions would undoubtedly emerge. All cancer fatalities are not the same; informed people would surely make distinctions between those that involve long periods of suffering and those that do not. If agencies are really interested in basing VSL on WTP, then a uniform number, treating all statistically identical mortality risks as the same, is too crude.

2. *Practice.* When I worked in the Obama Administration, we did not distinguish among mortality risks, and the same is true of my predecessors at OIRA. But at least in principle, such variations might be seriously considered. In the context of arsenic regulation, for example, the EPA was alert to some such variations. Hence its own sensitivity analysis for arsenic suggested the need for an upward revision of 7 percent because of the involuntariness and uncontrollability of the risk. In fact some people believe that this adjustment might be too low. Law professor Richard Revesz suggests that "the value of avoiding a death from an involuntary, carcinogenic risk should be estimated as four times as large as the value of avoiding an instantaneous workplace fatality."[43] Under this approach, the VSL, in the context of arsenic, would jump from $6.1 million to $24.3 million. I am not arguing that $24.3 million is the correct number; I am suggesting only that VSL, based on WTP, is almost certainly risk specific.

3. *Qualifications.* Three qualifications are important. First, psychological studies showing heightened public concern about particular risks may not translate into higher WTP. Social scientists might be able to show that certain qualitative factors make people especially concerned about certain risks, but it is an independent question whether and how much their WTP increases as a result. A number of studies of WTP at

least suggest affirmative answers to that question, raising the possibility that VSL should vary significantly across risk types.[44]

Second, there is no simple or rigid distinction between the involuntary/uncontrollable and the voluntary/controllable. It is a mistake to believe that risks can be neatly separated into the two categories. Are the risks from air pollution in Los Angeles involuntarily incurred? The answer might seem to be affirmative, but people can choose whether to live in Los Angeles. Are the risks of airplane travel uncontrollable? Many people think so, but the decision to fly is certainly under human control. Death from an asteroid seems to be a model case of involuntariness, at an opposite pole from hang gliding. But exactly why?

In deciding whether a risk is faced involuntarily or whether it is within personal control, the underlying issues seem to be whether those exposed to the risk are exposed knowingly and whether it is costly or otherwise difficult for people to avoid the risk. In general, the question would be whether WTP varies across risks because of factors of this kind, and on that question, evidence is crucial. When risks are approached in these terms, it is likely that some risks are worse than others, even if the probability of harm is identical. This point is enough to raise questions about a unitary VSL.

Third, it is possible that extreme aversion to certain risks reflects a form of bounded rationality—and it might be doubted whether bounded rationality should be allowed to play a role in regulatory policy. Suppose, for example, that people really are willing to pay twice as much to avoid a cancer risk as to avoid a sudden, unanticipated death. Is it so clear that these numbers must be decisive for purposes of policy, assuming that the contingent valuation study is reliable? They might not be *if* there is reason to believe that the WTP figures are not accurately measuring people's welfare; cancer is very bad, of course, but perhaps the WTP figures are suggesting an excessively large difference between cancer risks and other fatal or potentially fatal risks. Maybe people are in some sense phobic about cancer, and the phobia is inflating their answers beyond reasonable bounds. And is it even plausible to think that the "cancer premium" is so high that it actually doubles the cost of death? Is it reasonable to think that a death from cancer is actually *twice* as bad as a death that is sudden and unanticipated?

To be sure, a degree of pain and suffering typically accompanies cancer, and that fact illustrates the obtuseness of using the same number for cancer risks as for risks of sudden, unanticipated deaths. But it is not easy to defend the set of (exotic) values that would lead to the conclusion that the relevant pain and suffering is as bad as death itself. If WTP does not accurately measure welfare in the case of cancer, and if the inflated numbers for cancer deaths are a product of an intuitive recoil or terror at the idea of cancer, then regulators may not want to use what are, by hypothesis, the unrealistically high monetary values.

For those who emphasize autonomy rather than welfare, perhaps this point does not amount to an objection to the use of WTP. If the goal is to respect people's autonomy, regulators may defer to their judgments even if those judgments are mistaken. But if people show an especially high WTP because of a visceral reaction to cancer, or because of insufficiently thoughtful assessments of the stakes, then it is not clear that respect for autonomy requires regulators to track WTP. Government does not respect people's autonomy if it follows their uninformed choices, and this proposition raises doubts about government's use of uninformed WTP.

The central conclusions are simple. The least controversial uses of WTP numbers involve informed, rather than reflexive, judgments about the nature of the harms involved. Insofar as informed judgments point to different values for different risks, it makes sense for regulators to consider using different values. The best argument for caution is not one of principle. It involves the question about whether we know enough to include those differences.

PERSONS

Even when risks are identical, people differ in their values and their preferences. Everyone should agree that in workplaces and elsewhere, individual WTP is highly variable. Some of the variability stems from different degrees of aversion to different risks. Some people are especially concerned to avoid the dangers associated with pesticides, whereas others focus on the risks of air travel. Some of these differences are a product of beliefs about existing risk levels, while others result from different tastes and values.

So too, people with high levels of background risk should be expected to be willing to pay less to avoid an additional risk of 1/100,000 than those with low levels of background risk. If a relevant population lives in dangerous conditions, and faces fifty different annual mortality risks of 1/10,000 or higher, it should be expected to show a lower VSL with respect to a new risk of 1/100,000 than a population that lives in safe conditions and whose background risks are less serious.[45] The difference between the VSL of people in wealthy nations and that of people in poor nations, taken up below, is partly a product of the fact that the latter group generally faces far higher background risks.

It is likely that WTP varies with respect to age as well. It is reasonable to predict that other things being equal, older people will show a lower WTP and hence a lower VSL, simply because they have fewer years left. One study finds that the VSL of a forty-eight-year-old is 10 percent lower than that of a thirty-six-year-old; another finds that people under forty-five have a VSL twenty times higher than people over sixty-five.[46] A careful analysis suggests that VSL peaks around age thirty, stays constant for about a decade, but declines from that point, so much so that the VSL for a sixty-year-old is approximately half of that of a person between thirty and forty.[47] Existing evidence does suggest the likelihood of a lower VSL for those in the very last stages of life than for those who have many decades to live—and perhaps this difference ought to be reflected in regulatory policy.

These findings raise particular conundrums in the case of children. How should government proceed if the VSL for those between infancy and fifteen years of age is low, simply because they have little or no money? It is implausible to use a tiny VSL for them, but what number should be used, and why? In terms of government practice, little progress has been made on this question,[48] as agencies use the ordinary, uniform number for children as for everyone else. But some research suggests that this is a mistake and that children should be valued more highly.[49] There is evidence that parents would pay twice as much to avoid a statistical risk faced by a child as a statistical risk faced by an adult. If the standard VSL is $9 million, then we might expect a VSL of $18 million for children. Indeed, this number is based on parents' willingness to pay, and it might seem too low (and perhaps far too low) insofar as it does not include the welfare loss that would be experienced by children themselves. On the other hand, the relevant evidence comes from contingent valuation studies, which are of uncertain reliability and which typically find a lower VSL than do revealed preference studies, which account for the $9 million figure.

Along the same lines, many analysts suggest that regulatory policy should focus not on the value of statistical lives but on the value of statistical life years (VSLY).[50] Suppose that they are right. If so, then the statistical lives of young people are likely to be worth more than the statistical lives of older people. The government's interest in focusing on VSLY led to widespread public objections to what, under one proposal, was characterized by critics as a "senior death discount." That discount would have valued someone over seventy as "worth" $0.62 on the dollar.[51] At first glance, it seems unacceptable to value older people at some fraction of the value assigned to younger people. But if we assume that people over seventy are willing to pay about 62 percent, on average, of what younger people are willing to pay, the theory that underlies current practice justifies exactly this disparity. If the theory is right (a question to which I will turn), then a disparity between older people and younger people makes perfect sense if and to the extent that the WTP figures justify it.

As I have suggested, those with little money will show a far lower VSL than those who have plenty. WTP depends on ability to pay, and when ability to pay is low, WTP will be low as well, holding preferences constant. For this reason, the VSL of people with an annual income of $50,000 will be lower than that of people with an annual income of $150,000. People in the former category might be willing to pay no more than $25 to reduce a risk of 1/100,000, whereas people in the latter group might be willing to pay as much as $100. If so, government should not require everyone to pay $100; its decision to do so would harm those unwilling to pay that amount, by requiring them to pay more for safety than they want.

A uniform VSL, of the sort that government now uses, threatens to "overprotect" the poor, in a way that might well be harmful to them, because it will prevent them from using their limited resources on other goods (including risk reduction). At the same time, the uniform VSL threatens to underprotect the wealthy, in a way that is highly likely to be harmful to them.[52] In making these points, I am not attempting to reach final conclusions, but to establish that a uniform number, indifferent to disparities in wealth, can cause serious trouble.

As a simple matter of fact, it would be expected that unionized workers would receive more compensation for incurring risks—and studies almost always show a higher VSL for unionized workers, with amounts as high as $12.3 million, $18.1 million, and even $44.2 million.[53] Large differences across nations would also be expected, with VSL being higher in rich countries than in poor ones. And in fact, studies find a VSL as low as $200,000 for Taiwan, $500,000 for South Korea, and $1.2 million for India—but $21.7 million for Canada and $19 million for Australia.[54] Consider, for purposes of illustration, table 4.2.[55]

It would follow that within the United States, wealthy populations would show a higher VSL than poorer populations. If a program is designed to combat health risks in wealthy suburbs, the VSL should be above the population-wide median. If the protected population is mostly in poor areas, the VSL should be below this median. Currently agencies pay no attention to this possibility in undertaking cost-benefit analysis.

What about the controversial categories of race and gender? Some studies show significant differences. Using workplace data from 1996 to

TABLE 4.2: VSL across Nations

Nation and Year of Study	VSL (in 2000 US$)
Taiwan (1997)	.2–.9 million
South Korea (1993)	.8 million
India (1996/97)	1.2–1.5 million
Hong Kong (1998)	1.7 million
Canada (1989)	3.9–4.7 million
Switzerland (2001)	6.3–8.6 million
Japan (1991)	9.7 million
Australia (1997)	11.3–19.1 million
United Kingdom (2000)	19.9 million

1998, Professors Leeth and Ruser find that women's VSL ranges from $8.1 million to $10.2 million, whereas men's VSL is less than half that amount, ranging from $2.6 million to $4.7 million.[56] Leeth and Ruser find that Hispanic males show a slightly higher VSL than white males ($5 million compared to $3.4 million).[57] Most strikingly, they find that African Americans receive *no* compensation for workplace risks, producing a VSL of zero.[58] Using workplace data from 1992 through 1997, Professor Viscusi also finds a significant disparity across racial lines, though his numbers are quite different from those found by Leeth and Ruser.[59]

In Viscusi's study, the VSL is highest for white males and lowest for African American males, with white and African American females falling between the poles. More particularly, Viscusi finds that the overall white VSL is $15 million, whereas the overall African American VSL is $7.2 million.[60] For white females, the overall VSL is $9.4 million, compared to $18.8 million for white males. For African American females, the overall VSL is $6.9 million, compared to $5.9 million for African American males.[61] Another study by Viscusi finds a VSL of $7 million for blue-collar males and $8.5 million for blue-collar females.[62]

What accounts for these somewhat puzzling differences? It might not be altogether surprising that whites as a class will show a higher WTP and hence VSL than African Americans as a class. Simply because whites are wealthier, and because African Americans have been subject to discrimination, the WTP of whites might well turn out to be higher. Might the same be expected not only across the general population but also within specific job categories? Perhaps the answer is yes, if past or present discrimination, or different starting points, produce racial disparities in compensation for risk within similar jobs. The precise causes and levels of the disparities are unclear, and the differences between Professors Leeth and Ruser, on the one hand, and Professor Viscusi, on the other, remain a puzzle. There is no a priori reason to think that men or women would show a higher VSL. If the relevant group of women is wealthier, then its WTP should be higher too. And if women are more averse to mortality risks than men, they will show a higher WTP, just because they will demand a higher premium. For my purposes, the central point is that demographic differences in VSL are entirely to be expected, and they are found in both studies.

Theory and Practice

If the foregoing points are put together, it is apparent that there is not one VSL, but an exceptionally large number of VSLs. In fact each of us has not one VSL but a number of them, targeted to each risk that each of us faces. A policy that truly tracked WTP, and based VSL on WTP, would seek to provide all people with the level of protection for which they are willing to pay to reduce each risk. Tracking WTP is the goal that underlies current practice; and apart from questions of administrability, it calls for a very high level of individuation.

A thought experiment. As a thought experiment, suppose that an all-knowing regulator could costlessly identify each person's WTP for each statistical risk that she faces—and perfectly match the level of regulatory protection to that WTP. In these circumstances, the regulator should give every person no more and no less than her WTP for each risk that they face. (In cases in which people's WTP was low because they were poor, they might be subsidized; but they would not be forced to purchase goods for an amount in excess of their WTP. I will return to this point, but subsidies are not my topic here.) Under this approach, regulatory benefits would be treated the same as every other commodity that is traded on markets, including safety itself.

To be sure, many people face serious problems in dealing with risk, stemming both from an absence of information and from bounded rationality. The all-knowing regulator would overcome these problems and provide people with what they would want if they did not suffer from them. If agencies could do this, then the current theory would be perfectly implemented. It would follow that with full individuation, overall WTP would be lower for poor people than for wealthy people, for African Americans than for whites, and (possibly) for men than for women.

Under this thought experiment, however, government would not discriminate against groups. For example, it would neither decide on high VSLs for programs predominantly benefiting whites nor decide on low VSLs for programs predominantly benefiting African Americans. The difference would be a product of aggregation of fully individual VSLs—aggregation of the kind that most conventional markets, including those for automobiles and consumer goods, now provide. Recall that the use of WTP is justified because of its connection with welfare and individual autonomy. If so, then fully individual VSLs are justified on those same grounds.

Of course there are two practical problems with taking the thought experiment seriously. The first is that agencies do not know the WTP of every individual, and as a practical matter, it is not (yet) possible to find out. The second problem is that regulatory benefits are often collective goods—goods that cannot feasibly be provided to one without also being provided to many. In the context of air pollution, for example, it is not possible to provide cleaner air for some without providing cleaner air for many or all. In regulating air pollution and water pollution, individuation is simply not an option.

These problems are fatal objections to *full* individuation. But they are not fatal objections to *more* individuation. At a minimum, agencies might be encouraged to take account of existing research in their sensitivity analyses, which would result (for example) in increased "upper bound" estimates for cancer risks. In addition, disparities in VSL findings might be mapped onto different agency estimates, producing reasonable rather than arbitrary differences in VSL across agencies.

If, for example, the risks of death from workplace accidents produce a lower number than the risks of death from consumer products, then the Occupational Safety and Health Administration should use a lower VSL than the Consumer Products Safety Commission. It is easy to imagine a research program that would attempt to elicit far more information on VSL across different risks. A movement in this direction need not raise troubling ethical questions.

It would be far more controversial to suggest that agencies should adopt different VSLs depending on whether the affected population is especially wealthy or especially poor. But at the very least, agencies should adjust VSL to changes in national wealth over time, producing a higher amount than would result from inflation adjustments alone. In the Obama Administration, agencies did precisely this, producing increases in VSL not because of fundamental reassessments of any kind, but as a result of incorporating changes in national wealth.

Or suppose, more controversially, that a regulation is designed to protect migrant farmworkers, who are expected to show a low VSL. Current studies in fact estimate the relationship between income and WTP,[63] allowing agencies to make suitable adjustments to their VSLs. And when the population is relatively wealthy, the agency might adopt a higher VSL. For present purposes, I am suggesting only that an approach of this kind is indicated by the theory that government now uses. I will shortly turn to the larger questions that such an approach would make it necessary to answer.

Optimal individuation: An intermediate approach. The larger question is simple: What is the optimal level of individuation with respect to the value of life? The answer depends in part on how much is known. Even in markets, individuals are not usually asked, or charged, their particular WTP. In real estate markets, negotiations between individuals are the usual practice. But for ordinary consumer goods—cereal, soap, books, subscriptions to magazines—a standard price emerges from the forces of supply and demand.

It is also clear that full individuation is not feasible. The appropriate approach depends on two familiar variables: the costs of decisions and the costs of errors. In the early years of cost-benefit analysis, a uniform number was probably the best that agencies could do. As better information emerges about different VSLs across risks and persons, the use of a uniform number might well turn out to be increasingly difficult to support. If those differences are substantial, the argument for further differentiation will be strengthened. A uniform number might be seen as a plausible "first-generation" response to the problems posed by cost-benefit analysis. The second generation is now well underway, and hence finer distinctions might be increasingly hard to resist.

Administrative law. How would the use of more individuated VSLs bear on the legality of agency action? Courts have started to develop principles by which to review agency decisions about how to assess the costs and benefits of regulation.[64] Some statutes explicitly require agencies to balance costs against benefits, and under such statutes an agency's choices about valuation might be challenged as unreasonable or arbitrary.[65] If an agency used a VSL of $200,000, it would almost certainly be assigning an arbitrarily and hence unlawfully low monetary value. If it used a VSL of $40 million, its selection would be arbitrarily high. In all cases agencies are required to produce a reasonable explanation for why they have proceeded one way rather than another.

In view of the arguments made thus far, it is easy to imagine legal challenges to agency decisions. Suppose that the EPA uses a VSL of $9 million based on workplace studies. The agency's decision would be vulnerable on several grounds. First, it might be too low in light of the growth in national income. Second, it would fail to account for evidence that pollution risks, especially if cancer is involved, might produce a higher VSL than workplace risks. Third, it would not, on the facts stated, come to terms with the possibility that the protected group might be wealthier or poorer than the group involved in the workplace studies.

All of these challenges are not implausible under existing law. As new and better data emerge, they become stronger still. It is certainly possible that a decade from now, the use of a uniform figure will seem obtuse, even indefensible.

Is there anything that agencies might say in defense of a uniform VSL? They might urge, reasonably enough, that the existing evidence is too ambiguous and contestable to justify a change in current practice. Most studies based on more recent data do find a VSL in the range of $9 million. With respect to cancer, the EPA's Science Advisory Board (SAB) rejected an upward revision for especially dread illnesses, finding that the existing literature did not justify any such revision;[66] and some evidence supports the view of the SAB.[67] To be sure, it is more than plausible to think that VSL is wealth dependent; but the EPA might contend that a uniform number is preferable on moral and distributive grounds and is not greatly out of line with existing evidence. In any case, a single number might have the advantage of easy administrability—and produce results that in general would be the same as those produced by imaginable variations. Most of the time, the agency's choice will not be affected if it selects a VSL of $6 million or $10 million; in such situations, a uniform number seems acceptable.

In many cases, it is unclear that these responses are fully convincing as a matter of policy. But in light of the properly limited role of courts in the oversight of agency action, they are convincing as a matter of law. Courts should allow agencies considerable room to maneuver here, at least until the evidence against a uniform VSL becomes overwhelming. Permission to adopt such a number has an important corollary: an agency would be on firm legal ground if it attempted to make adjustments of the sort that I have suggested, even if current evidence does not unambiguously support those adjustments. The underlying questions are technical and difficult. They should be resolved by agencies, not by federal judges.

FIVE

Valuing Life, 2: Solutions

Notwithstanding what has been said thus far, the most fundamental questions remain. Why should government conduct cost-benefit analysis with such close reference to VSL? What is the argument for relying on people's WTP in regulatory policy? Why should government care about WTP at all? In chapter 4, I sketched arguments involving welfare and autonomy. But to say the least, those arguments are not self-evidently correct.

It is now time to explore these issues in more detail. I begin by discussing what I shall call the "Easy Cases," in which those who benefit from regulatory protection must pay for it. I contend that in such cases, WTP is usually the right foundation for VSL, because beneficiaries are hardly helped by being forced to pay for regulatory programs that they believe not to be in their interests. The major qualifications here involve lack of information and bounded rationality, potentially in the form of "behavioral market failures." But with those qualifications, the argument for using VSL, and indeed an individualized VSL, is quite powerful in the Easy Cases on grounds of both welfare and autonomy.

The analysis is much less straightforward in harder cases, in which beneficiaries pay little or none of the cost of what they receive. In such cases, the underlying considerations are regrettably complex, and it will be useful to summarize them here.

In the hard cases as I defined them, beneficiaries are likely to be net winners from regulation. They are receiving benefits, and they are paying little or nothing for them. Unlike in the Easy Cases, arguments from welfare and autonomy do not lead in any clear direction. As we shall see (and this is a more subtle point), it is possible that regulation is justified on welfare grounds even if the cost-benefit analysis (based on VSL) suggests that it is not. The reason is that in terms of welfare, the winners may win more than the losers lose. Suppose that poor workers gain a great deal in terms of safety while (wealthy) consumers have to pay more for the goods that they produce. Even if the monetized costs exceed the monetized benefits, the welfare gains to workers might be higher than the welfare losses to consumers.

To be sure, it is not easy to measure welfare gains and losses directly, and because of the measurement problem, regulators might ultimately want to ignore the point. But the theoretical point nonetheless holds. In such cases, it is also possible that regulation is justified on redistributive grounds, if it helps those who need help while hurting those who are well-off.

It is important to see that the best response to unjustified inequality is a redistributive income tax, not regulation—which is, as we will see, a crude and potentially counterproductive redistributive tool. But suppose that we are dealing with the harder cases and that a nation lacks an optimal income tax and seeks greater redistribution. If so, it is possible (though far from inevitable) that regulation is justified—and that the use of a VSL that exceeds the WTP of the beneficiaries will produce desirable redistribution or be justified on welfare grounds. I outline the circumstances in which this conclusion might hold.

I conclude that in the Easy Cases, the argument for using VSL, and even a disaggregated VSL, is fairly secure, even if it is based on WTP. In the harder cases, it is of course simplest to use a unitary VSL, and for reasons discussed in chapter 4, a disaggregated VSL has considerable appeal. The problem is that in such cases, either a unitary or disaggregated VSL may produce a cost-benefit analysis that fails to point in the right directions. At the same time, it is exceedingly difficult to measure welfare directly, and regulation is at best an imperfect redistributive tool. In the hard cases, I suggest that regulators should depart from the outcome of cost-benefit analysis, based on VSL, only when there is compelling reason to believe that the regulation is nonetheless justified on the ground that it will promote welfare or achieve important redistributive goals.

Easy Cases

For the sake of simplicity, assume a society in which people face multiple risks of 1/100,000, and in which every person is both adequately informed and willing to pay no more and no less than $60 to eliminate each of those risks. Assume too that the cost of eliminating these 1/100,000 risks is widely variable, ranging from close to zero to many billions of dollars. Assume finally that the cost of eliminating any risk is *borne entirely by those who benefit from eliminating that risk*. For example, people's water bills will entirely reflect the costs of a policy that eliminates a 1/100,000 risk of getting cancer from arsenic in drinking water. If the per-person cost is $100, each water bill will be increased by exactly that amount.

Welfare and Autonomy (Again)

With these assumptions, the argument for using WTP to calculate VSL is straightforward. Regulation amounts to a forced exchange. It tells people that they must purchase certain benefits for a certain amount. Why should government force people to pay for things that they do not want?

Welfare. Begin with welfare. Let us understand that term in a capacious sense, capturing essentially everything that choosers care about. They might focus on subjective well-being, understood as their personal hedonic states; they might want their lives to have meaning; they might want to serve others; they might focus mostly on their family. Their own ends define their welfare. The question is what approach will promote their welfare, broadly understood.[1]

By hypothesis, a forced exchange on terms that people dislike will make them worse off. It will require them to buy something that they do not want, undoubtedly because they want other things more. They might want to use the relevant money not to eliminate a mortality risk of 1 in 100,000, but to buy food or education or medical care, to help their favorite charity, or to eliminate a mortality risk of 1 in 20,000 or

1 in 10,000. At first glance, use of WTP, on the assumptions that I am making, seems hard to contest. In free societies that are concerned with people's welfare, we should begin by asking people what they want, and if people do not want certain goods, we should presume that they know their own priorities. A forced exchange will decrease their welfare. Indeed, a forced exchange would violate John Stuart Mill's Harm Principle (requiring respect for private choices in the absence of harm to others) without apparent justification.[2]

For purposes of evaluating regulation, it does not matter if the existing distribution of income is unjust or if poor people are, in some intelligible sense, coerced to run certain risks (as they might be if they live in bad or desperate conditions and have few, and bad, opportunities). The remedy for unjust distributions, and for that form of coercion, is hardly to require people to buy regulatory benefits on terms that they find unacceptable. Suppose that people are willing to pay only $60 to eliminate a 1/100,000 risk because they are not rich, and that if they had double their current wealth, they would be willing to pay $120. Government does people no favors by forcing them to pay the amount that they would pay if they had more money. It does not help them. On the contrary, it hurts them.

It follows that in the Easy Cases, it is true but irrelevant that willingness to pay is dependent on ability to pay. Suppose that certain people are willing to pay a very small amount to eliminate a 1/100,000 mortality risk, not because they would not obtain much welfare from eliminating that risk, but because they have little money to spend. It might be thought that the welfare gain is not captured by the very small amount that they are willing to pay. That thought should not be used to collapse two different questions. (a) Should government force people to spend more than the very small amount that they are willing to pay, because the welfare gain would not be trivial? (b) Should government itself, through a compelled expenditure from consumers or taxpayers, be willing to spend more than poor people are willing to pay to reduce a risk, because the welfare gain would not be trivial?

The answer to (b) is not clear, and if government is concerned with welfare, it might well answer in the affirmative. (One question of course is what other uses might be found for the money.) But (a) is a quite different question. Unless there is a problem of lack of information or bounded rationality, the answer to (a) is clearly no. The welfare gain would not justify the welfare loss. That is the beauty of the WTP approach, which offers an automatic test of the welfare consequences of regulation.

Autonomy. In chapter 4, I suggested that considerations of autonomy point in exactly the same direction. Those who refuse to pay a certain amount to eliminate a risk of 1/100,000 might want to use their resources for other things—medical care, children, food, recreation, entertainment, savings. If people in a free society are entitled to have a kind of sovereignty over the conduct of their own lives, then they should be permitted to make such allocations as they choose. It is usual to justify use of WTP on welfare grounds, but the same approach is at least equally defensible as a means of respecting the autonomy of persons.

When people decline to devote more than $60 to the elimination of a 1/100,000 risk, it is because they would like to spend the money in a way that seems to them more desirable. If regulators do not use people's actual judgments, then they are insulting their autonomy. Suppose that people in a free society are entitled to have a kind of mastery over the conduct of their own lives. If so, then they should be permitted to make such allocations as they choose. It is usual to justify use of WTP on welfare grounds, but the same approach is at least equally defensible as a means of respecting the autonomy of persons.

Disaggregating VSL

Consider how this argument works with respect to risks and persons. Suppose, for example, that people are willing to pay no more than $50 to avoid a 1/100,000 risk of dying in a car crash, but that they are willing to pay up to $100 to avoid a 1/100,000 risk of dying of cancer. If government uses a WTP for both risks of $75, it will force people to pay more than they want to avoid the risks associated with car crashes, and less than they want to avoid risks of cancer. Why should government do that? And if the argument is convincing in this example, it should apply in numerous cases in which WTP and hence VSL vary across mortality

risks. The central question would not be conceptual but instead empirical: How does VSL vary, depending on the nature of the particular risk
at issue?

With respect to persons, the central idea is that different people
should be expected to have a different WTP to avoid mortality risks,
and to the extent feasible, regulators should not use a "mass" VSL, but
should instead attempt to individuate.[3] This argument is more controversial, among other things because it might well treat children differently
from adults[4] and the elderly differently from the young,[5] and because it
would certainly treat poor people as less valuable (in the relevant sense)
than rich people. The reason is that because they have less money, poor
people would have a lower VSL than wealthy people. (Similarly, poor
areas, and poor nations, would have a lower VSL than wealthier ones.[6])
But so long as we are dealing with Easy Cases, differences appear to be
appropriate here as well.

The reason is not that poor people are less valuable than rich people.
It is that *no one, rich or poor, should be forced to pay more than she is willing to pay for the reduction of risks.* In fact this idea embodies a norm of
equality (and the right one). If poor people are unwilling to pay much
for the reduction of serious risks, and if government wants to help, the
appropriate response is not a compelled purchase, but a subsidy, perhaps in the form of cash payments. We might even say that part of the
right conception of risk equity is that people should not be compelled
to pay more than they are willing to pay to reduce risks (unless there is a
lack of information or a problem of bounded rationality).[7]

Suppose, for example, that each member of a group of relatively poor
people, earning less than $30,000 annually, is willing to pay only $45
to eliminate a risk of 1/100,000—one-half, suppose, of the nation's
population-wide median of $90. Should regulators require every citizen,
including those in the relatively poor group, to pay $90? Government
should not force poor people to pay more than their WTP to eliminate
statistical risks; forced exchanges of this kind do poor people no good
and some harm.

It is tempting to defend a uniform VSL, one that does not distinguish
between rich and poor, on the ground that it embodies the right conception of risk equity, treating every person as equal to every other person

and redistributing resources in the direction of poor people. But this is an error. In the Easy Cases, a uniform VSL, taken from a population-wide median, does not produce redistribution toward the poor, any more than any other kind of forced exchange. Government does not require people to buy Volvos, even if Volvos would reduce statistical risks. If government required everyone to buy Volvos, it would not be producing desirable redistribution.[8] A uniform VSL has some of the same characteristics as a policy that requires people to buy Volvos. In principle, the government should force exchanges only on terms that people find acceptable, at least if it is genuinely concerned with their welfare. That principle is the correct conception of risk equity.

Note, once again, that the argument for using WTP does not imply satisfaction with the existing distribution of wealth. The problem with forced exchanges is that they do nothing to alter existing distributions. In fact they make poor people worse off, requiring them to use their limited resources for something that they do not want to buy.

Are There Easy Cases?

Do the Easy Cases seem implausibly unrealistic? In many contexts, they are not likely to match reality. The costs of air pollution regulation, for example, are not fully borne by its beneficiaries.[9] Under some provisions of the Clean Air Act, relatively poor people receive disproportionate benefits, and they do not have to pay the full costs of those benefits. But for workers' compensation regulation, the situation is very different. With the enactment of workers' compensation programs, nonunionized workers faced a dollar-for-dollar wage reduction, corresponding almost perfectly to the expected value of the benefits that they received.[10] For drinking water regulation, something similar is involved. The entire cost of regulation is passed onto consumers in the form of higher water bills.[11]

Hence the Easy Cases find a number of real-world analogues. And even where beneficiaries do not pay the full cost of what they obtain, they might pay a substantial portion of it, and for such cases, the analysis of the Easy Cases is at least a place for the analysis to start.

Objections

There are several plausible objections to the use of WTP to calculate VSL, even in the Easy Cases. They point to some important qualifications of the arguments thus far, and they suggest some puzzles that deserve continuing empirical and conceptual attention.

"MISWANTING"

The first objection is that people may suffer from a problem of "miswanting."[12] They want some things that do not promote their welfare (as they understand it), and they do not want some things that would promote their welfare (also as they understand it). In many settings, people's decisions appear not to make them happier or better off, even when alternative decisions would do so.[13] *Predicted welfare*, or welfare at the time of decision, may be very different from *experienced welfare*, or welfare as life is actually lived.[14] If this is so, then WTP loses much of its underlying justification. People's choices do not actually promote their welfare.[15] If government can be confident that people are not willing to pay for goods from which they would greatly benefit, perhaps government should abandon WTP.

A more specific concern is that people's preferences may have adapted to existing opportunities, including deprivation.[16] Thus Tocqueville writes, "Shall I call it a blessing of God, or a last malediction of his anger, this disposition of the soul that makes men insensible to extreme misery and often gives them a sort of depraved taste for the cause of their afflictions?"[17] Perhaps people show a low WTP for environmental goods, including health improvements, simply because they have adjusted to environmental bads, including health risks. Perhaps people's WTP reflects an effort to reduce cognitive dissonance through the conclusion that risks are lower than they actually are.[18] It is not a lot of fun to think that you face serious dangers, and some people undoubtedly develop an unduly optimistic account of their actual situation[19] (a problem to which I will return).

In some contexts, the idea of miswanting raises serious problems for neoclassical economics and for unambivalent enthusiasm for freedom of choice.[20] As Daniel Kahneman and Carol Varey have suggested, "if people do not know their future experience utilities, or if their preferences of the moment do not accurately reflect what they do know, a case can be made for using experience utility rather than preference as the unit of account in utilitarian calculations."[21] If the basis for use of WTP is welfare, there is a real difficulty, because use of WTP may be imperfectly connected with promoting people's welfare.

Recall that in making these claims, I do not mean to take a contentious position on the nature of welfare. People want their lives to go well, but their understandings of what it means for their lives to go well are diverse, and include an assortment of different goods. Hedonic states are important, but they are hardly all that matters. People choose certain activities not because they are fun or joyful, but because they are right to choose, perhaps because they are meaningful. People want their lives to have purpose; they do not want their lives to be simply happy.[22] People sensibly, even virtuously, choose things that they will not in any simple sense "like."[23]

For example, they may want to help others even when they do not enjoy doing that. They may want to do what they are morally obliged to do, even if they do not like it. An important survey suggests that people's projected choices are *generally* based on what they believe would promote their subjective well-being—but that sometimes people are willing to make choices that would sacrifice their happiness in favor of promoting an assortment of other goals, including (1) promoting the happiness of their family, (2) increasing their control over their lives, (3) increasing their social status, or (4) improving their sense of purpose in life.[24] The point here is not that people seek to promote a narrow conception of welfare, but that whatever their preferred conception, they make mistakes, and these mistakes can be implicated in the use of WTP.

These points have implications for autonomy as well. The idea of autonomy requires not merely respect for whatever preferences people happen to have, but also for preferences that are actually informed, and for social conditions that allow preferences to be developed in a way that does not reflect coercion or injustice.[25] With respect to some risks, the relevant preferences are nonautonomous. Consider the fact that many women face a risk of male harassment or domination (or even violence) under circumstances in which they believe that little can be done—and hence adapt.[26]

In the context of ordinary regulatory policy, however, the objection from "miswanting" probably has more theoretical than practical interest. Typically regulation involves the reduction of low-level mortality risks (say, 1/100,000). In the abstract, there is no reason to believe that the use of people's WTP (say, $90) is a product of adaptive preferences or a problem of miswanting. It is true that when WTP does result from adaptive preferences or miswanting, the judgment about the Easy Cases must be revised—but in the real world of regulatory practice, we do not yet have good reason to think that problem arises often, or that it is sufficient to "impeach" the evidence on which regulators rely in using VSL.

INFORMATION AND BEHAVIORAL MARKET FAILURES

A closely related objection would point to an absence of information and to bounded rationality, meant as an umbrella concept for a wide range of findings from behavioral sciences, including behavioral economics.[27] We can use the term "behavioral market failures" to refer to a set of problems that may make markets work imperfectly, including unrealistic optimism, myopia, and self-control problems.

Here is a way to make the point. Imagine a population of people. Let us call them Simpsons (after the character Homer Simpson in the television show of that name).[28] Simpsons make choices, but the choices reflect systematic errors, in the sense that they are unrealistically optimistic, neglectful of the long term, and reckless. The Simpsons will have an identifiable WTP to avoid mortality risks (and other risks). By hypothesis, the WTP and the corresponding VSL will be low. But the fact that it is low does not mean that for the Simpsons, the government should use a low VSL in regulatory policy. What matters is the welfare of the population, and the Simpsons' welfare is not adequately captured by the Simpsons' WTP. Regulators should use preferences that are informed and rational and that extend over people's life histories. The Simpsons' preferences do not satisfy those criteria.[29]

No nation is the Simpsons, but as behavioral economists have shown, people often have difficulty in dealing with low-probability events.[30] If people are not aware of the risks that they actually face, or if they have a poor understanding of such risks, their WTP, as measured by market evidence, might be too low. Suppose that workers receive a $90 wage premium for risks of 1 in 100,000. What does this mean, concretely? Are workers actually trading off risks and money? Do they even know about the relevant probabilities? If these questions do not have clear answers, the market evidence might not be reliable. (Note that this is not an objection to basing VSL on informed WTP; it is merely a concern that existing evidence does not allow us to be certain that we are eliciting informed WTP.)

Or perhaps the availability heuristic will lead people to underestimate mortality risks. If people cannot recall a case in which some activity produced illness or death, they might conclude that a risk is trivial even if it is not. Perhaps market evidence will reflect such mistakes. Or perhaps the same heuristic, and probability neglect,[31] will lead people to exaggerate risks, producing a WTP that is inflated in light of reality. And if people are unable to understand the meaning of ideas like "one in fifty thousand," or to respond rationally to such ideas, then there are serious problems with relying on contingent valuation studies to produce WTP.

It is also possible that people's WTP reflects excessive discounting of future health benefits. If workers are disregarding the future, or applying an implausibly high discount rate, then there is a good argument for not relying on their WTP, at least with respect to mortality risks that will not come to fruition in the short term. Young smokers, for example, undoubtedly give too little attention to the long-term health risks associated with smoking. Those who choose a poor diet and little exercise often fail to consider the long-term effects of their behavior.[32] Self-control problems are an important part of bounded rationality. If a low WTP shows a failure to give adequate attention to the future, then there is reason not to use WTP.

To be sure, a dollar today is worth less than a dollar tomorrow, in part because a dollar today can be invested and made to grow. For money, some kind of discount rate makes a great deal of sense. And for rational reasons, people might prefer welfare today to welfare tomorrow; for example, there is at least some chance of death tonight, which argues for welfare today. The question how rational people distribute welfare (as opposed to money) over time does not admit of an easy answer. But if people care very little about their future selves, and are willing to impose a great deal of future suffering in return for a small benefit in the present, something has likely gone wrong.[33] An appealing welfarist approach emphasizes preferences that are fully informed and fully rational, and that extend over life histories.[34] If people's choices do not satisfy these constraints, they are "impeached" from the standpoint of welfare.

When a behavioral market failure is involved, appropriate adjustments should be made to WTP, and the VSL that emerges from WTP should be corrected accordingly. It is possible, of course, that across large aggregations of workers, behavioral market failures are not a serious problem, and hence existing numbers are trustworthy. As noted, no nation consists of Simpsons. But further conceptual and empirical work needs to be done on these issues.

RIGHTS

A quite different objection would point to people's rights. Perhaps people have a right not to be subjected to risks of a certain magnitude, and the use of WTP will violate that right. It is tempting to think that, whatever their WTP, human beings should have a right not to be subject to risks above a particular level. Imagine, for example, that poor people live in a place where they face a 1/20 annual risk of dying from water pollution. That risk seems intolerably high. It makes sense to say that the government, or perhaps the international community, should consider taking steps to reduce that risk even if the relevant population is poor, even if people are willing to pay only $1 to eliminate it, and even if the per-person cost is $10.

As an abstract claim about people's rights, the objection may be correct. Something has gone badly wrong if people are exposed to serious risks and their WTP prevents them from doing anything in response. It would be foolish to suggest that WTP is determinative of the appropriate use of government resources. (Would it make sense to say that government would give poor people a check for $100 only if they were willing to pay $100 for the check?) And in many cases, people are subject to risks whose magnitude is indeed a violation of their rights. But for several reasons, this point has little force against my conclusions for the Easy Cases.

The initial problem with this objection is that, in the cases under discussion, rights of this kind are usually not involved; we are speaking here of statistically small risks. Suppose that this initial response is unconvincing[35] and that rights are indeed involved. If so, there is a still more fundamental response. When rights are involved, the proper response is not to force people to buy protection that they do not want, but to provide a subsidy that will give them the benefit for free, or enable them to receive the benefit at what is, for them, an acceptable price. Nothing here is meant to deny the possibility that government should provide certain goods via subsidy, or indeed that subjection to risks above a certain level is a violation of rights. The question instead is one of regulation under the stated assumptions. So long as that is the question, use of WTP does not violate anyone's rights.

DEMOCRACY AND MARKETS

An independent objection would stress that people are citizens, not merely consumers. It would urge that regulatory choices should be made after citizens have deliberated with one another about their preferences and values.[36] The argument against forced exchanges treats people as consumers; it sees their decisions about safety as the same as their decisions about all other commodities.[37] For some decisions, this approach is badly misconceived. Well-functioning constitutional systems are deliberative democracies,[38] not maximization machines, and many social judgments should be made by citizens engaged in deliberative discussion with one another, rather than by aggregating the individual choices of consumers.

Consider some examples:

· The permissible level of race and sex discrimination is not set by using market evidence, or contingent valuation studies, to see how much people would be willing to pay to discriminate (or to be free from discrimination). Such discrimination is banned, even if discriminators would be willing to pay a lot to avoid associating with members of unpopular groups. Through democratic processes, citizens have decided that certain forms of discrimination are illicit, whatever people's WTP.

· The prohibition against sexual harassment does not emerge from consulting people's WTP. Many potential harassers would be willing to pay something, perhaps a great deal, for the privilege of harassing. In imaginable circumstances, the harassers' WTP might exceed their victims' WTP to prevent harassment. Nonetheless, harassment is forbidden. One reason is that a goal of the civil rights laws is to alter existing preferences and beliefs, not entrench them.

· Laws that forbid cruelty to animals, and that impose affirmative duties of protection on human beings, stem not from WTP, but from a belief that morality justifies such laws. When laws require protection of animals against cruelty or suffering, it is not decisive that those who are regulated may be willing to pay a significant amount to avoid the regulation. Of course the cost of the regulatory burden might play an important role in deciding whether to impose it. But the underlying moral judgment is rooted in a belief in the prevention of suffering that does not essentially turn on WTP.

Emphasizing the limits of any approach that takes "preferences" to be the foundation of regulatory policy, Amartya Sen argues that "discussions and exchange, and even political arguments, contribute to the formation and revision of values."[39] He urges that in the particular context of environmental protection, solutions require regulators "to go beyond looking only for the best reflection of given individual preferences, or the most acceptable procedures for choices based on those preferences."[40]

Sen's claims are both fundamental and correct. They point to some serious limitations on the use of WTP. But it is important not to read such objections for more than they are worth. In trading off safety and health in their private lives, people do not have static values and preferences. Much of the time, human choices are a product of reflection, even if choosers are simply acting as consumers. Reflection and deliberation, including reflection and deliberation with other people, are hardly absent from the market domain. To be sure, moral questions should not be resolved by aggregating private WTP. Sometimes people's preferences, even though backed by WTP, are morally off-limits (consider sexual harassment), and policy should not take account of them. In addition, people may be unwilling to pay a great deal for goods that have strong moral justifications; animal welfare is a potential example. In these circumstances, the market model is inapplicable and WTP reveals very little.

But what about the Easy Cases? Do these arguments suggest that government should override individual choices about how much to spend to eliminate low-level risks, even when those choices are adequately informed? For environmental protection generally, it is indeed important to go beyond "the best reflection of given individual preferences." But this point does not mean that people should be required to pay $100 to eliminate mortality risks of 1/100,000 when they are willing to pay only $75. If people's WTP reflects an absence of information, bounded rationality, or insufficient deliberation, then it is important for other people, in government and elsewhere, to draw attention to that fact. And in some cases, a low WTP might be overridden on the ground that it is rooted in errors, factual or otherwise. But these points should not be taken as a general objection to my conclusion about the Easy Cases, or to suggest that government should force people to reduce statistical risks at an expense that they deem excessive.

VERY LOW PROBABILITIES AND CATASTROPHIC RISKS

Suppose that everyone in the United States faces an annual death risk of 1/10 million—and that this risk, if it comes to fruition, will kill every person in the country. The expected number of annual deaths is a little more than thirty, which would produce expected annual costs in excess of $270 million, assuming a VSL of $9 million. But if the government attempted to elicit each individual's WTP to avoid a risk of 1/10 million, it might well produce a number very close to zero. How much would you be willing to spend to avoid a risk of 1/10 million? If you say "nothing," you might well be like most people. And if most people really are like that, the supposed risk of 1/10 million, applicable to everyone in the United States, yields both thirty expected annual fatalities and expected annual costs very close to zero—an especially odd result in light of the fact that there is a 1/10 million risk not simply that *each* American will die, but that *every* American will die.

This result does seem anomalous. For one thing, is it really sensible to conclude that the prevention of thirty deaths is worth nothing, or close to it? An affirmative answer is suggested by a perspective that is fully based on people's WTP to avoid very low probability risks. But assigning a value near zero, for the prevention of dozens of deaths, seems quite implausible. In cases of this kind, there is a serious problem with using WTP to calculate the benefit of avoiding that risk.

This conclusion actually understates the problem. In the case at hand, the risk is potentially catastrophic. I have said that if the 1/10 million chance is realized, every American will be dead. Even if people show a WTP near zero to avoid a risk of that size, it does not seem right to think that the nation should spend almost nothing to prevent it. The point has a general bearing on precautions against low-probability risks of catastrophe: some degree of prevention should be undertaken even if WTP numbers do not justify it. Part of the problem with those numbers is that individual behavior will not reflect the "catastrophe premium" or "extermination premium" that would almost certainly emerge if it were possible to test for it. People may be unwilling to pay anything to avoid a risk of 1/100 million that they themselves face; but if they were told that every person in the nation faced this risk, they might come up with a significantly higher figure. It would only take the right question to produce the higher numbers. Another part of the problem is that WTP is not an adequate measure of social responses to catastrophes—perhaps because people are not familiar with making choices about risks of that sort.

In my view, this is a sound objection to the use of a low or near-zero VSL in the context of catastrophic risks, even if the WTP calculation would produce that VSL. As Judge Richard Posner has shown,[41] this is an important point when government is considering how to respond to small risks of catastrophic harm. But notice that the objection applies in very few contexts (fortunately!) and thus has serious limitations. It does not apply to the overwhelming number of cases in which VSL is used. In those cases, the risks in question are 1/10,000 to 1/100,000, and no large-scale catastrophe is at issue. Here, then, is a limitation on the use of WTP, but the domain of the objection is severely restricted.

THIRD-PARTY EFFECTS

A final objection would point to effects on third parties. If outsiders would be adversely affected by the undervaluing of a particular risk, and if their welfare is not being considered, then the WTP calculus is seriously incomplete. This point demonstrates a general and neglected problem for WTP as it is currently used: agencies consider people's

WTP to eliminate statistical risks, without taking account of the fact that others—especially family members and close friends—would also be willing to pay something to eliminate those risks.

John might be willing to pay \$25 to eliminate his own risk of 1/100,000, but his wife, Jane, might be willing to pay \$25 to eliminate John's risk also. When John is hurt or killed, John is not the only person who pays the price. If regulators add the WTP, on John's behalf, of John's friends and relatives, the total WTP might soon exceed \$100. This is a real problem for existing uses of WTP. In principle, regulators should consider the full range of people who are adversely affected, not only the person directly at risk.[42] A great deal of work remains to be done on this topic.[43]

This is a legitimate point, but thus far the discussion has been assuming that there are no third-party effects. In the Easy Cases, the argument for using WTP, on the stated assumptions, is that government should not force people to buy goods that are not worthwhile for them. At least at first glance, this argument seems sound with respect to statistical risks of the kind on which I am focusing.

Harder Cases

There is an obvious artificiality in the assumptions thus far. Most important, people do not always bear the full social costs of the regulatory benefits that they receive. Sometimes they pay only a fraction of those costs—or possibly close to nothing. When this is so, the analysis is much more complicated.[44]

WELFARE AND DISTRIBUTION

We have seen that in the context of air pollution regulation, there is a complex set of distributional effects, and on balance, poor people, and members of minority communities, may well be net gainers. Suppose that the result of an air pollution regulation is to improve public health in poor communities, and that those who benefit pay only a small part of the cost. Suppose too that strictly in terms of welfare, they benefit a great deal, perhaps because they are less likely to get sick, perhaps because they live longer lives. Suppose that most of the cost is paid by people who can easily bear it (and hence do not much suffer from paying). A cost-benefit analysis, based on WTP, might not produce an adequate account of the welfare effects of air pollution regulation. The reason is that in terms of welfare, the people who gain may end up gaining more than the people who lose end up losing. Use of WTP, and hence of VSL, may produce a cost-benefit analysis suggesting that the regulation is a net loser—but on welfare grounds, the analysis might be misleading. It might point in the wrong direction.

The case of rich and poor may be the most vivid, but it is merely illustrative. We could imagine many cases in which cost-benefit analysis, based on WTP, produces outcomes that do not promote welfare. A safety regulation, designed to protect workers, might increase welfare even if the cost-benefit analysis suggests otherwise. This is true not only if and because WTP does not capture informed, rational preferences over a lifetime,[45] but also if and because the welfare effects are not sufficiently captured by the monetary figures. Of course it may also be true that a regulation that has positive net benefits is also bad from the standpoint of promoting welfare. Indeed, we could distinguish among four kinds of cases: (1) net monetary benefits and net welfare benefits; (2) net monetary benefits but net welfare costs; (3) net monetary costs and net welfare costs; and (4) net monetary costs but net welfare benefits. For present purposes, cases (2) and (4) are the interesting ones.

In any case, the welfare effects might not resolve the question about what to do, because the distributional gains are important to consider. Recall that Executive Order 13563 explicitly makes "distributional impacts" relevant. If poor people are gaining a great deal, and wealthy people are losing slightly more, the regulation might be justified on distributional grounds. Consider the idea of prioritarianism, which suggests that the social goal should be to increase overall welfare, but with priority given to the most disadvantaged.[46]

Here is what distinguishes the Easy Cases from the harder ones. We have seen that in the Easy Cases, it does not make much sense to require people to pay more than they are willing to pay. But in the harder cases, people are not paying all of the cost of the benefits that they receive. If so, it is quite possible that they will gain on balance from the relevant regulation, even if their WTP is significantly lower than the cost of the regulation. The more relevant possibility is that, on net, society will gain in terms of welfare as well.[47] The point suggests a potentially serious limitation to the use of WTP in regulatory policy when those who benefit from regulations do not pay for them. In such cases, even a unitary VSL may produce misleading results if welfare is our guide. And a more disaggregated VSL, suggesting a lower figure for poor people, may be especially misleading if poor people stand to gain a great deal in terms of welfare.

Indeed, the use of a unitary rather than disaggregated VSL, in which poor people are given more than they are willing to pay for, might be justified in such circumstances. Thus W. Kip Viscusi suggests that, by "using a uniform VSL across different populations, agencies engage in an implicit form of income redistribution, as benefits to the poor receive a greater weight than is justified by their VSL and benefits to the rich are undervalued."[48] The use of a uniform VSL will not always promote desirable redistribution, but if poor people are receiving benefits at less than their cost, and if the losses are borne by those who are well-off, it may well do so.

Some of the most intuitively plausible defenses of cost-benefit analysis speak in terms of the Kaldor-Hicks criterion (sometimes called potential Pareto superiority), which asks whether the winners win more than the losers lose.[49] The central idea is that if the winners could compensate the losers, and there would be a surplus, satisfaction of the Kaldor-Hicks criterion shows a net welfare gain. The criterion raises many doubts and puzzles,[50] but let us simply stipulate that regulation is ordinarily justified if it produces such a welfare gain. The problem is that under certain circumstances, a net loss, in terms of cost-benefit analysis, may coexist with a net gain, in terms of welfare. Because welfare is the master concept, and because monetized numbers are mere proxies, it would seem clear that the proxies would have to yield in favor of the master concept.

It is sometimes argued that if agencies use cost-benefit analysis, everyone, or almost everyone, will benefit in the long run. Hicks so argued about the Kaldor-Hicks criterion, suggesting that "although we could not say that all the inhabitants of that community would be necessarily better off than they would have been if the community had been organized on some different principle, nevertheless there would be a strong probability that almost all of them would be better off after the lapse of a sufficient amount of time."[51] Note that this argument is about analysis of welfare, not about cost-benefit analysis, and it would take a great deal of work to make plausible the view that if agencies use cost-benefit analysis, based on VSL, as the criterion of decision, almost everyone "would be better off after the lapse of a sufficient length of time." More generally, there is good reason to question Hicks's argument on its own terms.[52]

In the harder cases, it is much harder to argue that the use of cost-benefit analysis promotes autonomy. If poor people do not bear all of the costs of programs that benefit them, the autonomy argument for use of WTP is greatly weakened. Poor people are enjoying a benefit (in whole or in part) for free. It does not insult people's autonomy to give them a good on terms that they find acceptable.

Insofar as regulation is motivated by distributional impacts, it is natural to respond that if redistribution is the goal, then it should be produced not through regulation but through the tax system, which is a much more efficient way of transferring resources to people who need help.[53] In general, the point is correct. But suppose that redistribution is not possible through the tax system. If so, then regulation in the harder cases cannot be ruled off-limits (despite its inefficiency). To be sure, the fact that a regulation is helpful to the most disadvantaged is not decisive in its favor. It is necessary to provide an account by which to measure benefits to the most disadvantaged against costs to others. If a regulation is trivially helpful to the most disadvantaged, and if it inflicts huge costs on everyone else, little can be said for it. But everything depends on the magnitude of the relevant effects. A program that produces large gains for the least well-off might well be justified even if it imposes, in terms of WTP, somewhat higher costs than benefits on balance. As we have seen, it might be justified either because it promotes net welfare gains or because the distributional impacts are sufficient to tip the balance.

OPTIMAL TAXATION AND ADMINISTRABILITY

Notwithstanding these considerations, regulators do not make direct inquiries into welfare. And while Executive Order 13563 allows them to take account of distributional effects, they do not often do so. Why?

One answer involves administrability, or more particularly, the best way to minimize decision costs and error costs. In the real-world cases, regulators might well think that a direct inquiry into welfare, bypassing WTP, would be extremely difficult or perhaps even impossible to operationalize (even bracketing, as I have throughout, the problem of inter-personal comparisons of well-being[54]). Regulators might rely on WTP not because it is perfect as a proxy for welfare, or even very close to it, but because any more direct welfare inquiry is not tractable.[55] Regulators lack welfare meters, and for that reason alone, they might be inclined to use standard cost-benefit analysis instead. Alternative approaches, departing from the standard analysis, impose large information-gathering burdens on agencies, and they might create errors of their own.[56]

The point deserves emphasis. Public officials are inevitably working with incomplete information, and the cost-benefit framework has the advantage of administrability and feasibility (and an established track record). Alternative approaches must be carefully assessed to see if they have that advantage as well. However intriguing and even promising, they may not be ready for official use. Direct assessment of welfare continues to present quite serious challenges, though perhaps those challenges can be met over time.

If regulators decide that distributional considerations are relevant, some regulators might fear that interest-group warfare would be the consequence, rather than distribution to those who particularly need and deserve help. The larger point is that it is not easy to identify many regulations for which poor people are the clear beneficiaries while wealthy people foot the bill. It is far more usual for the costs and benefits of regulations to be widely distributed, so that a variety of demographic groups both enjoy the benefits and pay the costs. A great deal of additional work needs to be done on this topic, in order to specify distributional effects with more precision than has been done to date.

Under current circumstances, a reasonable approach would be for regulators to use WTP as the foundation for decisions, and generally to follow the results of cost-benefit balancing, but to inquire into welfare or distribution in cases in which there is compelling reason to do so. Consider cases in which the monetized benefits are only modestly higher than the monetized costs, but in which the costs are borne by those who are well-off, and the benefits are enjoyed mostly by those who are struggling. Regulators might decide to proceed in such circumstances. In fact this is generally the correct approach, because it is right in principle, and because it does not impose undue information-gathering burdens on regulators. But as more information becomes available, it may well become possible to assess welfare and distributional consequences more directly and accurately, and to give them a greater role.

What are the implications for individuation of VSL? It remains true that according to the theory that underlies agency valuations, a higher degree of individuation would be desirable. It also remains true that with respect to risks, individuation is appropriate insofar as valuations differ depending on the nature of the risk at stake. The principal qualification is that a uniform VSL—one that gives disadvantaged people regulatory protection in excess of their WTP—might turn out to have fortunate distributional consequences in the harder cases. This is an important point, but regulators should be careful with it. It will not always hold, and if the goal is to provide more assistance to those in need, a uniform VSL is hardly the best way to achieve that goal.

Global Risk Regulation and Cross-National Valuations

The analysis thus far has significant implications for global risk regulation and cross-cultural variations in WTP and VSL. I now turn to those implications.[57] My central claim is that poor countries should use a lower VSL than wealthy countries, and that people in poor countries are not helped if the United States, or an international body, insists on a high one. But the analysis must be different if the question is the behavior of donors or donor nations. Nations who are most in need deserve help, even if their WTP is low. For purposes of regulation, however, insistence on a high VSL will not provide that help. I begin with the distinction between donor practices and government regulation and then turn to the practical question of cross-national valuations.

ARE INDIAN LIVES WORTH LESS THAN AMERICAN LIVES? CLIMATE CHANGE AND BEYOND

In chapter 4, I suggested that people in poor nations show a lower WTP and hence VSL than people in wealthy nations (see table 4.1). Because poor people have less money than rich people, this finding should not be at all surprising. Building on evidence of this kind, some assessments of the effects of climate change find far higher monetized costs from deaths of people in rich countries than from deaths of people in poor countries.[58]

In its Second Report in 1995, for example, the Intergovernmental Panel on Climate Change calculated that a life in an industrialized country was worth $1.5 million, whereas a life in a developing country was worth only $150,000.[59] These assessments proved highly controversial. The philosopher John Broome notes that, under this approach, an American life is worth ten or twenty Indian lives, a judgment that he deems "absurd."[60] As a result, some analysts, including the Intergovernmental Panel, have opted for a worldwide VSL of $1 million, a choice that seems quite arbitrary and potentially harmful to people in rich and poor nations alike.

The issue raises important dilemmas. How should global institutions assess the monetary value of human lives? What are the monetized costs of (say) ten thousand worldwide deaths from climate change, deaths that include (say) eight thousand people from poor countries and two thousand from wealthy ones? The discussion thus far suggests that there is no sensible abstract answer to these questions; it is crucial to know what, in particular, the answer is *for*. If a general question is asked, outside of any particular context, about the monetary value of a stated number of deaths in 2050, it is best left unanswered (except perhaps with laughter). The appropriate assessments of VSL, and variations across countries, depend on their intended use. If disparate numbers are meant to identify the actual monetary values of human lives, and to suggest that people in Canada are "worth" much more than people in Argentina or that poor people are "worth" less than rich ones, the numbers are ludicrous as well as offensive.

It is possible to go further. If the disparate numbers are meant to suggest the appropriate amount that donor institutions should spend to reduce mortality risks, they make little sense. The fact that a poor person in a poor nation would be willing to pay $1 to eliminate a risk of 1/10,000, whereas a wealthy person in a wealthy nation would be willing to pay $100, cannot plausibly be used to defend the view that an international agency should devote its resources to the latter rather than the former. To illustrate this point, imagine choosing between two programs:

A. Program A would eliminate (at a stated cost of $500) a 1/10,000 risk faced by fifty poor people in Costa Rica, each willing to pay $2 to eliminate that risk.

B. Program B would eliminate (also at a stated cost of $500) a 1/10,000 risk faced by fifty wealthy people in France, each willing to pay $350 to eliminate that same risk.

In principle, there is no reason to think that a donor should prefer to save the French, even though their WTP is far higher than that of the Costa Ricans. In fact, Program A has much higher priority, because it would help people who are facing extreme deprivation. What is true at the individual level is true across nations as well. Program A might well be better on welfarist grounds than Program B. Even if they are equal on welfarist grounds, and indeed even if B is better on those grounds, there are strong arguments, prioritarian in nature, on behalf of Program A.

But now consider a different issue. The government in a poor nation is deciding on appropriate policy to reduce workplace risks. What VSL should it use? At least under the assumptions that I have given thus far, such a government would do well to begin by using the admittedly low WTP of its own citizens. If citizens in that nation show a WTP of $2 to eliminate risks of 1/10,000, then their government does them no favors by requiring them to pay $50 or $10 for that protection. This is the sense in which VSL properly varies across nations, and in which citizens of poor nations have lower VSLs than citizens of wealthy ones.

The point has strong implications for international labor standards. It is tempting to suggest that workers in poor countries, for example, China and India, should receive the same protection as those in the United States. Why should a worker in Beijing be subject to significantly higher death risks than a worker in Los Angeles? The answer is that so long as the distribution of global income has the form that it does, a system that gives Indian workers the same protection as American workers is not in the interest of Indian workers—assuming, as I am, that the cost of that protection is borne by workers themselves.

Requiring Indian workers to have the same level of protection as Americans amounts to a forced exchange on terms that Indian workers reject. In these circumstances, it is unsurprising that workers in wealthy nations, not in poor ones, sometimes clamor the loudest for greater health and safety protection of workers in poor nations. Workers in wealthier nations might be the principal beneficiaries of such regulation, which would protect them against competition from those in poorer nations (who are not willing to pay so much to eliminate low-level risks, and who would prefer to have money instead). The idea that workers in poor nations should have the "same" protection as workers in wealthy nations is an error, rooted in a "moral heuristic" involving the equal worth of all human lives—a heuristic that sometimes works well but that also misfires (see chapter 6). The real question is the real effects of different numbers for actual human beings.

If the Indian government uses a VSL of $9 million, on the theory that its citizens should not be valued "less" than those of wealthy nations, harm will almost inevitably result to the citizens of India. In the Easy Cases, the forced exchanges will be harmful to the people whom they are supposed to help. In the hard cases, in which the beneficiaries pay only a fraction of the cost (which will mostly be borne by others in the same nation), the nation might well be spending far too much of its money on risk reduction (or more precisely, on reducing the particular risks that happen to get onto the regulatory agenda). The inefficiency of an extremely high VSL could be felt acutely and in many forms, including reduced growth, higher prices, and decreased employment. (The analysis is the same as if the United States used an inefficiently high VSL of, say, $21 million.)

If, by contrast, the costs of risk reduction would be paid by third parties—for example, wealthy nations—then people in the poor country would be helped even if risk reduction is based on a high VSL. Of course the citizens of poor nations would almost certainly be helped even more if they were given cash rather than in-kind benefits. But if cash redistribution is not possible, regulatory benefits, provided for free or for a fraction of their cost, remain a blessing. If, for example, a global institution uses a worldwide VSL of $5 million, and if that amount exceeds the domestic VSL of people in poor nations, poor people will gain a great deal if the resources for risk reduction are provided by wealthy nations. But to make the point once more: Regulation is not a subsidy. If a poor nation uses a high VSL, and if that nation is footing the bill, it is most unlikely to be helping its own citizens.

Policy and Practice

In this chapter and in chapter 4, my largest goal has been to inquire into the theory behind current practice and to show its roots in plausible ideas about both welfare and autonomy. I have also sought to draw attention to the limits of the prevailing theory. Finally, I have suggested that however regulators deal with distributional problems and the hardest cases, that theory calls for more individuation of VSL than regulators currently provide.

Nothing that I have said here is meant to suggest approval of existing distributions of wealth and resources. Certainly poor people are not "worth less" than wealthy ones, and it is often appropriate for government to provide resources directly to poor people or to subsidize the provision of regulatory benefits. But we have seen that forced exchanges are not a good way to assist poor people and that a uniform VSL may be a perverse response to inequality.

Of course full individuation is not practicable. Government lacks the necessary information about individual risk preferences; categorical judgments are inevitable. In any case, many of the benefits provided by regulation are collective in character. Regulators cannot feasibly provide protection to one person without simultaneously providing protection to many. But it is nonetheless important to see what the current theory counsels in principle, and to understand that the limitations are practical ones, some of which may be overcome as knowledge progresses. Even with the practical limitations, a uniform VSL is increasingly difficult to justify.

SIX

The Morality of Risk

Pioneering the modern literature on the use of heuristics in cognition, Amos Tversky and Daniel Kahneman contended that "people rely on a limited number of heuristic principles which reduce the complex tasks of assessing probabilities and predicting values to simpler judgmental operations."[1] A great deal of controversy has developed over the virtues and vices of the heuristics, most of them "fast and frugal," that play a role in many areas.[2] When people use simple heuristics, or mental shortcuts, it is generally because they work well, in the sense that they enable us to make good decisions. But even if heuristics usually work well, they can lead to big errors. When we make inaccurate assessments of probabilities, it may well be because simple heuristics are leading us astray (see chapter 7 for more details).

The relevant literature is only starting to investigate the possibility that in the moral and political domain, people also rely on simple rules of thumb that often work well but that sometimes misfire. In fact the central point seems obvious. Much of everyday morality consists of simple, highly intuitive rules that generally make sense but that fail in certain cases. It is wrong to lie or steal, but if a lie or a theft would save a human life, lying or stealing is probably obligatory. Not all promises should be kept.

One of my major goals in this chapter is to identify a set of heuristics that influence not only factual but also moral judgments, especially in the domain of risk, and to try to demonstrate that some widely held practices and beliefs are a product of those heuristics. Often risk-related heuristics represent generalizations from a range of problems for which they are indeed well suited, and hence most of the time, such heuristics work well. They have "ecological rationality" in the sense that they produce sensible judgments to the contexts to which they ordinarily apply. They make life simpler, easier, and better.

The problem comes when the generalizations are wrenched out of context and treated as freestanding or universal principles, applicable to situations in which their justifications no longer operate. Because the generalizations are treated as freestanding or universal, their application seems obvious. Those who reject them appear morally obtuse, possibly even monstrous. I want to urge that the appearance is misleading and even productive of moral mistakes. There is nothing obtuse or monstrous about refusing to apply a generalization in contexts in which its rationale is absent.

To the extent that Kahneman and Tversky were dealing with probability judgments, they could demonstrate that the heuristics sometimes lead to errors. Unfortunately, that cannot easily be demonstrated here. In the moral and political domains, it is hard to come up with unambiguous cases where the error is both highly intuitive and on reflection uncontroversial—where people can ultimately be embarrassed about their own intuitions. Nonetheless, I hope to show that whatever one's moral commitments, moral heuristics exist and indeed are omnipresent, with occasionally unfortunate effects on both individual and social reactions to risks.

Ordinary Heuristics, Probability, and an Insistent Homunculus

The classic work on heuristics and biases deals not with moral questions but with issues of fact, usually in the domain of probability judgments. In answering hard factual questions, those who lack accurate information use simple rules of thumb. How many words, in four pages of a novel, will have "ing" as the last three letters? How many words, in the same four pages, will have "n" as the second-to-last letter? Most people will give a higher number in response to the first question than in response to the second[3]—even though a moment's reflection shows that this is a mistake. People err because they use an identifiable heuristic—the availability heuristic—to answer difficult questions.

When people use this heuristic, they answer a question of probability by asking whether examples come readily to mind. How likely is a flood, an airplane crash, a traffic jam, a terrorist attack, or a disaster at a nuclear power plant? Lacking statistical knowledge, people try to think of illustrations. For people without statistical knowledge, it is far from irrational to use the availability heuristic. The problem is that this heuristic can lead to serious errors of fact, in the form of excessive fear of small risks and neglect of large ones.

Or consider the representativeness heuristic, in accordance with which judgments about probability are influenced by assessments of resemblance (the extent to which A "looks like" B). The representativeness heuristic is famously exemplified by people's answers to questions about the likely career of a hypothetical woman named Linda, described as follows: "Linda is 31 years old, single, outspoken, and very bright. She majored in philosophy. As a student, she was deeply concerned with issues of discrimination and social justice and also participated in anti-nuclear demonstrations."[4] People were asked to rank, in order of probability, eight possible futures for Linda. Six of these were fillers (such as psychiatric social worker and elementary school teacher); the two crucial ones were "bank teller" and "bank teller and active in the feminist movement."

Most people say that Linda is more likely to be a bank teller and active in the feminist movement than to be a bank teller. This is an obvious mistake, a "conjunction error," in which characteristics A and B are thought to be more likely than characteristic A alone. The error stems from the representativeness heuristic. Linda's description seems to match "bank teller and active in the feminist movement" far better than "bank teller." In a funny and illuminating reflection on the example, Stephen Jay Gould observes that "I know [the right answer], yet a little homunculus in my head continues to jump up and down, shouting at me—'but she can't just be a bank teller; read the description.'"[5] Because Gould's homunculus is especially inclined to squawk in the moral domain, I shall return to him.

The principal heuristics should be seen in light of dual-process theories of cognition.[6] Those theories distinguish between two families of cognitive operations, sometimes labeled System 1 and System 2. System 1 is intuitive. It is rapid, automatic, and effortless (and it features

Gould's homunculus). System 2, by contrast, is reflective. It is slower, self-aware, calculative, and deductive. System 1 proposes quick answers to problems of judgment, and System 2 operates as a monitor, confirming or overriding those judgments.

Consider, for example, someone who is flying from New York to London in the month after an airplane crash. This person might make a rapid, barely conscious judgment, rooted in System 1, that the flight is quite risky; but there might well be a System 2 override, bringing a more realistic assessment to bear. System 1 often has an emotional component, but it need not. For example, a probability judgment might be made quite rapidly and without much emotion or affect at all (see chapter 7 for more details).

There is growing evidence that people often make automatic, largely unreflective moral judgments, for which they are sometimes unable to give good reasons.[7] System 1 is operative here as well, and it may or may not be subject to System 2 override. Consider the incest taboo. People have moral revulsion against incest even in circumstances in which the grounds for that taboo seem to be absent. They are subject to "moral dumbfounding,"[8] that is, an inability to give an account for a firmly held intuition. It is plausible, at least, to think that System 1 is driving their judgments, without System 2 correction. The same is true in legal and political contexts relating to risk as well.

Heuristics and Morality

To show that heuristics operate in the moral domain, we have to specify some benchmark by which we can measure moral truth. On these questions I want to avoid any especially controversial claims. Whatever one's view of the foundations of moral and political judgments, I suggest, moral heuristics are likely to be at work in practice.

Many people are utilitarians, and many utilitarians, including the philosophers John Stuart Mill and Henry Sidgwick, argue that ordinary morality is based on simple rules of thumb that generally promote utility but that sometimes misfire.[9] On this view, ordinary morality actually is utilitarian, but imperfectly so. For example, Mill emphasizes that human beings "have been learning by experience the tendencies of experience," so that the "corollaries from the principle of utility" are being progressively captured by ordinary morality.[10] Is ordinary morality a series of heuristics for what really matters, which is utility? Utilitarians are likely to think so.

To say the least, deontologists will not agree. They insist that morality requires us to do what is right, and what is right may not promote utility. It is usually wrong to lie, to cheat, or to inflict suffering, even if doing so would be justified on utilitarian grounds. Deontologists might insist that ordinary morality is based on simple rules of thumb that generally point in the right direction but that sometimes misfire.[11] On this view, ordinary morality is deontological, but imperfectly so.

Utilitarians might well insist that the views held by deontologists are heuristics for what morality requires, which is promoting utility. Deontologists might well turn the tables and urge that exactly the opposite is true. These large debates are not easy to resolve, for utilitarians and deontologists are most unlikely to be convinced by the suggestion that their defining commitments are mere heuristics. Here there is a large difference between moral heuristics and the heuristics uncovered in the relevant psychological work, where the facts or simple logic provide a good test of whether people have erred. If people tend to think that more words, in a given space, end with the letters "ing" than have "n" in the next-to-last position, something has clearly gone wrong. If people think that some person Linda is more likely to be "a bank teller who is active in the feminist movement" than a "bank teller," there is an evident problem. In the moral domain, factual blunders and simple logic do not provide such a simple test.

My goal here is therefore not to say anything controversial about the correct general theory with respect to morality or risks, but to suggest more cautiously that, in many particular cases, moral heuristics are at work—and that this point can be accepted by people with diverse general theories, or with grave uncertainty about which general theory is correct. In the cases cataloged below, I contend that it is possible to conclude that a moral heuristic is at work without accepting any especially controversial moral claims. In several of the examples, that claim can be accepted without accepting any contestable moral theory at all. Other examples will require acceptance of what I shall call "weak consequentialism," in accordance with which the social consequences of the legal system are relevant, other things being equal, to what law and government ought to be doing.

Of course some deontologists will reject any form of consequentialism altogether. But weak consequentialism seems to me sufficiently nonsectarian, and attractive to sufficiently diverse people, to make plausible the idea that in the cases at hand, moral heuristics are playing a significant role. And for those who reject weak consequentialism, it might nonetheless be productive to ask whether, from their own point of view, certain moral judgments about risks are reflective of heuristics that sometimes produce serious errors.

The Asian Disease Problem and Moral Framing

In a finding closely related to their work on heuristics, Kahneman and Tversky themselves find "moral framing" in the context of what has become known as "the Asian disease problem."[12] Framing effects do not involve heuristics, but because they raise obvious questions about the nature and rationality of moral intuitions, they provide a valuable backdrop. Here is the first component of the problem:

> Imagine that the U.S. is preparing for the outbreak of an unusual Asian disease, which is expected to kill 600 people. Two alternative programs to combat the disease have been proposed. Assume that the exact scientific estimates of the consequences are as follows:
>
> If Program A is adopted, 200 people will be saved.
>
> If Program B is adopted, there is a one-third probability that 600 people will be saved and a two-thirds probability that no people will be saved.
>
> Which of the two programs would you favor?

Most people choose Program A.

But now consider the second component of the problem, in which the same situation is given but followed by this description of the alternative programs:

If Program C is adopted, 400 people will die.

If Program D is adopted, there is a one-third probability that nobody will die and a two-thirds probability that 600 people will die.

Most people choose Problem D. But a moment's reflection should be enough to show that Program A and Program C are identical, and so too for Program B and Program D. These are merely different descriptions of the same programs! The purely semantic shift in framing is sufficient to produce different outcomes.

Apparently people's judgments about which program is preferable depend on whether the results are described in terms of "lives saved" or instead "lives lost." What accounts for the difference? The most sensible answer begins with the fact that human beings are pervasively averse to losses (hence the robust cognitive finding of loss aversion[13]). With respect to either self-interested gambles or fundamental moral judgments, loss aversion plays a large role in people's decisions. But what counts as a gain or a loss depends on the baseline from which measurements are made. Purely semantic reframing can alter the baseline and hence alter moral intuitions.

Moral framing has been demonstrated in the important context of obligations to future generations,[14] a much-disputed question of morality, politics, and law. To say the least, the appropriate discount rate for those yet to be born is not a question that most people have pondered, and hence their judgments are highly susceptible to different frames. From a series of surveys, Maureen Cropper and her coauthors suggest that people are indifferent between saving one life today and saving forty-five lives in one hundred years.[15] They make this suggestion on the basis of questions asking people whether they would choose a program that saves "one hundred lives now" or a program that saves a substantially larger number "one hundred years from now."

It is possible, however, that people's responses depend on uncertainty about whether people in the future will otherwise die later (perhaps technological improvements will extend lives?). Other ways of framing the same problem yield radically different results.[16] For example, most people consider "equally bad" a single death from pollution next year and a single death from pollution in one hundred years. This finding implies no preference for members of the current generation. The simplest conclusion is that people's moral judgments about obligations to future generations are very much a product of framing effects.

Of course skeptics might question whether people actually err when they make different judgments in response to logically identical descriptions of risk-related problems. Perhaps the change from logical form A to logically equivalent form B has the effect of altering the subject's understanding of the substance of the problem, in a way that does introduce ethical differences. Certainly this is possible if the change alters the pragmatics of communication; we might distinguish here between truth-value and speech-act. If a doctor says that five years after a certain operation, "90 percent of patients are alive," the speech-act is different from what it is if the doctor says that after a certain operation, "10 percent of patients die"—even though the truth-value remains the same. With the "90 percent are alive" frame, the doctor is suggesting his belief that the operation is worth a try, while the "10 percent die" frame suggests a degree of pessimism. I do not believe that such explanations are adequate to account for framing effects. But it is not necessary to reject them to suggest that moral intuitions are highly susceptible to frames.

As a further example, consider the question whether government should consider not only the number of "lives" but also the number of "life years" saved by regulatory interventions. The difference might well matter. Some regulations save an impressively large number of lives, but not such an impressive number of life years, because the people who are being helped are quite old. Other regulations save a relatively small number of lives, but a lot of life years, because the people who are being helped are quite young. If the government focuses on life years, a program that saves children will be worth far more attention than a similar program that saves senior citizens. Is this immoral?

People's moral intuitions very much depend on how the question is framed. Consider this question: *Do you favor valuing an older person's life less than a younger person's life?* People will predictably reject an approach that would count every old person as worth "less" than what every young person is worth. But consider this question: *Would you favor (a) a regulation that would save the lives of 105 people over the age of 80 or (b) a regulation that would save the lives of 100 people under the age of 10?* If people are asked whether they would favor a policy that saves 105 old people or 100 young people, many will favor the latter, in a way that suggests a willingness to pay considerable attention to the number of life years at stake.

At least for unfamiliar questions of morality, politics, and law, people's intuitions are very much affected by framing. In the domain of risk, it is effective to frame certain consequences as "losses" from a status quo. When losses are so framed, people's moral concern becomes significantly elevated. It is for this reason that political actors often phrase one or another proposal as "turning back the clock" on some social advance. The problem is that for many social changes, the framing does not reflect social reality, but is simply a verbal manipulation.

Let us now turn to examples that are more controversial.

Cost-Benefit Analysis

An automobile company is deciding whether to take certain safety precautions for its cars. In deciding whether to do so, it conducts a cost-benefit analysis, in which it concludes that certain precautions are not justified—because, say, they would cost $100 million and save only four lives, and because the company has a "ceiling" of $15 million per life saved (a ceiling that is, as we have seen, significantly higher than the amount the U.S. Environmental Protection Agency uses for a statistical life, which is about $9 million). How will ordinary people react to this decision?

The answer is that they will not react favorably.[17] In fact they tend to punish companies that base their decisions on cost-benefit analysis, even if a high valuation is placed on human life. By contrast, they impose less severe punishment on companies that are willing to impose a "risk" on people but that do not produce a formal risk analysis that measures lives lost and dollars, and compares one to another.[18] The oddity here is that under tort law, it is unclear that a company should be liable at all if it has acted on the basis of a competent cost-benefit analysis; such an analysis might even insulate a company from a claim of negligence. What underlies people's moral judgments, which are replicated in actual jury decisions?[19]

It is possible that when people disapprove of trading money for lives, they are generalizing from a set of moral principles that are usually sound, and even important, but that work poorly in some cases. Consider the following moral principle: *Do not knowingly cause a human death.* In ordinary life, you should not engage in conduct with the knowledge that several people will die as a result. If you are playing a sport or working on your yard, you ought not to continue if you believe that your actions will kill others. Invoking that idea, people disapprove of companies that fail to improve safety when they are fully aware that deaths will result. By contrast, people do not disapprove of those who fail to improve safety while believing that there is a "risk" but appearing not to know, for certain, that deaths will ensue. When people object to risky action taken after cost-benefit analysis, it seems to be partly because that very analysis puts the number of expected deaths squarely "on screen."[20]

Companies that fail to do such analysis, but that are aware that a "risk" exists, do not make clear, to themselves or to anyone else, that they caused deaths with full knowledge that this was what they were going to do. People disapprove, above all, of companies that cause death knowingly. There may be a kind of "cold-heart heuristic" here: Those who know that they will cause a death, and do so anyway, are regarded as cold-hearted monsters.[21] On this view, critics of cost-benefit analysis might be seen as appealing to System 1 and as speaking directly to the homunculus. Their question is this: *Is a corporation or public agency that endangers us to be pardoned for its sins once it has spent $9 million per statistical life, and no more, on risk reduction?*[22] Their answer is a firm "no." My suggestion is that the answer is based on a moral heuristic—one that usually works well but that also misfires.

Note that it is easy to reframe a probability as a certainty and vice versa; if I am correct, the reframing is likely to have large effects. Consider two cases:

A. Company A knows that its product will kill ten people. It markets the product to its ten million customers with that knowledge. The cost of eliminating the risk would have been $100 million.

B. Company B knows that its product creates a 1 in 1 million risk of death. Its product is used by ten million people. The cost of eliminating the risk would have been $100 million.

I have not collected data, but I am willing to predict that Company A would be punished more severely than Company B, even though there is no difference between the two. A moral heuristic is at work, one that imposes moral condemnation on those who knowingly engage in acts that will result in human deaths.

Of course this heuristic does a great deal of good. The problem is that it is not always unacceptable to cause death knowingly, at least if the deaths are relatively few and an unintended byproduct of generally desirable activity. When government allows new highways to be constructed, it knows that people will die on those highways. When government allows new coal-fired power plants to be built, it knows that some people will die from the resulting pollution. When companies produce tobacco products, and when government does not ban those products, hundreds of thousands of people will die. The same is true for alcohol. Of course it would make sense, in all of these domains, to take extra steps to reduce risks. But that proposition does not support the implausible claim that we should disapprove, from the moral point of view, of any action taken when deaths are foreseeable.

I believe that it is impossible to vindicate, in principle, the widespread social antipathy to cost-benefit balancing. But here too, "a little homunculus in my head continues to jump up and down, shouting at me" that corporate cost-benefit analysis, trading dollars for a known number of deaths, is morally unacceptable. The voice of the homunculus, I am suggesting, is not reflective, but instead a product of System 1, and a crude but quite tenacious moral heuristic.

Betrayals and Betrayal Risk

To say the least, people do not like to be betrayed. A betrayal of trust is likely to produce a great deal of outrage. If a babysitter neglects a child, or if a security guard steals from his employer, people will be angrier than if the identical acts are performed by someone in whom trust has not been reposed. So far, perhaps, so good: When trust is betrayed, the damage is worse than when an otherwise identical act has been committed by someone who was not a beneficiary of trust. And it should not be surprising that people will favor greater punishment for betrayals than for otherwise identical wrongs.[23]

Perhaps the disparity can be justified on the ground that the betrayal of trust is an independent harm, one that warrants greater deterrence and retribution—a point that draws strength from the fact that trust, once lost, is not easily regained. A family robbed by its babysitter might well be more seriously injured than a family robbed by a thief. The loss of money is compounded, and possibly dwarfed, by the violation of a trusting relationship. The consequence of the violation might also be more serious. Will the family ever feel entirely comfortable with babysitters? It is bad to have an unfaithful spouse, but it is even worse if the infidelity occurred with your best friend, because that kind of infidelity makes it harder to have trusting relationships with friends in the future.

In this light it is possible to understand why betrayals produce special moral opprobrium and (where the law has been violated) increased punishment. But consider a finding that is much harder to explain: *People are especially averse to risks of death that come from products (like airbags) designed to promote safety.*[24] The aversion is so great that people have been found to prefer a higher chance of dying, as a result of accidents from a crash, to a significantly lower chance of dying in a crash as a result of a malfunctioning airbag.

The relevant study involved two principal conditions. In the first, people were asked to choose between two equally priced cars, Car A and Car B. According to crash tests, there was a 2 percent chance that drivers of Car A, with Air Bag A, will die in serious accidents as a result of the impact of the crash. With Car B, and Air Bag B, there was a 1 percent chance of death, but also an additional chance of 1 in 10,000 (0.01 percent) of death *as a result of deployment of the air bag.* Similar studies involved vaccines and smoke alarms.

The result was that most participants (over two-thirds) chose the higher risk safety option when the less risky one carried a "betrayal risk." A control condition demonstrated that people were not confused about the numbers. When asked to choose between a 2 percent risk and a 1.01 percent risk, people selected the 1.01 percent risk so long as betrayal was not involved. In other words, people's aversion to betrayals is so great that they will increase their own risks rather than subject themselves to a (small) hazard that comes from a device that is supposed to increase safety! "Apparently, people are willing to incur greater risks of the very harm they seek protection from to avoid the mere possibility of betrayal."[25] Remarkably, "betrayal risks appear to be so psychologically intolerable that people are willing to double their risk of death from automobile crashes, fires, and diseases to avoid incurring a small possibility of death by safety device betrayal."

What explains this seemingly bizarre and self-destructive preference? I suggest that a heuristic is at work: *Punish, and do not reward, betrayals of trust.* The heuristic generally works well. But it misfires in some cases, as when those who deploy it end up increasing the risks they themselves face. An airbag is not a security guard or a babysitter, endangering those whom they have been hired to protect. It is a product, to be chosen if and only if it decreases aggregate risks. If an airbag makes people safer on balance, it should be used, even if in a tiny percentage of cases it will create a risk that would not otherwise exist.

Of course it is true that some kinds of death are reasonably seen as worse than others. It is not absurd to prefer one kind of death to another. But betrayal aversion is not adequately explained in these terms. The experimental work suggests that people are generalizing from a heuristic.

A skeptic might respond that the special antipathy to betrayal risks should be seen to involve not a moral heuristic but a taste. In choosing products, people are not making pure moral judgments. They are choosing what they like best, and it just turns out that a moral judgment, involving antipathy to betrayals, is part of what they like best. But why? On what grounds is this a reasonable choice? To be sure, it would be useful to design a further test of moral judgments, one that would ask people not about their own safety but about that of others—for example, whether people are averse to betrayal risks when they are purchasing safety devices for their friends or family members. There is every reason to expect that it would produce substantially identical results to those in the experiments just described.

Closely related experiments support that expectation.[26] In deciding whether to vaccinate their children from risks for serious diseases, people show a form of "omission bias." Many people are more sensitive to the risk of the vaccination than to the risk from the diseases against which the vaccination would provide protection—so much so that they will expose their children to a greater risk from "nature" than from the vaccine. (There is a clear connection between omission bias and trust in nature and antipathy to "playing God," as discussed below.) The omission bias, I suggest, is closely related to people's special antipathy to betrayals. It leads to moral errors, in the form of vaccination judgments (and undoubtedly others) by which some parents increase the fatality risks faced by their own children.

Emissions Trading

Through what mechanisms should regulators attempt to reduce social risks? In the last decades, those involved in enacting and implementing environmental law have experimented with systems of "emissions trading." In those systems, polluters are typically given a license to pollute a certain amount, and the licenses can be traded on the market. The advantage of emissions trading systems is that if they work well, they will ensure emissions reductions at the lowest possible cost.

Is emissions trading immoral? Is this a morally unacceptable means of reducing the risks associated with pollution? Many people believe so. Political theorist Michael Sandel, for example, urges that trading systems "undermine the ethic we should be trying to foster on the environment."[27] Sandel contends:

> [T]urning pollution into a commodity to be bought and sold removes the moral stigma that is properly associated with it. If a company or a country is fined for spewing excessive pollutants into the air, the community conveys its judgment that the polluter has done something wrong. A fee, on the other hand, makes pollution just another cost of doing business, like wages, benefits and rent.

In the same vein, Sandel objects to proposals to open carpool lanes to drivers without passengers who are willing to pay a fee. Here, as in the environmental context, it seems unacceptable to permit people to do something that is morally wrong so long as they are willing to pay for the privilege.

I suggest that like other critics of emissions trading programs, Sandel is using a moral heuristic. In fact he has been fooled by his homunculus.

The heuristic is this: *People should not be permitted to engage in moral wrongdoing for a fee.* You are not allowed to assault someone so long as you are willing to pay for the right to do so; there are no tradable licenses for rape, theft, or battery. The reason is that the appropriate level of these forms of wrongdoing is zero (putting to one side the fact that enforcement resources are limited; if they were unlimited, we would want to eliminate, not merely to reduce, these forms of illegality).

But pollution is an altogether different matter. At least some level of pollution is a byproduct of desirable social activities and products, including automobiles and power plants. Of course certain acts of pollution are morally wrong; but the same cannot be said of pollution as such. When Sandel objects to emissions trading, he is treating pollution as equivalent to a crime, in a way that overgeneralizes a moral intuition that makes sense in other contexts. There is no moral problem with emissions trading as such. The insistent objection to emissions trading systems stems from a moral heuristic.

Unfortunately, that objection has appeared compelling to many people, so much so as to delay and to reduce the use of a pollution reduction tool that is, in many contexts, the best available. Here, then, is a case in which a moral heuristic has led to political blunders, in the form of policies that impose high costs for no real gain.

The Precautionary Principle and Loss Aversion

In many nations, risk regulation is undertaken with close reference to the Precautionary Principle.[28] The Precautionary Principle has no canonical formulation, but in its strongest and most distinctive forms, it is designed to insert a "margin of safety" into all decision making, and to impose a burden of proof on proponents of activities or processes to establish that they are "safe." Thus understood, the Precautionary Principle is taken to have important consequences. For example, it is thought to raise serious questions about DDT, genetically modified organisms, nuclear power, electromagnetic fields, and the emission of greenhouse gases.

On reflection, however, it should be clear that, in its strong forms, the Precautionary Principle is incoherent. It condemns the very measures that it requires. The reason is that risk regulation often introduces risks of its own. Sometimes it does so because it eliminates the risk reduction benefits associated with the activity against which it imposes precautions. Regulation of DDT, for example, can increase the risk of malaria—and thus violates the Precautionary Principle. In other contexts, precautionary steps give rise to substitute risks. For example, regulation of nuclear power might increase the likelihood that societies will depend on fossil fuels, which create air pollution and emit greenhouse gases. In any event, precautionary steps sometimes create risks merely by virtue of their expense. For example, regulatory controls on asthma medicine that emit chemicals that deplete the ozone layer might increase the likelihood that asthmatics will have trouble finding inexpensive, effective medicines. By its very nature, costly regulation threatens to increase unemployment and poverty, and both of these increase risks of mortality.

If we are truly serious about the Precautionary Principle, we will condemn measures that increase such risks by virtue of their expense—and hence condemn the very measures that the Precautionary Principle requires. A vivid example involves the risks associated with preemptive war. President George W. Bush justified the war in Iraq on precautionary grounds, as a way of eliminating the danger from Saddam Hussein. The problem is that the war offered risks of its own. Whether or not the war was ultimately justified, no precautionary principle would suffice to support it.

Why, then, is the principle widely thought to give guidance? I suggest that two mechanisms are at work. The first is the availability heuristic. Sometimes a certain risk, said to call for precautions, is cognitively available, whereas other risks, including those associated with regulation itself, are not. In many cases where the Precautionary Principle seems to offer guidance, some of the relevant risks are available while others are barely visible. And if one nation is concerned with the risk of terrorism and another is not, availability is likely to provide a large part of the reason. (See chapter 7.)

The second mechanism involves loss aversion. As I have noted, human beings are typically averse to losses, which they dislike more than they like corresponding gains. When the Precautionary Principle seems coherent, it is often because the status quo is taken as the baseline for its operation; losses "code" as especially troublesome, whereas foregone opportunities do not. This point helps explain intense disapproval, in some quarters, of genetically modified organisms and food. The potentially large social benefits of genetic modification, perhaps saving numerous lives, are not much on the public view screen.

I do not mean to deny the possibility that the Precautionary Principle can be reconstructed in coherent terms, nor do I contend that in all imaginable forms, the principle becomes operational only because of the availability heuristic and loss aversion. But most of the time, a senseless idea—that it is possible to be precautionary *in general*—appears sensible only because people operate with selective blinders, focusing on some but not all of the universe of relevant risks.

There is a much broader point in the background. Precautionary thinking often involves a form of the act-omission distinction, in a way that seems to reflect a moral heuristic, and a potentially destructive one. Both regulators and ordinary people often worry that they will be blamed for licensing a potentially dangerous process, activity, or product (such as a drug) that might cause deaths—while showing much less concern about the failure to prevent deaths through their refusal to license a process, activity, or product that is potentially beneficial. At times, the result has been a precautionary stance that imposes undue barriers to life-saving processes, activities, or products.

To be sure, the act-omission distinction might be plausibly defended on consequentialist or deontological grounds, at least in many contexts in ordinary life. But for risk regulators, the distinction seems to operate as a kind of heuristic, one that misfires in many cases. I believe that in the general context of risk reduction, intense concern about potentially harmful acts, and relative indifference to the effects of relatively harmful omissions, can sometimes be seen as the squawking of an internal homunculus on the part of regulators and their constituents—very much like Gould's in the context of the representativeness heuristic.

Rules and Blunders

I have argued here that moral judgments about risks, no less than probability judgments, are often a product of heuristics, and that they often misfire. To the extent that moral heuristics operate as rules, they might be defended in the way that all rules are—better than the alternatives even if productive of error in imaginable cases. As I have noted, moral heuristics might show a kind of "ecological rationality," working well in most real-world contexts.[29] Recall the possibility that human beings live by simple heuristics that make us good.

My suggestion is not that the moral heuristics, in their most rigid forms, are worse than the reasonable alternatives. It is hard to resolve that question in the abstract. I am claiming only that such heuristics lead to real errors and significant confusion in thinking about risk. After all, regulators are not in the position of ordinary people, with limited time and in need of simple rules of thumb. They typically have significant resources, including significant time, and they can do far better than to rely on heuristics.

If it is harder to demonstrate that heuristics are at work in the domain of morality than in the domain of facts, this is largely because we are able to agree about what constitutes factual error, and often less able to agree about what constitutes moral error. With respect to the largest disputes about what morality requires, it may be too contentious to argue that one side is operating under a heuristic, whereas another side has it basically right. But I hope that I have said enough to show that, in particular cases, sensible rules of thumb lead to demonstrable errors not merely in probability judgments, but in moral assessments as well.

SEVEN

What Scares Us

When fear is widespread, it is often because of one or more of three features of human psychology. The first two are well known. The third is less so, and it will be my principal emphasis here. Because the three features are related, they should be identified at the outset.

As behavioral scientists have demonstrated, and as we saw in chapter 6, people assess probabilities through the use of various heuristics, most notably the availability heuristic, in accordance with which probability is measured by asking whether a readily available example comes to mind.[1] In the aftermath of a terrorist act, for example, that act is likely to be both available and salient, and thus to make people fear that another such act may well occur, even if it is highly unlikely to do so. One or two horrific incidents—an airplane accident, an environmental disaster, a crime—can have a significant impact on both thought and behavior, with exaggerated risk perceptions a likely result of the substantial publicity given to such incidents.

Floods, earthquakes, and other catastrophes tend to have large and immediate effects on people's behavior, even if the risk of another incident is low. In short, a highly publicized event may well produce unrealistically inflated fear. For those with imperfect information, use of the availability heuristic may be consistent with rational learning, and sometimes the resulting fear is justified. But there is no question that the availability heuristic can produce significantly exaggerated judgments about probable harm.

The second point is that people show a disproportionate fear of risks that seem unfamiliar and hard to control.[2] Such risks may well receive far more attention than is warranted by the sheer numbers. Indeed, the law itself tends to regulate new hazards far more aggressively than old ones.[3] Hence it is possible that a hurricane, a flood, an act of terrorism, or other terrible events will cause large changes in private and public behavior, even if the magnitude of the risk does not justify those changes, and even if statistically equivalent risks occasion little or no concern. And if a risk appears hard to control, people will be especially concerned about it, possibly even terrified. The purpose and effect of terrorism, for example, may be to make people fear that they "cannot be safe anywhere." For this reason, isolated acts of terrorism, involving a small subset of the population, can cause far more serious dislocations than are warranted by the statistical risk.

The third problem, and my principal claim here, is that people are prone to what I shall call *probability neglect*, especially when their emotions are intensely engaged. People fall victim to probability neglect if and to the extent that the intensity of their reaction does not greatly vary even with large differences in the likelihood of harm. When probability neglect is at work, people's attention is focused on the bad outcome itself, and they are inattentive to the fact that it is unlikely to occur. Probability neglect may well occur in the aftermath of horrific events of all kinds. At the same time, those in the private and public sectors may be able to take steps to counteract that form of neglect (as happened in the aftermath of the bombings at the end of the Boston marathon in 2013).

I will offer a good deal of evidence of probability neglect, suggesting in particular that substantial variations in probability do not greatly affect people's judgments, at least when the outcome engages people's emotions. An understanding of probability neglect has several implications for law and policy. In the aftermath of a serious terrorist attack, for example, the public may well alter its behavior and demand a substantial governmental response—even if the magnitude of the risk does not warrant that response, and even if the danger is far less than that presented by other hazards that do not greatly concern people.

Hence terrible events can have a large number of "ripple effects," including a demand for legal interventions that might not reduce risks and that might in fact make things worse. Consider, for example, the possibility that excessive security precautions at airports will lead people to drive rather than to fly. Because flying is much safer than driving, such precautions might sacrifice many lives on balance.

If probability neglect leads the public to be excessively concerned about terrorism-related risks, should government respond? At first glance, the answer would appear to be negative. Private and public resources should not be devoted to small problems, even if some members of the public are demanding action. But the negative answer is far too simple. Fear, whether rational or not, is itself a cost, and it is likely to lead to a range of other costs, in the form of ripple effects, perhaps including a reluctance to fly or to appear in public places. If government is able to reduce the level of fear produced by probability neglect, it should do so, at least if the costs outweigh the benefits.

Probability Neglect: Theory and Practice

Probability neglect, as I understand it here, should be distinguished from three other phenomena, all of them quite well known and also bearing on the demand for law in the aftermath of a terrorist attack. As I have suggested, the availability heuristic is used strategically by many people, including terrorists.[4] Indeed "availability entrepreneurs" take advantage of the availability heuristic by producing or publicizing particular risk-related events, perhaps to seek legislation that they favor (as environmentalists do), perhaps to promote either selfish or altruist goals. Terrorists are extreme examples of availability entrepreneurs, hoping to produce fear that greatly outruns statistical reality. Because of social interactions, knowledge of terrorist incidents spreads rapidly through the population, producing social cascades that greatly aggravate fear.

It is also well known that people are insensitive to significant variations in *low* probabilities. In an illuminating study, the economist Howard Kunreuther and his coauthors found that people's willingness to pay for insurance premiums did not vary among risks of 1 in 100,000, 1 in 1 million, and 1 in 10 million.[5] They also found little difference in people's willingness to pay for insurance premiums for risks ranging from 1 in 650, to 1 in 6,300, to 1 in 68,000. This is a striking form of probability neglect. But insensitivity to variations among low probabilities is different from the more extreme form of insensitivity that I will be emphasizing here.

Prospect theory is an influential account of how people make decisions under circumstances of risk, and it can also be taken to show a form of probability neglect.[6] For present purposes, what is most important about prospect theory is that it offers an explanation for simultaneous gambling and insurance. With respect to low-probability risks, the key finding is that most people prefer a certain loss of X to a gamble with an expected value less than X, *if the gamble involves a small probability of catastrophe.* (Hence the purchase of insurance.) Prospect theory predicts that people will overreact to a small probability of bad outcomes. And if that aspect of prospect theory is emphasized, it may be possible to understand some aspects of federal risk regulation, which sometimes shows what seems to be an exaggerated response to low-probability catastrophes.[7] Just as people buy expensive insurance against low-probability risks, so may regulators adopt a kind of regulatory insurance, even if it is expensive.

The same understanding helps illuminate official responses to terrorism and other low-probability risks. Prospect theory suggests that people will seek regulation, as a form of insurance, to prevent harms that are grave but that are highly unlikely to occur. This point helps explain the demand for protection against small risks of catastrophic attacks. But in making this descriptive claim, prospect theory does not set out any special role for emotions, and it does not predict that people will react in any special way to emotionally gripping risks. On the contrary, prospect theory predicts the same reaction to risks that produce strong emotional reactions and to statistically equivalent risks that do not produce such reactions. Prospect theory is both more specialized and more general than the phenomenon to which I seek to draw attention here.

Electric Shocks

To see how probability neglect operates, consider a study of people's willingness to pay to avoid electric shocks.[8] The central purpose of the study was to test the relevance of variations in probability to highly emotional (or "affect rich") decisions. The most important experiment attempted to see whether varying the probability of harm would matter more, or less, in settings that trigger strong emotions than in settings that seem relatively emotion free.[9]

In the relatively emotion-free setting, participants were told that the experiment entailed some chance of a $20 penalty. Some participants were informed that there was a 1 percent chance of receiving the bad outcome (the $20 loss). Others were informed that the chance was 99 percent. Participants were asked to say how much they would be willing to pay to avoid participating in the experiment. For the cash penalty, the difference between the median payment for the 1 percent chance of loss and the median payment for the 99 percent of loss chance was predictably large and indeed consistent with the standard economic model: $1 to avoid a 1 percent chance and $18 to avoid a 99 percent chance. So far, so good.

In the "strong emotion" setting, participants were asked to imagine that they would participate in an experiment involving some chance of a "short, painful, but not dangerous electric shock." Here again, some participants were told that there was a 1 percent chance of receiving the bad outcome (the electric shock). Others were told that the chance was 99 percent. But in this setting, the difference in probability made strikingly little difference to median willingness to pay: $7 to avoid a 1 percent chance of an electric shock, and $10 to avoid a 99 percent chance! Hence people's responses to emotion-free harms were highly sensitive to differences in probability—whereas for harms that triggered stronger emotions, their responses were remarkably flat across the two probability conditions. In the emotional conditions, probability did not matter; people's answers were driven by the bad outcome, not the likelihood that it would occur.

This is a striking demonstration of probability neglect in action. What is observed for bad events can be found for good ones as well. In the same set of studies, people were found not to pay a lot of attention to probability when the question involved the opportunity to meet and kiss their favorite movie star. What got their attention was the outcome, not the statistical likelihood that it would come to fruition. Those who sell lottery tickets exploit the same phenomenon, drawing people's attention to "easy street" while downplaying the question of probability.

In the context of other emotionally gripping evidence, such as flood, earthquakes, and terrorism, the implication is clear. The risks associated with (for example) terrorist attacks are highly likely to trigger strong emotions, in part because of the sheer vividness of the bad outcome and the associated levels of outrage and fear. It follows that even if the likeli-hood of a terrorist attack is extremely low, people may well be willing to do and pay a great deal to avoid it. In October 2002, the significant and often expensive precautions taken against possible sniper attacks, by citizens of the Washington, D.C., area, attest to the phenomenon of probability neglect in the face of vivid bad outcomes.

Cancer

To explore the phenomenon of probability neglect, Harvard economist Richard Zeckhauser and I conducted several experiments.[10] The sub-jects were students in a class in Administrative Law—for second- and third-year students—at Harvard Law School. All students were required to participate. The participants were randomly sorted into four groups, representing the four conditions in a 2×2 experiment, where both the probability and the description of the risk varied. In the first condition, people were asked to state their maximum willingness to pay to elimi-nate a cancer risk of 1 in 1 million. In the second condition, people were asked to state their maximum willingness to pay to eliminate a cancer risk of 1 in 100,000.

In the third condition, people were asked the first question (how much would they pay to eliminate a cancer risk of 1 in 1 million), but the cancer was described in vivid terms, as "very gruesome and intensely painful, as the cancer eats away at the internal organs of the body." In the fourth condition, people were asked the second question (how much they would pay to eliminate a risk of 1 in 100,000), but the cancer was described in the same vivid terms as in the third condition.

In each condition, participants were asked to check off their will-ingness to pay among the following options: $0, $25, $50, $100, $200, $400, and $800 or more. Notice that the description of the cancer in the "highly emotional" conditions added little information, simply describ-ing many cancer deaths, though admittedly some participants might well have learned that these were especially horrific deaths.

The first hypothesis, consistent with the probability weighting func-tion of prospect theory, was that the tenfold difference in probabilities—

TABLE 7.1: Willingness to Pay in Dollars for Elimination of Arsenic Risks

Harvard Law School Results, 2008
Mean (Median)
[Number of Subjects]

Probability	Unemotional description	Emotional description
1/100,000	241.25 (100)	250 (100)
	[20]	[13]
1/1,000,000	59.21 (25)	211.67 (200)
	[19]	[15]

between 1/100,000 and 1/1 million—would generate much less than a tenfold difference in willingness to pay. The second hypothesis was that the probability variations would matter less in the highly emotional conditions than in the less emotional conditions. More specifically, we predicted that the descriptions in the highly emotional conditions would overshadow differences in probability, whereas such differences would have greater importance in the less emotional condition. The results are presented in table 7.1.

As hypothesized and found, the valuations for the emotional description did not much differ even though risks differed by a factor of ten. By contrast, and also as expected, the difference for the unemotional description was highly significant, with the 1/100,000 payment higher ($z = 3.398, p < 0.001$). Comparing the two results showed that the unemotional description gave a greater differential, one that was highly statistically significant. (It is important to note that the difference in WTP, even for the unemotional description, was far below the 10 to 1 odds ratio; for means it was roughly 4 to 1.)

Both hypotheses were therefore supported. First, varying the probability had an effect on WTP that was much less than standard decision theory would predict. (Future research should assess whether merely mentioning the word "cancer" induced sufficient emotion to reduce a 10 to 1 ratio to 4 to 1; recall the discussion of cancer risks in chapters 4 and 5.) Second, increasing the probability by a factor of ten had an effect that was highly significant in the unemotional condition—but completely insignificant in the emotional condition. When the cancer was described in emotionally gripping terms, people were insensitive to probability variations.

This study has two implications for the public reaction to emotionally gripping events. It suggests, first, that simply because such events arouse strong feelings, they are likely to trigger a larger behavioral response than do statistically identical risks that do not produce emotional reactions. Here, as in the experiment, there will be a kind of "emotion premium." The study suggests, second, that probability neglect might well play a role in the government's reaction to emotionally gripping events, in part because many people will focus on the badness of the outcome, rather than on its likelihood.

Fear, Outrage, and Probability

Probability neglect, when strong emotions are involved, has been found in many other studies.[11] Consider another set of experiments designed to test levels of anxiety in anticipation of a painful electric shock of varying intensity, to be administered after a "countdown period" of a stated length. In these studies, the stated intensity of the shock had a significant effect on physiological reactions. But the probability of the shock had no effect. "Evidently, the mere thought of receiving a shock was enough to arouse subjects, and the precise likelihood of being shocked had little impact on their arousal level."[12]

A related study asked people to provide their maximum buying prices for risky investments, which contained different stated probabilities of losses and gains of different magnitudes.[13] Happily for the standard theory, maximum buying prices were affected by the size of losses and gains and also by probabilities. (Note that, for most people, this experiment did not involve an affect-rich environment.) But—and this is the key point—reported feelings of *worry* were not much affected by probability levels. In this study, then, probability did affect behavior, but it did not affect emotions. The point has independent importance for potentially catastrophic events, to which I will return: Worry and anxiety are individual losses, and potentially big ones, even if they do not ultimately affect behavior.

Several studies have tested the effect of *outrage* on people's reactions to risks and explored how outrage interacts with variations in probability.[14] Here it is hypothesized that certain low-probability risks, such as those associated with nuclear waste radiation, produce outrage, whereas other low-probability risks, such as those associated with radon exposure, do not. Of course terrorism can be seen as the most extreme example of risks that produce outrage. A central finding is consistent with that stressed here: a large difference in probability had no effect in the "high outrage" condition, with people responding the same way to a risk of 1 in 100,000 as to a risk of 1 in 1 million.[15]

Even when the statistical risk was identical in the high outrage (nuclear waste) and low outrage (radon) cases, people in the nuclear waste case reported a much greater perceived threat and a much higher intention to act to reduce that threat. Indeed, "the effect of outrage was practically as large as the effect of a 4000-fold difference in risk between the high-risk and low-risk conditions."[16]

Efforts to communicate the meaning of differences in risk levels, by showing comparisons to normal risk levels, reduced the effect of outrage. But even after those efforts, outrage had nearly the same effect as a two-thousand-fold increase in risk. A great deal of information appears to be necessary to counteract the effects of strong emotions—showing that people are not impervious to such information, but that when emotions are involved, a great deal of careful work has to be done.

It should not be surprising, in this light, that visualization or imagery matters a great deal to people's reactions to risks.[17] When an image of a bad outcome is easily accessible, people will become greatly concerned about a risk, holding probability constant.[18] Consider the fact that when people are asked how much they will pay for flight insurance for losses resulting from "terrorism," they will pay more than if they are asked how much they will pay for flight insurance from all causes.[19] An evident explanation for this peculiar result is that the word "terrorism" evokes vivid images of disaster, thus crowding out probability judgments. Note also that when people discuss a low-probability risk, their concern rises even if the discussion consists mostly of apparently trustworthy assurances that the likelihood of harm really is infinitesimal.[20] One reason is that the discussion makes it easier to visualize the risk and hence to fear it.

Probability neglect should be sharply distinguished from use of the availability heuristic, which leads people not to neglect the issue of probability, but to answer the question of probability by substituting a hard question (what is the statistical risk?) with an easy question (do salient examples readily come to mind?). The central point here is not that visualization makes an event seem more probable (though this is also often true and highly relevant to the impact of terrorism), but that visualization, if productive of strong emotions, makes the issue of probability less relevant or even irrelevant. (Many people who are fearful of admittedly low-probability risks, such as those associated with flying in airplanes, report that they visualize the worst-case outcome and do not give adequate attention to the issue of likelihood, which they acknowledge to be low.) In theory, the distinction between use of the availability heuristic and probability neglect should not be obscure. In practice, of course, it will often be hard to know whether the availability heuristic or probability neglect is influencing behavior.

The most sensible conclusion is that with respect to risks of injury or harm, vivid images and concrete pictures of disaster can "crowd out" other kinds of thoughts, including the crucial thought that the probability of disaster is really small. With respect to hope, those who operate gambling casinos are well aware of the underlying mechanisms. They play on people's emotions in the particular sense that they conjure up palpable pictures of victory and prosperity, thus encouraging people to neglect the question of probability. With respect to risks, insurance companies, environmental groups, and terrorists do exactly the same. The point explains "why societal concerns about hazards such as nuclear power and exposure to extremely small amounts of toxic chemicals fail to recede in response to information about the very small probabilities of the feared consequences from such hazards."[21]

Limitations and Heterogeneity

Of course the phenomenon of probability neglect has limitations. A great deal depends on context. Under certain circumstances, the initial act of terrorism (for example) may well produce more in the way of probability neglect than the second, and certainly more than the third or fourth, simply because people may become acclimated. Some risks, even terrible ones, can become part of life's furniture, and while the risk of terrorism is not likely to become furniture, people can adjust to it. I have referred to the 2013 bombing at the Boston marathon, which, however tragic, did not make Bostonians feel that they "cannot be safe anywhere." As noted, however, context is important, and several incidents of terrorism might serve to heighten rather than diminish probability neglect, perhaps especially if they occur in short succession.

Moreover, many people do attend to issues of probability even when their emotions are running high. Recall from chapter 6 that the social science literature, authoritatively discussed by Daniel Kahneman in his masterful *Thinking, Fast and Slow*,[22] distinguishes between two families of cognitive operations, called System 1 and System 2. System 1 is responsible for probability neglect, and System 2 can provide a corrective. Hence there is considerable heterogeneity in the data, with many subjects attending to probability even when the harm is described in the most graphic terms. For them, System 2 is operating at all times. These points raise a question about whether education and "debiasing" are possible. If people are made alert to probability neglect, will they be less likely to neglect probability? We do not yet have a clear answer to that question.

What Drives the Demand for Law?

If people show unusually strong reactions to low-probability catastrophes, a democratic government might well act accordingly. In the environmental area, there has been an intense debate about whether the National Environmental Policy Act requires federal agencies to discuss the worst-case scenario in environmental impact statements.[23] Environmental groups sought to ensure discussion of that scenario. They did so in part to stimulate public concern, with the knowledge that the worst case might well have a great deal of salience, even if it is highly unlikely. For its part, the government originally required discussion of the worst case, but changed in its mind, with the apparent understanding that people are too likely to overreact.[24] Hence the current approach, upheld by the Supreme Court, requires consideration of low-probability events, but only if they are not entirely remote and speculative.

At first glance the current approach, and the Supreme Court's decision, seem entirely reasonable. If there is only a miniscule chance that the worst case will come to fruition, it need not be discussed in environmental impact statements. The principal effect of the discussion would be to activate public fear, which is by hypothesis unwarranted by the facts. But there is an important qualification. While probability neglect makes worst-case analysis easy to criticize, such analysis might be defended if regulators are operating under conditions of uncertainty rather than risk (see chapter 3). Under conditions of uncertainty, probabilities cannot be assigned at all, and in such cases it may be reasonable to follow the maximin principle (choose the option that has the least-bad worst outcome).[25] If we are dealing with uncertainty rather than risk, worst-case analysis can be defended on these standard grounds, simply because it identifies the approach that should be favored by those applying the maximin principle. What I am suggesting is that in the context of terrorism and other emotionally laden hazards, people neglect probability even when the evidence suggests that it is quite low.

A good deal of legislation and regulation can be explained in part by reference to probability neglect when emotions are running high. Consider a few examples:

1. In 1976, there were a number of frightening news reports about serious adverse health effects allegedly caused by abandoned hazardous waste in Love Canal, an abandoned waterway that feeds into the Niagara River in New York State. In response to those reports, the government engaged in a number of efforts to assure the public that the probability of harm was low. In fact little was accomplished by those efforts.[26] When the local health department publicized controlled studies showing little evidence of adverse effects, the publicity did not dampen concern, because the numbers "had no meaning."[27] In fact the numbers seemed to aggravate fear: "One woman, divorced and with three sick children, looked at the piece of paper with numbers and started crying hysterically: 'No wonder my children are sick. Am I going to die? What's going to happen to my children?'"[28]

Questions of this sort contributed to the enactment of new legislation to control the environmental risks associated with abandoned hazardous waste sites—legislation that was well justified in principle, but that did not require careful consideration of the probability of significant health or environmental benefits from particular actions. At least until recently, the government has not taken sufficient account of the probability of significant harm in making cleanup decisions.[29]

2. In 1989, there was a highly publicized campaign designed to show a connection between Alar, a pesticide, and cancer in children. For a time, the national media paid a great deal of attention to the campaign. The public demand for action was not much affected by the EPA's suggestion that children were highly unlikely to get cancer as a result of Alar.[30] The mere idea that children might die as a result of apple consumption had a significant effect on behavior, with statistical information seeming not to reduce people's fears.

3. In the fall of 2001, vivid images of shark attacks created a public outcry about potential risks for ocean swimmers.[31] The public outcry occurred notwithstanding the fact that a shark attack was highly improbable, and the absence of any reliable evidence of an increase in shark attacks in the summer of 2001. Predictably, there was considerable discussion of new legislation to control the problem, and eventually such legislation was enacted in Florida. Public fear was not impervious to the fact that the underlying risk was miniscule; but the fear greatly outran the statistical risk.

4. For a variety of reasons, jury behavior is not likely to be greatly affected by assurance that the underlying risk was unlikely to come to fruition, even if the issue of probability is legally relevant.[32] In cases involving low-probability risks of emotionally gripping harms, it might not be difficult to convince jurors to offer high damage awards. Litigators therefore do well to try to engage jurors' emotions by pointing to the worst case. Even if the law asks the jury to balance the benefits of the defendant's action against the costs, the jury might disregard the issue of probability if its attention is focused on an outcome that triggers strong emotions.

5. An understanding of probability neglect helps explain the finding, in both experimental and real-world settings, that juries do not respond favorably to a demonstration that the defendant performed

a cost-benefit analysis before proceeding, even if the analysis places a high value on human life (see chapter 6).[33] The reason is that jurors will be focusing on the badness of the outcome, not the low (ex ante) probability that it would have occurred.

6. With respect to terrorism, consider the anthrax scare of October 2001, which was based on relatively few incidents. Four people died of the infection; about a dozen others fell ill. The probability of being infected was exceedingly low. Nonetheless, fear proliferated, with people focusing their attention on the outcome rather than the low probability of the harm. The government responded accordingly, investing significant resources in ensuring against anthrax infections. Private institutions reacted the same way, asking people to take substantial care in opening the mail even though the statistical risks were small.

To say this is not to suggest that extensive precautions were clearly unjustified in this case. Private and public institutions faced an unknown probability of a major health problem. But it is hard to deny that the public fear was disproportionate to its cause, and that the level of response was disproportionate too. The extraordinary ripple effects attest to the intensity of that fear.

In the context of the terrorist attacks of September 11, 2001, of course, public fear led to private and public costs that (whether or not justified) were significantly higher than the costs of the attacks themselves, and that are best explained in part by reference to probability neglect. The same might be said about the extraordinary public fear produced by the sniper attacks in the Washington, D.C., area in October 2002. The extent of the fear is hard to understand without an appreciation of probability neglect.

What Should Be Done?

I have noted that discussions of low-probability risks tend to heighten public concern, even if those discussions consist largely of reassurance. In some contexts, the most effective way of reducing fear of a low-probability risk may be to discuss something else and to let time do the rest. (Recall in this regard President Bush's effort, in the aftermath of the terrorist attacks of 9/11, not to emphasize that the statistical risks were low, but to treat flying as a kind of patriotic act, one that would prevent terrorists from obtaining victory.) Of course, media attention can undermine this approach.

With respect to regulatory policy, institutional safeguards might well be the best way of ensuring against the harmful consequences of probability neglect. A general requirement of cost-benefit balancing should provide a check on regulations that cannot be grounded in objective fact—and also as an impetus to preventative measures that the public might not seek. If government wants to avoid excessive responses, analytic requirements and institutional checks will provide a start (see chapters 1 and 2). We might well see such requirements and checks as providing a kind of System 2 check on the operation of System 1. Consider a striking (and profound) demonstration of the relationship between System 1 and System 2: Some of the most important cognitive errors identified by behavioral economists *disappear when people are using a foreign language*.[34] Asked to resolve problems in a language that is not their own, people are less likely to blunder. In an unfamiliar language, they are more likely to get the right answer. How can this be?

The answer is straightforward. When people are using their own language, they think quickly and effortlessly, and so System 1 has the upper hand. When they are using a foreign language, System 1 is a bit overwhelmed, and System 2 is given a serious boost. Rapid, intuitive reactions are slowed down when people are using a language with which they are not entirely familiar, and they are more likely to do some calculating and to think deliberatively—and to give the right answers. In a foreign language, people have some distance from their intuitions, and that distance can stand them in good stead. We do not have evidence that probability neglect diminishes when people speak in a foreign language, but it would not be at all surprising to find that it does.

There is a large lesson here about the importance of approaches to policy and regulation that emphasize careful consideration of costs and benefits. Such approaches do not (exactly) use a foreign language, but they do ensure a degree of distance from people's initial judgments and intuitions, thus constraining the mistakes associated with System 1. At first glance, then, analytic checks, measuring outcomes and probabilities, are indispensable safeguards. We have seen some serious challenges with quantification in this context (see chapter 3), but they are nonetheless the place to start.

But public fear raises independent problems. Suppose that people are greatly concerned about a risk that has a small or even miniscule probability of occurring—perhaps anthrax in the mail, sniper attacks at gas stations, or terrorism on airplanes. If government is confident that it knows the facts, and if people are far more concerned than the facts warrant, should the government respond, via regulation, to their concerns? Or should it ignore them, if and on the ground that the concerns are excessive and unjustified?

Consider the individual analogy first. Even if your fear is excessive, it might be entirely rational for you to take account of your fear in your behavior, at least if you cannot talk yourself out of being afraid. Of course you should try to calm your fears. But if you are afraid to fly, and if your fear is hard to dislodge, you might decline to do so, on the ground that your fear will make the experience dreadful (not only while flying but while anticipating it). In certain periods in the last decade, some people have declined to travel to certain nations, not because they believe that the risks are statistically large, but because they anticipate their own (less than rational) anxiety, and because they seek, rationally, to avoid an anxiety-pervaded experience. Some kind of informal cost-benefit analysis is involved, and it takes account of fear itself.

So too at the social level. Suppose, for example, that people are afraid of certain risks and that they demand steps to reduce those risks. There is a strong argument that government should not respond if the relevant risks are very small and if the requested steps have costs in excess of benefits. By hypothesis, however, the fear is real. If people are fearful that some product or activity is "not safe," they are, simply for that reason alone, experiencing a significant loss. In many domains, widespread fear is not merely a loss in itself (one for whose reduction people would be willing to pay), but also leads to an array of additional problems, produced by changed behavior.

In the context of terrorism, for example, fear is likely to make people reluctant to engage in certain activities, such as flying on airplanes and appearing in public places. The resulting costs may not be low. It is plausible to suggest that government should attempt to reduce fear, just as it attempts to produce other gains to people's well-being.

It is obvious that if government is able to inform and educate people, it should respect public fear through that route; it should not impose otherwise unjustified regulatory controls. But whether information and education will work is an empirical question and in the presence of probability neglect, it may not be so easy to educate people. Certainly public officials should try, and perhaps they will succeed. But if information and education do not work, government might be willing to consider regulatory responses to fears that are not fully rational, but real and by hypothesis difficult to eradicate. Recall that fear is a real social cost and that it is likely to lead to other social costs. If people are afraid to fly, the economy will suffer in multiple ways; so too if people are afraid to send or to receive mail. The reduction of even baseless fear is a social good.

Even if it is clear that government should respond, many questions remain. How and how much should government respond? The answer must depend on the extent and cost of the fear and the effect and cost of the response. If the cost of an effective response is very high, a refusal to respond might well make sense. With this point, the analysis of appropriate action becomes similar to the analysis of risks in many other settings. We need to know how much good, and how much harm, would be done by the action in question. A special difficulty here consists in the problem of quantifying and monetizing fear and its consequences.

Vividness and Probability

In this chapter, my central claim has been that when emotions are running high, people might well neglect the question of probability. Probability neglect is especially likely in the context of emotionally gripping events. If a flood, a hurricane, or a terrorist attack is easy to visualize, significant changes in thought and behavior may occur, even if the statistical risk is lower than that associated with many activities that do not produce public concern. The point helps explain public overreaction to highly publicized, low-probability risks.

It follows that if a private or public actor is seeking to convince the public to attend to a neglected risk, it is best to provide vivid, even visual images of the worst that might happen. It also follows that government regulation, affected as it is by the public demand for law, might neglect probability too. At first glance, the government should not capitulate if the public is demonstrating probability neglect and showing an excessive response to small risks. The best response is information and education. But public fear is itself a problem, and sometimes a quite serious one. If that fear cannot be alleviated without risk reduction, then government should consider risk reduction, at least if the relevant steps are justified by an assessment of costs and benefits, including those associated with fear itself.

EPILOGUE

Four Ways to Humanize the Regulatory State

This book has covered a lot of territory. By way of conclusion, it will be useful to say a few brief words about the central themes.

To decide how to handle social problems, governments should focus on the human consequences of their decisions. To do that, they have to rely on both science and economics. If a regulation would reduce risks in the food supply, it is important to know the magnitude of the reduction—the number of lives saved and the number of illnesses prevented. If a regulation would reduce the risk of a financial crisis, it is important to try to specify the nature and extent of the contribution. If a regulation would impose costs on businesses large and small, it is important to quantify those costs. When costs are high, real people have to bear them, and the results may include higher prices, lower wages, and fewer jobs. As I have emphasized, higher prices will be especially unwelcome to those at the bottom of the economic ladder.

At the present time, cost-benefit analysis—a form of political algebra—is the best way we have of accounting for the consequences of regulation.[1] It should be humanized in four different ways. First, it should see costs and benefits not as arithmetic abstractions, but as efforts to capture qualitatively diverse goods and to promote sensible trade-offs among them. The use of a unitary metric is designed to ensure sensible balancing, not to efface qualitative differences. Recall John Stuart Mill's powerful attack on Jeremy Bentham, emphasizing those qualitative differences.

Second, it should take account of values that are difficult or impossible to quantify. Such values include human dignity, which plays a crucial role in regulations designed to protect privacy, to reduce rape, and to prevent discrimination on the basis of race, sex, sexual orientation, and disability. Nonquantifiable values do present serious challenges for cost-benefit analysis. I have suggested possible ways of meeting those challenges, above all through the use of upper and lower bounds. Whether or not those methods work, we cannot lose sight of nonquantifiable values, which are sometimes the impetus behind regulatory policies.

Third, regulatory choices and cost-benefit analysis should be behaviorally informed, in the sense that they take account of the many differences between *Homo sapiens* and *Homo economicus*. Behavioral scientists have shown that people use heuristics, or mental shortcuts, in assessing risks, and that their intuitive judgments can go badly wrong, not least in trying to account for human consequences. A disciplined analysis does far much better than intuition. And when people fear when they need not, and are fearless when fear is appropriate, analysis of consequences can provide a lot of help.

People use heuristics, or mental shortcuts, not merely in assessing facts but also in assessing what morality requires. As with heuristics about facts, moral heuristics generally work well. But in important areas, they can misfire. For many moral (and political) problems, strong intuitions seem to tell us plainly about what morality requires. It is exceedingly hard to resist strong intuitions. They create a powerful tug. But if we really seek to value life, we will sometimes reject our intuitions, and try to provide a more disciplined account of the human consequences of alternative courses of action.

Fourth, policies and regulations need to benefit from the dispersed information of a wide variety of human beings. This book began with a glimpse inside of the federal government. When things go well there, it is in large part because of institutional safeguards that ensure that a lot of people, in both the public and the private sectors, are invited to provide information about the likely consequences. For all that public officials know, private citizens know far more. They are indispensable to a full accounting. The best response is for officials to draw on the dispersed information of members of the public (while enlisting market mechanisms, and allowing private flexibility, wherever possible).

Two of the inspirations for this book are especially important (as reflected in the epigraphs), and it is time to acknowledge them explicitly. The first is Amartya Sen, who has written illuminatingly about cost-benefit analysis and consequentialism, emphasized the centrality of freedom and "government by discussion," and stressed the need not to displace markets, but to supplement them. The second is Friedrich Hayek, who emphasized the dispersed nature of human knowledge, and who celebrated the price system on the ground that it collects and incorporates more information than any group of planners or bureaucrats, however well motivated and expert, can possibly assemble.

Sen and Hayek are two of history's very greatest economic thinkers, but they are not often paired. I think that they should be. In an illuminating and even moving appreciation, Sen praised Hayek for drawing attention to the intimate relationship between markets and freedom (and not only prosperity).[2] Because Hayek celebrated markets and decentralization, it is an understatement to say that he would not have endorsed all of the arguments of this book (much less all of the regulations that the United States has issued in the name of public health, safety, and environmental protection). There is a clear and powerful Hayekian objection to the use of cost-benefit analysis, rooted in the serious challenges that officials face in assessing both costs and benefits. I have been acutely aware of that objection here (if perhaps not acutely enough). But I like to think that Hayek might have appreciated some of the central themes of this book—enlisting the evidence of the market in deciding on appropriate values, acquiring dispersed information, acknowledging trade-offs, and making choices with careful reference to both freedom and prosperity.

APPENDIX A

Executive Order 13563 of January 18, 2011

Improving Regulation and Regulatory Review

By the authority vested in me as President by the Constitution and the laws of the United States of America, and in order to improve regulation and regulatory review, it is hereby ordered as follows:

Section 1. *General Principles of Regulation.* (a) Our regulatory system must protect public health, welfare, safety, and our environment while promoting economic growth, innovation, competitiveness, and job creation. It must be based on the best available science. It must allow for public participation and an open exchange of ideas. It must promote predictability and reduce uncertainty. It must identify and use the best, most innovative, and least burdensome tools for achieving regulatory ends. It must take into account benefits and costs, both quantitative and qualitative. It must ensure that regulations are accessible, consistent, written in plain language, and easy to understand. It must measure, and seek to improve, the actual results of regulatory requirements.

(b) This order is supplemental to and reaffirms the principles, structures, and definitions governing contemporary regulatory review that were established in Executive Order 12866 of September 30, 1993. As stated in that Executive Order and to the extent permitted by law, each agency must, among other things: (1) propose or adopt a regulation only upon a reasoned determination that its benefits justify its costs (recognizing that some benefits and costs are difficult to quantify); (2) tailor its regulations to impose the least burden on society, consistent with obtaining regulatory objectives, taking into account, among other things, and to the extent practicable, the costs of cumulative regulations; (3) select, in choosing among alternative regulatory approaches, those approaches that maximize net benefits (including potential economic, environmental, public health and safety, and other advantages; distributive impacts; and equity); (4) to the extent feasible, specify performance objectives, rather than specifying the behavior or manner of compliance that regulated entities must adopt; and (5) identify and assess available alternatives to direct regulation, including providing economic *incentives* to encourage the desired behavior, such as user fees or marketable permits, or providing information upon which choices can be made by the public.

(c) In applying these principles, each agency is directed to use the best available techniques to quantify anticipated present and future benefits and costs as accurately as possible. Where appropriate and permitted by law, each agency may consider (and discuss qualitatively) values that are difficult or impossible to quantify, including equity, human dignity, fairness, and distributive impacts.

SEC. 2. *Public Participation.* (a) Regulations shall be adopted through a process that involves public participation. To that end, regulations shall be based, to the extent feasible and consistent with law, on the open exchange of information and perspectives among State, local, and tribal officials, experts in relevant disciplines, affected stakeholders in the private sector, and the public as a whole.

(b) To promote that open exchange, each agency, consistent with Executive Order 12866 and other applicable legal requirements, shall endeavor to provide the public with an opportunity to participate in the regulatory process. To the extent feasible and permitted by law, each agency shall afford the public a meaningful opportunity to comment through the Internet on any proposed regulation, with a comment period that should generally be at least 60 days. To the extent feasible and permitted by law, each agency shall also provide, for both proposed and final rules, timely online access to the rulemaking docket on regulations.gov, including relevant scientific and technical findings, in an open format that can be easily searched and downloaded. For proposed rules, such access shall include, to the extent feasible and permitted by law, an opportunity for public comment on all pertinent parts of the rulemaking docket, including relevant scientific and technical findings.

(c) Before issuing a notice of proposed rulemaking, each agency, where feasible and appropriate, shall seek the views of those who are likely to be affected, including those who are likely to benefit from and those who are potentially subject to such rulemaking.

SEC. 3. *Integration and Innovation.* Some sectors and *industries* face a significant number of regulatory requirements, some of which may be redundant, inconsistent, or overlapping. Greater coordination across agencies could reduce these requirements, thus reducing costs and simplifying and harmonizing rules. In developing regulatory actions and identifying appropriate approaches, each agency shall attempt to promote such coordination, simplification, and harmonization. Each agency shall also seek to identify, as appropriate, means to achieve regulatory goals that are designed to promote innovation.

SEC. 4. *Flexible Approaches.* Where relevant, feasible, and consistent with regulatory objectives, and to the extent permitted by law, each agency shall identify and consider regulatory approaches that reduce burdens and maintain flexibility and freedom of choice for the public. These approaches include warnings, appropriate default rules, and disclosure requirements as well as provision of information to the public in a form that is clear and intelligible.

SEC. 5. *Science.* Consistent with the President's Memorandum for the Heads of Executive Departments and Agencies, "Scientific Integrity" (March 9, 2009), and its implementing guidance, each agency shall ensure the objectivity of any scientific and technological information and processes used to support the agency's regulatory actions.

SEC. 6. *Retrospective Analyses of Existing Rules.* (a) To facilitate the periodic review of existing significant regulations, agencies shall consider how best to promote retrospective analysis of rules that may be outmoded, ineffective, insufficient, or excessively burdensome, and to modify, streamline, expand, or repeal them in accordance with what has been learned. Such retrospective analyses, including supporting data, should be released online whenever possible.

(b) Within 120 days of the date of this order, each agency shall develop and submit to the Office of Information and Regulatory Affairs a preliminary plan, consistent with law and its resources and regulatory priorities, under which the agency will periodically review its existing significant regulations to determine whether any such regulations should be modified, streamlined, expanded, or repealed so as to make the agency's regulatory program more effective or less burdensome in achieving the regulatory objectives.

APPENDIX B

The Social Cost of Carbon

Revised Social Cost of CO_2, 2010–50 (from 2013 Working
Group, in 2007 dollars per metric ton of CO_2)[1]

Discount Rate Year	*5.0% Avg.*	*3.0% Avg.*	*2.5% Avg.*	*3.0% 95th*
2010	11	33	52	90
2015	12	38	58	109
2020	12	43	65	129
2025	14	48	70	144
2030	16	52	76	159
2035	19	57	81	176
2040	21	62	87	192
2045	24	66	92	206
2050	27	71	98	221

Annual Social Cost of CO_2, 2010–50 (from 2010 Working Group, in 2007 dollars per metric ton of CO_2)[2]

Discount Rate Year	5% Avg.	3% Avg.	2.5% Avg.	3% 95th
2010	4.7	21.4	35.1	64.9
2011	4.9	21.9	35.7	66.5
2012	5.1	22.4	36.4	68.1
2013	5.3	22.8	37.0	69.6
2014	5.5	23.3	37.7	71.2
2015	5.7	23.8	38.4	72.8
2016	5.9	24.3	39.0	74.4
2017	6.1	24.8	39.7	76.0
2018	6.3	25.3	40.4	77.5
2019	6.5	25.8	41.0	79.1
2020	6.8	26.3	41.7	80.7
2021	7.1	27.0	42.5	82.6
2022	7.4	27.6	43.4	84.6
2023	7.7	28.3	44.2	86.5
2024	7.9	28.9	45.0	88.4
2025	8.2	29.6	45.9	90.4
2026	8.5	30.2	46.7	92.3
2027	8.8	30.9	47.5	94.2
2028	9.1	31.5	48.4	96.2
2029	9.4	32.1	49.2	98.1
2030	9.7	32.8	50.0	100.0
2031	10.0	33.4	50.9	102.0
2032	10.3	34.1	51.7	103.9
2033	10.6	34.7	52.5	105.8
2034	10.9	35.4	53.4	107.8
2035	11.2	36.0	54.2	109.7
2036	11.5	36.7	55.0	111.6
2037	11.8	37.3	55.9	113.6
2038	12.1	37.9	56.7	115.5
2039	12.4	38.6	57.5	117.4
2040	12.7	39.2	58.4	119.3
2041	13.0	39.8	59.0	121.0

Discount Rate Year	5% Avg.	3% Avg.	2.5% Avg.	3% 95th
2042	13.3	40.4	59.7	122.7
2043	13.6	40.9	60.4	124.4
2044	13.9	41.5	61.0	126.1
2045	14.2	42.1	61.7	127.8
2046	14.5	42.6	62.4	129.4
2047	14.8	43.2	63.0	131.1
2048	15.1	43.8	63.7	132.8
2049	15.4	44.4	64.4	134.5
2050	15.7	44.9	65.0	136.2

APPENDIX C

Estimated Benefits and Costs of Selected Federal Regulations

Major Rules Reviewed with Estimates of Both Annual Benefits and Costs,
October 1, 2010 – September 30, 2011 (billions of 2001 dollars)[1]

Agency	RIN	Title	Benefits	Costs
HHS	0910-AG41	Cigarette Warning Label Statements	0.2 Range: 0–9.0	<0.1
HHS	0938-AQ12	Administrative Simplification: Adoption of Authoring Organizations for Operating Rules and Adoption of Operating Rules for Eligibility and Claims Status (CMS-0032-IFC)	1.0 Range: 0.9–1.1	0.4 Range: 0.3–0.6
DOL	1210-AB07	Improved Fee Disclosure for Pension Plan Participants	1.6 Range: 0.8–3.3	0.3 Range: 0.2–0.4
DOL	1210-AB35	Statutory Exemption for Provision of Investment Advice	10.9 Range: 5.8–15.1	3.0 Range: 1.6–4.2
DOE	1904-AA89	Energy Efficiency Standards for Clothes Dryers and Room Air Conditioners	0.2 Range: 0.2–0.3	0.1 Range: 0.1–0.2

(continued)

Agency	RIN	Title	Benefits	Costs
DOE	1904-AB79	Energy Efficiency Standards for Residential Refrigerators, Refrigerator-Freezers, and Freezers	1.8 Range: 1.7–3.0	0.8 Range: 0.8–1.3
DOE	1904-AC06	Energy Efficiency Standards for Residential Furnaces, Central Air Conditioners and Heat Pumps	0.9 Range: 0.7–1.8	0.5 Range: 0.5–0.7
EPA	2040-AF11	Water Quality Standards (Numeric Nutrient Criteria) for Florida's Lakes and Flowing Waters	<0.1	0.1 Range: 0.1–0.2
EPA	2050-AG50	Oil Pollution Prevention: Spill Prevention, Control, and Countermeasure Rule Requirements—Amendments for Milk Containers	0	(0.1)
EPA	2060-AP50	Cross State Air Pollution Rule (CAIR Replacement Rule)	Range: 20.5–59.7	0.7
DOT	2125-AF19	Real-Time System Management Information Program	0.2	0.1
DOT	2127-AK23	Ejection Mitigation	1.5 Range: 1.5–2.4	0.4 Range: 0.4–1.4
DOT & EPA	2127-AK74; 2060-AP61	Commercial Medium- and Heavy-Duty On-Highway Vehicles and Work Truck Fuel Efficiency Standards	2.6 Range: 2.2–2.6	0.5 Range: 0.3–0.5

( ) indicates negative.

Major Rules Reviewed with Estimates of Both Annual Benefits and Costs,
October 1, 2009 – September 30, 2010 (billions of 2001 dollars)[2]

Agency	RIN	Title	Benefits	Costs
DOJ	1117-AA61	Electronic Prescriptions for Controlled Substances	Range: 0.3–1.3	<0.1
DOJ	1190-AA44	Nondiscrimination on the Basis of Disability in Public Accommodations and Commercial Facilities	1.1 Range: 1.0–2.1	0.6 Range: 0.5–0.7
DOJ	1190-AA46	Nondiscrimination on the Basis of Disability in State and Local Government Services	Range: 0.2–0.3	Range: 0.1–0.2
DOL	1218-AC01	Cranes and Derricks in Construction	0.2	0.1
DOE	1904-AA90	Energy Efficiency Standards for Pool Heaters and Direct Heating Equipment and Water Heaters	1.4 Range: 1.3–1.8	Range: 1.0–1.1
DOE	1904-AB70	Energy Conservation Standards for Small Electric Motors	Range: 0.7–0.8	0.2
DOE	1904-AB93	Energy Efficiency Standards for Commercial Clothes Washers	Range: 0–0.1	<0.1
EPA	2050-AG16	Revisions to the Spill Prevention, Control, and Countermeasure (SPCC) Rule	0	(0.1)
EPA	2060-AO15	NESHAP: Portland Cement Notice of Reconsideration	Range: 6.1–16.3	Range: 0.8–0.9
EPA	2060-AO48	Review of the National Ambient Air Quality Standards for Sulfur Dioxide[3]	10.5 Range: 2.8–38.6	0.7 Range: 0.3–2.0

(continued)

Agency	RIN	Title	Benefits	Costs
EPA	2060-AP36	National Emission Standards for Hazardous Air Pollutants for Reciprocating Internal Combustion Engines (Diesel)	Range: 0.7–1.9	0.3
EPA	2060-AQ13	National Emission Standards for Hazardous Air Pollutants for Reciprocating Internal Combustion Engines—Existing Stationary Spark Ignition (Gas-Fired)	Range: 0.4–1.0	0.2
EPA	2070-AJ55	Lead; Amendment to the Opt-out and Record-keeping Provisions in the Renovation, Repair, and Painting Program	Range: 0.8–3.0	0.3
DOT	2120-AI92	Automatic Dependent Surveillance—Broadcast (ADS-B) Equipage Mandate to Support Air Traffic Control Service	Range: 0.1–0.2	0.2
DOT	2126-AA89	Electronic On-Board Recorders for Hours-of-Service Compliance	0.2	0.1
DOT	2130-AC03	Positive Train Control	<0.1	0.7 Range: 0.5–1.3
DOT	2137-AE15	Pipeline Safety: Distribution Integrity Management	0.1	0.1
DOT & EPA	2127-AK50; 2060-AP58	Light-Duty Greenhouse Gas Emission Standards and Corporate Average Fuel Economy Standards[4]	11.9 Range: 3.9–18.2	3.3 Range: 1.7–4.7

( ) indicates negative.

Estimates of the Total Annual Benefits and Costs of Major Rules Reviewed
October 1, 2008 – September 30, 2009 (millions of 2001 dollars)[5]

Agency	Title	Benefits	Cost
DOE/ EE	Energy Efficiency Standards for Commercial Refrigeration Equipment	196 Range: 186–224	81 Range: 69–81
DOE/ EE	Energy Efficiency Standards for General Service Fluorescent Lamps and Incandescent Lamps	1,924 Range: 1,111–2,886	486 Range: 192–657
HHS/ AHRQ	Patient Safety and Quality Improvement Act of 2005 Rules	93 Range: 69–136	97 Range: 87–121
HHS/ CMS	Revisions of HIPAA Code Sets	209 Range: 77–261	217 Range: 44–238
HHS/ CMS	Updates to Electronic Transactions (Version 5010)	1,988 Range: 1,114–3,194	1,090 Range: 661–1,449
HHS/ FDA	Prevention of Salmonella Enteritidis in Shell Eggs	1,284 Range: 206–8,583	74 Range: 48–106
HUD/ OH	Real Estate Settlement Procedures Act (RESPA); To Simplify and Improve the Process of Obtaining Mortgages and Reduce Consumer Costs (FR-5180)	2,303	884
DOT/ FAA	Part 121 Pilot Age Limit	35 Range: 30–35	4
DOT/ FAA	Washington, DC, Metropolitan Area Special Flight Rules	239 Range: 10–839	92 Range: 89–382
DOT/ FMCSA	Hours of Service of Drivers	0–1,760	0–105
DOT/ FMCSA	New Entrant Safety Assurance Process	472–602	60–72

(*continued*)

Agency	Title	Benefits	Cost
DOT/ NHTSA	Passenger Car and Light Truck Corporate Average Fuel Economy Model Year 2011	1,665 Range: 857–1,905	979 Range: 650–1,910
DOT/ NHTSA	Reduced Stopping Distance Requirements for Truck Tractors	1,250 Range: 1,250–1,520	46 Range: 23–164
DOT/ NHTSA	Roof Crush Resistance	652 Range: 374–1,160	896 Range: 748–1,189
DOT/ PHMSA	Pipeline Safety: Standards for Increasing the Maximum Allowable Operating Pressure for Gas Transmission Pipelines	85 Range: 85–89	13 Range: 13–14
EPA/AR	Review of the National Ambient Air Quality Standards for Lead	455–5,203	113–2,241

APPENDIX D

Selected Examples of Breakeven Analysis

Rule	Cost	Benefit
Terrorism—Coast Guard[1]	$26.5 million annually at a 7 percent discount rate.	Rule would be cost-justified if it prevents one terrorist attack with consequence equal to the average every 130.9 years."[2]
Terrorism—Freight Trains[3]	Not yet calculated.	Not yet calculated.[4]
Terrorism—Aviation[5]	$285 million annually at a 7 percent discount rate.	Not yet calculated.[6]
Prison Rape[7]	$8.2 million per year annualized at a 7 percent discount rate.	Rule would be cost-justified if it reduces the annual number of sexual abuse incidents by 55.[8]
Terrorism—Highway Rail Crossings[9]	$1.52 million over 20 years at a 7 percent discount rate.	Rule would be cost-justified if there is a decrease of 0.015% of crossing accidents over twenty years.[10]
Emergency Preparedness—Trains[11]	Industry cost: $1.5 million over 10 years with a 7 percent discount rate.	Rule would be cost-justified if 3.84 injuries are prevented from increasing in severity.[12]
Prison Rape—PREA[13]	$468.5 million per year when annualized at a 7 percent discount rate.	Rule would be cost-justified if the annual number of prison rape victims is reduced by 1.671.[14]

(continued)

Rule	Cost	Benefit
Fire Suppression—Coast Guard[15]	$2.3 million over 10 years at a 7 percent discount rate.	Rule would be cost-justified if it prevents one fatality every 4–5 years.[16]
Rail Employee Safety—Employee Training[17]	$64.1 million over 20 years, discounted to present dollars at a 7 percent discount rate.	Rule would be cost-justified if it results in a 7% reduction in human factors–caused accidents.[18]
Rail—Emergency Systems[19]	$13.3 million over 20 years discounted to present dollars at a 7 percent discount rate.	Not explicitly stated.[20]
Commercial Motor Vehicles—Restrictions on Cell Phone Use[21]	$12.1 million per year discounted at 7 percent.	Rule would be cost-justified if it eliminates two fatalities per year.[22]
Airlines—Cargo Screening (this rule amends two provisions of the Air Cargo Screening Interim Final Rule [IFR] issued on September 16, 2009, and responds to public comments on the IFR)[23]	$178.1 million annualized and discounted at 7 percent.	Not explicitly stated.[24]
Terrorism—Ammonium Sale Restrictions[25]	$300 million to $1.041 billion over 10 years at a 7 percent discount rate.	Rule would be cost-justified if it prevents one terrorist attack every 14.1 years[26]
Nutrition Labeling—Restaurants[27]	$34.9 million to $130.1 million annualized at a 7 percent discount rate.	Rule would be cost-justified if 0.06 percent of the adult obese population reduces caloric intake by 100 calories per week.[28]

Rule	Cost	Benefit
Nutrition Labeling— Vending Machines[29]	$24.5 million annualized at a 7 percent discount rate.	Rule would be cost-justified if 0.02 percent of the adult obese population reduces caloric intake by 100 calories per week.[30]
Hazardous Materials Risk Assessment[31]	$3.5 million per year.	Rule would be cost-justified if it reduces risk of hazardous materials incidents by 40%.[32]
Food Safety Inspection—Catfish[33]	Present value $74.8 million over 10 years using a 7 percent discount rate.	Rule would be cost-justified if 790 salmonellosis illnesses are prevented.[34]
Food Shipping—Farm Bill[35]	Not yet estimated.	Not yet estimated.[36]
Expanded Field of View for Vehicles[37]	$19.7 million based on a 7 percent discount rate.	Rule would be cost-justified if nonquantified benefits to each vehicle are at least $65.[38]
Commercial Motor Vehicles—Rule Disqualifying Those with Traffic Offenses[39]	$3.8 million annually.	Rule would be cost-justified if it eliminates one fatality every year.[40]
Nutrition Labeling— Meat and Poultry[41]	Net present values of $316.99 million over 20 years using a 7 percent discount rate.	Rule would be cost-justified if 0.53 lives are saved annually.[42]
Airline Security—Security of Aircraft Repair Stations[43]	$45,200 for all respondents annualized over the next three years.	Rule would be cost-justified if one moderate terrorist attack is prevented every 92 years.[44]
Airlines—Baggage Screening[45]	Rule costs of $1.9 billion discounted by 7 percent. Industry costs for delayed shipment of cargo estimated at $203.1 million at a 7 percent discount rate.	Rule would be cost-justified if it prevents one attack every 2.6 years.[46]

(continued)

Rule	Cost	Benefit
Airline Crew Standards[47]	$7.7 million over 20 years using a 7% discount rate.	Rule would be cost-justified if it prevents at least 10 serious injuries over the period of analysis.[48]
Medication Labeling—Over the Counter Drugs[49]	$71.0 million at 7 percent discount rate.	Rule would be cost-justified if it prevents at least 2 deaths per year.[50]
Medication Labeling—Over the Counter Drugs[51]	One-time compliance costs of $32 million in the first year.	Rule would be cost-justified if it prevents 1 death per year for 10 years or 476 hospitalizations per year for 10 years.[52]

Values for Mortality and Morbidity

Health Endpoint	Central Estimate of Value per Statistical Life[1]	
	1990 Income Level	*2020 Income Level*
Premature Mortality (value of a statistical life)	$8,000,000	$9,600,000
Nonfatal Myocardial Infraction (heart attack)		
3% discount rate		
Age 0–24	$87,000	$87,000
Age 25–44	$110,000	$110,000
Age 45–54	$120,000	$120,000
Age 55–64	$200,000	$200,000
Age 65 and over	$98,000	$98,000
7% discount rate		
Age 0–24	$97,000	$97,000
Age 25–44	$110,000	$110,000
Age 45–54	$110,000	$110,000
Age 55–64	$190,000	$190,000
Age 65 and over	$97,000	$97,000

Hospital Admissions

	2000 Income Level	2020 Income Level
Chronic lung disease (18–64)	$21,000	$21,000
Asthma admissions (0–64)	$21,000	$21,000
All cardiovascular		
Age 18–64	$42,000	$42,000
Age 65–99	$41,000	$41,000
All respiratory (Age 65+)	$36,000	$36,000
Emergency department visits for asthma	$430	$430

Respiratory Ailments Not Requiring Hospitalization

	2000 Income Level	2020 Income Level
Upper respiratory symptoms	$31	$33
Lower respiratory symptoms	$20	$21
Asthma exacerbations	$54	$58

ACKNOWLEDGMENTS

This book has had an unusually long genesis. The original plan, developed about six years ago, was to focus on moral heuristics. Karen Darling, my terrific editor, and I devoted a great deal of time to that topic. Before I could complete the project, or even make significant progress, government service intervened, and from early 2009 to late 2012, the book was put on the back burner. When I returned to it in 2012, I decided that it would be best to venture a more general treatment of valuation, combining what I had learned in government with what I knew, or thought I knew, before I started. Moral heuristics are the subject of chapter 6, and in a way that topic continues to run throughout, but the focus is much broader. (A book remains to be written on moral heuristics, and while I am not sure whether I will write it, I do hope that someone does.)

A wise and supportive guide for many years, Karen deserves particular credit for making this book both possible and much better. I am also thankful to many people for valuable discussions and for comments on early versions of one or more of the chapters. For particular thanks, I single out Daniel Kahneman, Martha Nussbaum, Eric Posner, Richard Thaler, Adrian Vermeule, David Weisbach, and Richard Zeckhauser. Special thanks to my wife, Samantha Power, for her insistent emphasis on focusing on the human consequences of public policy, for her sharp critical eye, for her boundless generosity, and for much more.

The book is dedicated to Amartya Sen, an indispensable guide and true inspiration for many years. I suspect that he will not agree with everything said here, but I have benefited throughout from his extraordinary work on closely related topics.

The chapters in this book grow out of earlier work (though in many cases there have been substantial revisions). I am grateful to the following for permission to draw on the following essays here:

Chapter 1: *The Office of Information and Regulatory Affairs*, 126 HARVARD LAW REVIEW 1838 (2013).

Chapter 2: *The Real-World of Cost-Benefit Analysis*, 114 COLUMBIA LAW REVIEW 167 (2014).

Chapter 3: *Nonquantifiable*, CALIFORNIA LAW REVIEW (2014). (This essay is an initial basis for the Brennan Lecture, delivered at the University of California at Berkeley, and I am especially grateful to the editors of the CALIFORNIA LAW REVIEW for permission to publish an early version here. For a fuller account, readers are invited to see the final product.)

Chapters 4 and 5: *Valuing Life: A Plea for Disaggregation*, 54 DUKE LAW JOURNAL 385 (2004).

Chapter 6: *Moral Heuristics and Risk, in* EMOTIONS AND RISKY TECHNOLOGIES (Sabine Roeser ed. 2010). With kind permission from Springer Science+Business Media.

Chapter 7: *Terrorism and Probability Neglect*, 26 JOURNAL OF RISK AND UNCERTAINTY 121 (2003). With kind permission from Springer Science+Business Media.

NOTES

EPIGRAPHS

1. AMARTYA SEN, *The Discipline of Cost-Benefit Analysis, in* RATIONALITY AND FREEDOM 553, 561 (2002).
2. Friedrich Hayek, *The Uses of Knowledge in Society*, 35 AM. ECON. REV. 519, 519 (1945).

INTRODUCTION

1. BENJAMIN FRANKLIN, MR. FRANKLIN: A SELECTION FROM HIS PERSONAL LETTERS (Whitfield J. Bell Jr. & Leonard W. Labaree eds., 1956).
2. *See* OFFICE OF MGMT. & BUDGET, DRAFT 2013 REPORT TO CONGRESS ON THE BENEFITS AND COSTS OF FEDERAL REGULATIONS AND UNFUNDED MANDATES ON STATE, LOCAL, AND TRIBAL ENTITIES 54, *available at* http://www .whitehouse.gov/sites/default/files/omb/inforeg/2013_cb/draft_2013_cost _benefit_report.pdf.
3. An especially instructive discussion is MATTHEW D. ADLER, WELL-BEING AND FAIR DISTRIBUTION: BEYOND COST-BENEFIT ANALYSIS 92–114 (2011).
4. There are of course multiple ways to account for those consequences; cost-benefit analysis is only one such method. *See id.* I believe that, at present, cost-benefit analysis has the advantage of relative ease of administration, but the various alternatives and critiques, from within the consequentialist framework, deserve careful consideration. *See id.*
5. *See id.*
6. *See* RICHARD H. THALER & CASS R. SUNSTEIN, NUDGE (2008); CASS R. SUNSTEIN, SIMPLER (2013).

CHAPTER ONE

1. *See* Exec. Order No. 12,291 § 3, 3 C.F.R. 127, 128–29 (1981), *revoked by* Exec. Order No. 12,866 § 11, 3 C.F.R. 638, 649 (1993), *reprinted in* 5 U.S.C. § 601 (2000).

The so-called independent agencies are not subject to OIRA review, though President Obama did issue an important executive order asking such agencies to follow many of the principles that govern executive agencies. See Executive Order 13579. An early and still-valuable discussion of the original theory behind the OIRA process, written by two former OIRA Administrators, is Christopher DeMuth & Douglas Ginsburg, *White House Review of Agency Rulemaking*, 99 HARV. L. REV. 1075 (1986).

2. Executive Order 13563, section 1.

3. *See* Friedrich Hayek, *The Uses of Knowledge in Society*, 35 AM. ECON. REV. 519 (1945).

4. Frankfurter famously wrote, "The history of liberty has largely been the history of the observance of procedural safeguards." McNabb v. United States, 318 U.S. 332, 347 (1943).

5. *See* AMARTYA SEN, DEVELOPMENT AS FREEDOM (1990).

6. *Id.* A valuable discussion of some of the foundational issues is MATTHEW ADLER, WELL-BEING AND FAIR DISTRIBUTION: BEYOND COST-BENEFIT ANALYSIS (2011).

7. Exec. Order No. 12,866 § 6(b)(2)(B), 3 C.F.R. 638, 647 (1993), *reprinted as amended in* 5 U.S.C. § 601 (2006).

8. *See* http://www.reginfo.gov/public/do/eoCountsSearch.

9. The predecessor Executive Order 12291 had no such limitation, and hence OIRA reviewed far more rules in the period between 1981 and 1993.

10. The question of agency incentives may be complicated. In some cases, agencies may strongly favor OIRA review, as a way of obtaining comments through a formal process, of avoiding error, of ensuring that relevant officials are notified, and of eliciting interagency support. No agency would be comfortable "surprising" the Executive Office of the President with regulatory activity with which it should have been, but was not, aware. Of course there are many ways of providing relevant notice; the OIRA process is the most formal.

11. *See, e.g.*, Environmental Protection Agency and Department of Transportation, Revisions and Additions to Motor Vehicle Fuel Economy Label, 76 Fed. Reg. 39,478, 39,480 fig. I-1 (2011) (amending 40 C.F.R. pts. 85, 86, and 600).

12. Exec. Order No. 12,866 § 3(e), 3 C.F.R. at 641.

13. Memorandum from Peter R. Orszag, Director of Office of Mgmt. & Budget (Mar. 4, 2009), *available at* http://www.whitehouse.gov/sites/default/files/omb/assets/memoranda_fy2009/m09-13.pdf. It would be possible to object that OIRA has no authority to review regulatory actions that do not strictly meet the definition of "regulatory action" within Executive Order 12866. As noted, however, such review has occurred for a long period, and in any case the Office of Management and Budget is authorized to require such review so long as the requirement is not inconsistent with relevant statutes and Executive Orders. The issuance of the Memorandum cited in this note reflects broad support for such review within the Executive Office of the President.

14. *See, e.g.*, Appalachian Power Co. v. EPA, 208 F.3d 1015 (D.C. Cir. 2000).

15. It is not. *See* 5 U.S.C. § 553 (exempting guidance documents and interpretive rules from notice and comment requirements).

16. See, for example, the "dashboards" that show, in graphical forms, both rules and information collection requests under OIRA review.

17. *Cf.* Kenneth Shepsle, *Congress Is a "They," Not an "It": Legislative Intent as Oxymoron,* 12 INT'L REV. L. & ECON. 239 (1992); Adrian Vermeule, *The Judiciary Is a They, Not an It: Two Fallacies of Interpretive Theory* (2003), *available at* http://papers.ssrn.com/s013/papers.cfm?abstract_id=449860.

18. *See* the Regulatory Flexibility Act, 5 U.S.C. 601 et seq., an important statute that helps to define the role of the Office of Advocacy.

19. The President directed me to return the draft rule to the EPA Administrator for reconsideration. *See* http://www.whitehouse.gov/sites/default/files/ozone _national_ambient_air_quality_standards_letter.pdf.

20. *See, e.g.,* Eric Lipton, *Ties to Obama Aided in Access for Big Utility,* N.Y. TIMES, Aug. 22, 2012, http://www.nytimes.com/2012/08/23/us/politics/ties-to -obama-aided-in-access-for-exelon-corporation.html; RENA STEINZOR ET AL., CENTER FOR PROGRESSIVE REFORM, BEHIND CLOSED DOORS AT THE WHITE HOUSE (2011), *available at* http://www.progressivereform.org/articles/ OIRA_Meetings_1111.pdf.

21. I am grateful to Adrian Vermeule for this term.

22. *See* STEINZOR ET AL., *supra* note 20.

23. *Cf.* Russell Hardin, *The Crippled Epistemology of Extremism, in* POLITICAL EXTREMISM AND RATIONALITY (Albert Breton et al. eds., 2002) (discussing the limited information that gives rise to extremism).

24. See the overview in DANIEL KAHNEMAN, THINKING, FAST AND SLOW (2012).

25. *See, e.g.,* RICHARD REVESZ & MICHAEL LIVERMORE, RETAKING RATIONALITY (2008).

26. *See* Office of Mgmt. & Budget, Draft 2012 Report to Congress on the Benefits and Costs of Federal Regulations and Unfunded Mandates on State, Local, and Tribal Entities 54, *available at* http://www.whitehouse.gov/sites/default/ files/omb/oira/draft_2012_cost_benefit_report.pdf.

     For a checklist that provides a brief summary of the relevant questions in the analysis, *see* http://www.whitehouse.gov/sites/default/files/omb/inforeg/ regpol/RIA_Checklist.pdf. For a document that answers key questions about cost-benefit analysis, *see* http://www.whitehouse.gov/sites/default/files/ omb/assets/OMB/circulars/a004/a-4_FAQ.pdf. For a primer on such analysis, *see* http://www.whitehouse.gov/sites/default/files/omb/inforeg/regpol/ circular-a-4_regulatory-impact-analysis-a-primer.pdf.

27. It is exceedingly rare, however, for an agency to proceed when the monetized costs exceed the monetized benefits, and as noted, the usual reason involves legal requirements. An example is the "positive train control" rule, which requires certain technology to be placed on trains, in the interest of safety. *See* http://www.fra.dot.gov/roa/press_releases/fp_FRA%2017-12%20.shtml.

28. Executive Order 13563, section 1.

29. *See, e.g.,* Revisions and Additions to Motor Vehicle Fuel Economy Label, 76 Fed. Reg. 39,478, 39,480 fig. I-1 (2011) (to be codified at 40 C.F.R. pts. 85, 86, and 600).

30. National Standards to Prevent, Detect, and Respond to Prison Rape, 77 Fed. Reg. 37,106 (June 20, 2012).

31. *Id.*

32. *See OIRA Reports to Congress,* OFFICE OF MGMT. & BUDGET, http://www .whitehouse.gov/omb/inforeg_regpol_reports_congress/ (last visited Sep. 23, 2012).

33. *See* Richard Epstein, *Reforms? What Reforms?,* DEFINING IDEAS (May 31, 2011), http://www.hoover.org/publications/defining-ideas/article/80536. OIRA may make certain technical judgments, but it begins and usually ends with the numbers that the agency used publicly after the interagency process.

34. *See, e.g.,* Philip M. Kannan, *The Logical Outgrowth Doctrine in Rulemaking,* 48 ADMIN. L. REV. 213 (1996).

35. For a useful discussion, *see* Michael Asimow, *Interim-Final Rules: Making Haste Slowly,* 51 ADMIN. L. REV. 703 (1999).

36. 5 U.S.C. 601 et seq.

37. 44 U.S.C. 3501 et seq.

38. *See, e.g.,* Re-Election Strategy Is Tied to a Shift on Smog, N.Y. TIMES, Nov. 16, 2011, *available at* http://www.nytimes.com/2011/11/17/science/earth/policy -and-politics-collide-as-obama-enters-campaign-mode.html?pagewanted=all; http://www.progressivereform.org/OIRASpecInterests.cfm.

39. There is a great deal of academic discussion of whether the President may "overrule" those within the executive branch, including Cabinet heads, who may be delegated a degree of statutory discretion. See, e.g., Elena Kagan, *Presidential Administration,* 114 HARV. L. REV. 2245 (2001). The issue has more theoretical interest than practical importance. This is so for a simple reason: Those who work for the President want to act consistently with his goals, priorities, and views. If he favors a certain course of action, his subordinates agree to do as he wishes, and they do so voluntarily and generally without hesitation; and if there is any hesitation, it is likely to be brief. In addition, the leaders of various agencies and departments fully understand the OIRA process and the importance of addressing interagency concerns.

CHAPTER TWO

1. For relevant discussion, *see* RICHARD POSNER, CATASTROPHE: RISK AND RE-SPONSE (2005); CASS R. SUNSTEIN, WORST-CASE SCENARIOS (2007); Martin Weitzman, *Why the Far-Distant Future Should Be Discounted at Its Lowest Possible Rate,* 36 J. ENVTL. ECON. & MGMT. 201 (1998).

2. *See* FRANK KNIGHT, RISK, UNCERTAINTY, AND PROFIT (1921).

3. *See id.* For relevant discussion, with references to the economic and philosophical literature, *see* POSNER, *supra* note 1; SUNSTEIN, *supra* note 1.

4. For valuable discussion, *see* CHRISTIAN GOLLIER, PRICING THE PLANET'S FU-
   TURE: THE ECONOMICS OF DISCOUNTING IN AN UNCERTAIN WORLD (2012);
   Matthew A. Adler, *Future Generations: A Prioritarian View*, 77 G.W. L. Rev.
   1478 (2009).

5. *See* Martin L. Weitzman, *Additive Damages, Fat-Tailed Climate Dynamics,
   and Uncertain Discounting*, 3 ECON.: OPEN-ACCESS, OPEN-ASSESSMENT
   E-J. 2009–39, *available at* http://dx.doi.org/10.5018/economics-ejournal
   .ja.2009–39.

6. *See* Interagency Working Grp. on Soc. Cost of Carbon, U.S. Govt., Technical
   Support Document: Social Cost of Carbon for Regulatory Impact Analysis
   (2010), *available at* http://www.epa.gov/oms/climate/regulations/scc-tsd
   .pdf. *See also* Michael Greenstone et al., *Estimating the Social Cost of Carbon
   for Use in U.S. Federal Rulemakings* (Mass. Inst. Tech. Dep't of Econ., Working
   Paper No. 11–04, 2011), *available at* http://papers.ssrn.com/s013/papers
   .cfm?abstract_id=1793366. For assessments, *see* William Nordhaus, *Estimates
   of the Social Cost of Carbon* (Cowles Found., Discussion Paper No. 1826, 2011),
   available at http://dido.econ.yale.edu/P/cd/d18a/d1826.pdf; Jonathan Masur
   & Eric Posner, *Climate Change and the Limits of Cost-Benefit Analysis*, 99 CAL.
   L. REV. 1557 (2011).

7. Interagency Working Grp. on Soc. Cost of Carbon, U.S. Govt., Technical Support Document: Updated Social Cost of Carbon for Regulatory Impact Analysis Under Executive Order 12866 (2013), *available at* http://www.whitehouse
   .gov/sites/default/files/omb/inforeg/social_cost_of_carbon_for_ria_2013_
   update.pdf.

8. OFFICE OF MGMT. & BUDGET, EXEC. OFFICE OF THE PRESIDENT, CIRCULAR
   A-4, REGULATORY ANALYSIS (2003), *available at* http://www.whitehouse
   .gov/omb/circulars_a004_a-4 [hereinafter OMB CIRCULAR A-4]. The Obama
   Administration issued several documents that offer significant clarifications.
   See OFFICE OF INFO. & REGULATORY AFFAIRS, REGULATORY IMPACT ANALY-
   SIS: A PRIMER, *available at* http://www.whitehouse.gov/sites/default/files/
   omb/inforeg/regpol/circular-a-4_regulatory-impact-analysis-a-primer.pdf;
   OFFICE OF INFO. & REGULATORY AFFAIRS, REGULATORY IMPACT ANALYSIS:
   FREQUENTLY ASKED QUESTIONS (2011), *available at* http://www.whitehouse
   .gov/sites/default/files/omb/assets/OMB/circulars/a004/a-4_FAQ.pdf.

9. This is highly artificial. Typically agencies work to explore more than two
   alternatives, and the process of interagency review focuses on alternatives
   as well. See the emphasis on alternatives in Exec. Order No. 13,563, 76 Fed.
   Reg. 3821 (Jan. 18, 2011). Of course the law may narrow the range of available
   options. Note, however, that Regulatory Impact Analyses frequently discuss
   alternatives that the law does not permit agencies to select, just as agencies
   often discuss costs even when they are legally irrelevant. The reason for such
   discussions is to promote transparency: The public, and relevant policy mak-
   ers, ought to appreciate these facts even if agencies' hands are tied.

10. Note also that the numbers are subject to considerable internal and external

scrutiny, *see* chapter 1, and there is no evidence that agencies systematically
skew them in self-serving directions, *see* CASS R. SUNSTEIN, SIMPLER: THE
FUTURE OF GOVERNMENT (2013). Hence there is no support for the view
that the numbers are unreliable because agencies are regularly attempting to
support decisions made by political leaders. Nonetheless, ex ante and ex post
numbers often differ, and it remains important to continue to scrutinize rules
on the books and to reassess them in light of that scrutiny. This is a central goal
of Exec. No. Order 13,563, 76 Fed. Reg. 3821 (Jan. 18, 2011) and in particular
the important requirement of a periodic "regulatory lookback" at rules on the
books.

11. For discussion, *see* CASS R. SUNSTEIN, LAWS OF FEAR (2007).

12. Circular A-4 recommends a range of $1 million to $10 million. *See* OMB CIRCU-
LAR A-4, *supra* note 8.

13. *See, e.g.*, W. Kip Viscusi & Joseph Aldy, *The Value of a Statistical Life*, 27 J. RISK
& UNCERTAINTY 5 (2003); W. Kip Viscusi, *The Heterogeneity of the Value of a
Statistical Life*, 40 J. RISK & UNCERTAINTY 1 (2010) (noting median value of
$7 million to $8 million).

14. There is a well-known disparity between "willingness to pay" and "willingness to accept," with the latter number typically being higher. *See, e.g.*, Cass R.
Sunstein, *Endogenous Preferences, Environmental Law*, 22 J. LEGAL STUD. 217
(1993). To the extent that labor market studies are used to determine VSL,
agencies are relying on willingness to accept.

15. *See* OMB CIRCULAR A-4, *supra* note 8.

16. Two agencies, the EPA and the DOT, have developed official guidance on VSL.
In its 2011 update, the DOT adopted a value of $6.2 million (2011 dollars) and
requires all the components of the Department to use that value in their Regulatory Impact Analyses. *See* Memorandum from Polly Trottenberg, Asst. Sec'y
for Transp. Policy, U.S. Dep't of Transp., to Secretarial Officers and Modal
Adm'rs, Treatment of the Economic Value of a Statistical Life in Departmental
Analyses—2011 Interim Adjustment (July 29, 2011), *available at* http://www
.dot.gov/sites/dot.dev/files/docs/Value_of_Life_Guidance_2011_Update_07
-29-2011.pdf. The EPA has changed its VSL to an older value of $6.3 million
(2000 dollars) and adjusts this value for real income growth to later years. In its
Regulatory Impact Analysis for a new primary standard for nitrogen dioxide,
for example, the EPA adjusted this VSL to account for a different currency year
(2006) and for income growth to 2020, which yielded a VSL of $8.9 million.
U.S. Envt'l Prot. Agency, Final Regulatory Impact Analysis (RIA) for the No2
National Ambient Air Quality Standards (NAAQS) 4–8 n.11 (2010), *available at*
http://www.epa.gov/ttn/ecas/regdata/RIAs/FinalN02RIAfulldocument.pdf.
Although the Department of Homeland Security has no official policy on VSL,
it sponsored a report through its U.S. Customs and Border Protection and
has used the recommendations of this report to inform VSL values for several
recent rulemakings. This report recommends $6.3 million (2008 dollars) and
also recommends that DHS adjust this value upward over time for real income

growth (in a manner similar to EPA's adjustment approach). Lisa A. Robinson, Valuing Mortality Risk Reductions in Homeland Security Regulatory Analyses, at vi (2008), *available at* http://www.regulatory-analysis.com/robinson-dhs -mortality-risk-2008.pdf.

Other regulatory agencies that have used a VSL in individual rulemakings include DOL's Occupational Safety and Health Administration and HHS's Food and Drug Administration. In OSHA's rulemaking setting a Permissible Exposure Limit for Hexavalent Chromium, it specifically referred to EPA guidance to justify a VSL of $6.8 million (2003 dollars), as the types of air exposure risks regulated in this rulemaking were similar to those in EPA rulemakings. *See* 71 Fed. Reg. 10,100, 10,305 (Feb. 28, 2006) (to be codified at various parts of 29 C.F.R.). The FDA has consistently used values of $5 million and $6.5 million (2002 dollars) in several of its rulemakings to monetize mortality risks. *See* 68 Fed. Reg. 41,434, 41,490 (July 11, 2003) (to be codified at 21 C.F.R. pt. 101); 68 Fed. Reg. 6062, 6076 (Feb. 6, 2003) (to be codified at 21 C.F.R. pt. 201). But it also uses a monetary value of the remaining life years saved by alternative policies. This is sometimes referred to as a "Value of a Statistical Life Year" or VSLY. *See* Lisa A. Robinson, *How US Government Agencies Value Mortality Risk Reductions*, 1 Rev. Envt'l Econ. & Pol'y 283, 293 (2007).

17. There is a large and growing literature on this question. *See* U.S. Envtl. Prot. Agency, Valuing Mortality Risk Reductions for Environmental Policy: A White Paper (2010), *available at* http://yosemite.epa.gov/ee/ epa/eerm.nsf/vwAN/EE-0563-1.pdf/$file/EE-0563-1.pdf. *See also* Trudy Ann Cameron et al., Willingness to Pay for Health Reductions (June 2009) (unpublished manuscript), *available at* http://pages.uoregon.edu/cameron/vita/ Cameron_DeShazo_Johnson_0619091.pdf; Cass R. Sunstein, *Bad Deaths*, 14 J. Risk & Uncertainty 259 (1997).

Circular A-4 states: "The age of the affected population has also been identified as an important factor in the theoretical literature. However, the empirical evidence on age and VSL is mixed. In light of the continuing questions over the effect of age on VSL estimates, you should not use an age-adjustment factor in an analysis using VSL estimates." OMB Circular A-4, *supra* note 8. But it allows consideration of VSLY:

> Another way that has been used to express reductions in fatality risks is to use the life expectancy method, the "value of statistical life-years (VSLY) extended." If a regulation protects individuals whose average remaining life expectancy is 40 years, a risk reduction of one fatality is expressed as "40 life-years extended." Those who favor this alternative approach emphasize that the value of a statistical life is not a single number relevant for all situations. In particular, when there are significant differences between the effect on life expectancy for the population affected by a particular health risk and the populations studied in the labor market studies, they prefer to adopt a VSLY approach to reflect those differences. You should consider providing

estimates of both VSL and VSLY, while recognizing the developing state of knowledge in this area.

18. The EPA did such an analysis in the context of arsenic. *See* Cass R. Sunstein, *The Arithmetic of Arsenic*, 90 Geo. L.J. 2255 (2002).

19. Consider here the Department of Transportation's proposed rule to increase rear visibility in motor vehicles, which grapples with issues of this kind. *See* 75 Fed. Reg. 76,186, 76,238 ("[T]he quantitative analysis does not offer a complete accounting. We have noted that well over 40 percent of the victims of backover crashes are very young children (under the age of five), with nearly their entire life ahead of them.") Executive Order 12866 also refers explicitly to considerations of equity ("'[I]n choosing among alternative regulatory approaches, agencies should select those approaches that maximize net benefits (including * * * equity), and there are strong reasons, grounded in those considerations, to prevent the deaths at issue here.")

20. *See* Sean Williams, *Statistical Children*, Yale J. Reg. (forthcoming 2013), *available at* https://papers.ssrn.com/s013/papers.cfm?abstract_id=2176463.

21. *See* OMB Circular A-4, *supra* note 8: "The age of the affected population has also been identified as an important factor in the theoretical literature. However, the empirical evidence on age and VSL is mixed. In light of the continuing questions over the effect of age on VSL estimates, you should not use an age-adjustment factor in an analysis using VSL estimates. Another way that has been used to express reductions in fatality risks is to use the life expectancy method, the 'value of statistical life-years (VSLY) extended.' . . . Those who favor this alternative approach emphasize that the value of a statistical life is not a single number relevant for all situations. In particular, when there are significant differences between the effect on life expectancy for the population affected by a particular health risk and the populations studied in the labor market studies, they prefer to adopt a VSLY approach to reflect those differences. You should consider providing estimates of both VSL and VSLY, while recognizing the developing state of knowledge in this area. . . . In any event, when you present estimates based on the VSLY method, you should adopt a larger VSLY estimate for senior citizens because senior citizens face larger overall health risks from all causes and they may have accumulated savings to spend on their health and safety."

There were intense controversies over what was called the "senior death discount" in the Bush Administration. *See* Katharine Q. Seelye & John Tierney, *E.P.A. Drops Age-Based Cost Studies*, N.Y. Times (May 8, 2003), http://www.nytimes.com/2003/05/08/us/epa-drops-age-based-cost-studies.html. For discussion, *see* W. Kip Viscusi & Joseph Aldy, Labor Market Estimates of the Senior Discount for the Value of a Statistical Life (2006), *available at* http://www.rff.org/RFF/documents/RFF-DP-06-12.pdf; Joseph E. Aldy & W. Kip Viscusi, Age Differences in the Value of a Statistical Life (2007), *available at* http://www.rff.org/documents/RFF-DP-07-05.pdf.

22. Perhaps one or another end of the scale can be shown to be more probable. The use of the middle of the range seems to suggest some kind of Principle of Equal Probability, and it is not clear if that principle can be defended, even under circumstances of uncertainty. *See* SUNSTEIN, *supra* note 1, for citations and discussion.

23. *See* OMB CIRCULAR A-4, *supra* note 8.

24. This example is realistic. See the EPA's analysis in connection with its mercury rule, 77 Fed. Reg. 9304 (Feb. 16, 2012), *available at* http://www.gpo.gov/fdsys/pkg/FR-2012-02-16/pdf/2012-806.pdf.

25. Circular A-4 states: "Your analysis should look beyond the direct benefits and direct costs of your rulemaking and consider any important ancillary benefits and countervailing risks. An ancillary benefit is a favorable impact of the rule that is typically unrelated or secondary to the statutory purpose of the rule-making (e.g., reduced refinery emissions due to more stringent fuel economy standards for light trucks) while a countervailing risk is an adverse economic, health, safety, or environmental consequence that occurs due to a rule and is not already accounted for in the direct cost of the rule (e.g., adverse safety impacts from more stringent fuel-economy standards for light trucks)." OMB CIRCULAR A-4, *supra* note 8. Of course the agency should avoid double counting; the benefits must be genuinely attributable to the rule in question, and they must not be counted more than once in the analyses that accompany more than one rule. It would, for example, be a mistake to claim benefits from one rule when they are actually attributable to another, or to claim the same benefits twice. Because the benefits of particulate matter reductions are so large, and because they play a role in many important regulations, both the scientific and the accounting questions continue to deserve careful attention.

26. In its recent rule on fuel economy standards, the Department of Transportation did include additional costs from increased traffic congestion, vehicle accidents, and highway noise in its calculations. *See* 2017 and Later Model Year Light-Duty Vehicle Greenhouse Gas Emissions and Corporate Average Fuel Economy Standards, 77 Fed. Reg. 62,624, 62,999 (Oct. 15, 2012) (to be codified at 49 C.F.R. pts. 523, 533, 536, 537).

27. For a discussion of the energy paradox, *see* Adam B. Jaffe & Robert N. Stavins, *The Energy Paradox and the Diffusion of Conservation Technology*, 16 RESOURCE & ENERGY ECON. 91, 92–94 (1994).

28. For a valuable overview, showing the complexity of the underlying issues and the amount that remains to be learned, *see* Hunt Alcott & Michael Greenstone, *Is There an Energy Efficiency Gap?*, 26 J. ECON. PERSP. 3 (2012). For an important discussion of externalities and internalities, *see* Hunt Allcott et al., *Energy Policy with Externalities and Internalities* (Nat'l Bureau of Econ. Research, Working Paper No. 17977, 2012), *available at* http://www.nber.org/papers/w17977. On behavioral market failures, *see* Cass R. Sunstein, *The Storrs Lectures: Behavioral Economics and Paternalism*, 122 YALE L.J. 1826 (2013).

29. U.S. DEP'T OF TRANSP., NAT'L HIGHWAY TRAFFIC ADMIN., CORPORATE

AVERAGE FUEL ECONOMY FOR MY 2017—MY 2025, FINAL REGULATORY IMPACT ANALYSIS 983 (2012), *available at* http://www.nhtsa.gov/staticfiles/ rulemaking/pdf/cafe/FRIA_2017-2025.pdf. It is true that the underlying questions deserve continuing investigation. For a valuable overview, showing the complexity of these questions and the amount that remains to be learned, *see* Allcott & Greenstone, *supra* note 28. For an important discussion of externalities and internalities, *see* Alcott et al., *supra* note 28.

30. In a relevant rule, the EPA stated as follows:

> The central conundrum has been referred to as the Energy Paradox in this setting (and in several others). In short, the problem is that consumers appear not to purchase products that are in their economic self-interest. There are strong theoretical reasons why this might be so:
>
> · Consumers might be myopic and hence undervalue the long-term.
> · Consumers might lack information or a full appreciation of information even when it is presented.
> · Consumers might be especially averse to the short-term losses associated with the higher prices of energy efficient products relative to the uncertain future fuel savings, even if the expected present value of those fuel savings exceeds the cost (the behavioral phenomenon of "loss aversion").
> · Even if consumers have relevant knowledge, the benefits of energy-efficient vehicles might not be sufficiently salient to them at the time of purchase, and the lack of salience might lead consumers to neglect an attribute that it would be in their economic interest to consider.

Light-Duty Vehicle Greenhouse Gas Emission Standards and Corporate Average Fuel Economy Standards, 75 Fed. Reg. 25,324, 25,510–11 (May 7, 2010) (to be codified at 49 C.F.R. pts. 531, 533, 536, 537, and 538).

31. In particular, DOT did a sensitivity analysis with consumer welfare losses, finding that even if such losses are very high, the benefits of its fuel economy rules justify the costs. *See* U.S. DEP'T OF TRANSP., NAT'L HIGHWAY TRAFFIC SAFETY ADMIN., FINAL REGULATORY IMPACT ANALYSIS: CORPORATE AVERAGE FUEL ECONOMY FOR MY 2012–MY 2016 PASSENGER CARS AND LIGHT TRUCKS 419–33, 432 tbl. VIII-18 (2010), *available at* http://www.nhtsa.gov/ staticfiles/rulemaking/pdf/cafe/CAFE_2012-2016_FRIA_04012010.pdf.

32. OMB CIRCULAR A-4, *supra* note 8: "To the extent possible, agencies should estimate people's valuations of benefits and costs using revealed preference studies based on actual behavior. . . . If the goods or attributes of goods that are affected by regulation—such as preserving environmental or cultural amenities—are not traded in markets, it may be difficult to use revealed preference methods. . . . In the absence of an organized market, it is difficult to estimate

use and non-use values. When studies are designed to elicit such values either though indirect market studies or stated preference methods, agencies should pay careful attention to characterization of the uncertainties. However, overlooking or ignoring these values may significantly understate the benefits and/ or costs of regulatory action."

33. For recent discussion, *see* Jerry Housman, *From Dubious to Hopeless*, 26 J. ECON. PERSP. 43 (2012); Richard Carson, *Contingent Valuation: A Practical Alternative Where Prices Aren't Available*, 26 J. ECON. PERSP. 27 (2012).

34. *See* Adler, *supra* note 4.

35. *See* OMB Circular A-4: "The size of net benefits, the absolute difference between the projected benefits and costs, indicates whether one policy is more efficient than another. The ratio of benefits to costs is not a meaningful indicator of net benefits and should not be used for that purpose. It is well known that considering such ratios alone can yield misleading results."

36. *See supra* note 7. For an illuminating critique, *see* Nordhaus, *supra* note 6.

37. *See supra* note 6.

38. *See* Richard G. Newell & William A. Pizer, *Discounting the Distant Future*, 46 J. ENVTL. ECON. & MGMT. 52 (2003).

39. On some of the complexities here, *see* Gollier, *supra* note 4.

40. *See* OMB CIRCULAR A-4, *supra* note 8 ("If your rule will have important intergenerational benefits or costs you might consider a further sensitivity analysis using a lower but positive discount rate in addition to calculating net benefits using discount rates of 3 and 7 percent.")

41. *See, e.g.*, Nordhaus, *supra* note 6; Weitzman, *supra* note 5; Masur & Posner, *supra* note 6.

42. William Samuelson & Richard Zeckhauser, *Status Quo Bias in Decision Making*, 1 J. RISK & UNCERTAINTY 7 (1988).

CHAPTER THREE

1. OFFICE OF MGMT. & BUDGET, EXEC. OFFICE OF THE PRESIDENT, CIRCULAR A-4, REGULATORY ANALYSIS (2003), *available at* http://www.whitehouse .gov/omb/circulars_a004_a-4 [hereinafter OMB CIRCULAR A-4], which provides authoritative guidance on regulatory impact analysis, states: "It will not always be possible to express in monetary units all of the important benefits and costs. When it is not, the most efficient alternative will not necessarily be the one with the largest quantified and monetized net-benefit estimate. In such cases, you should exercise professional judgment in determining how important the non-quantified benefits or costs may be in the context of the overall analysis. If the non-quantified benefits and costs are likely to be important, you should carry out a 'threshold' analysis to evaluate their significance. Threshold or 'break-even' analysis answers the question, 'How small could the value of the non-quantified benefits be (or how large would the value of the

non-quantified costs need to be) before the rule would yield zero net benefits?' In addition to threshold analysis you should indicate, where possible, which non-quantified effects are most important and why."

2. *See* Richard A. Posner, *A Theory of Negligence*, 1 J. LEGAL STUD. 29 (1972).

3. *See* Jeffrey Zients, Memorandum to the Heads of Executive Agencies and Departments, *available at* http://www.whitehouse.gov/sites/default/files/omb/memoranda/2012/m-12-14.pdf.

4. For relevant discussion, *see* MATTHEW ADLER & ERIC POSNER, NEW FOUNDATIONS OF COST-BENEFIT ANALYSIS (2006); MATTHEW ADLER, WELL-BEING AND FAIR DISTRIBUTION: BEYOND COST-BENEFIT ANALYSIS (2011).

5. *See* W. KIP VISCUSI, FATAL TRADEOFFS (1992) for an influential account of the basic theory.

6. *See, e.g.*, FRANK ACKERMAN & LISA HEINZERLING, PRICELESS (2004).

7. *See* W. KIP VISCUSI, RATIONAL RISK POLICY (1998).

8. *See* Elizabeth Hoffman & Matthew Spitzer, *Willingness to Pay vs. Willingness to Accept: Legal and Economic Implications*, 71 WASH. U. L.Q. 59 (1993).

9. *See* Thomas Kniesner et al., *Willingness to Accept Equals Willingness to Pay for Labor Market Estimates of the Value of Statistical Life* (2012), *available at* http://papers.ssrn.com/s013/papers.cfm?abstract_id=2221038. There is also a question about whether bounded rationality of various sorts—for example, unrealistic optimism, *see* TALI SHAROT, THE OPTIMISM BIAS (2010)—might "impeach" the numbers that emerge from revealed preference studies.

10. The Department of Justice did explore that question in the context of an important regulation. *See* DEPARTMENT OF JUSTICE: DISABILITY RIGHTS SECTION OF THE CIVIL RIGHTS DIVISION, FINAL REGULATORY IMPACT ANALYSIS OF THE FINAL REVISED REGULATIONS IMPLEMENTING TITLES II AND III OF THE ADA, INCLUDING REVISED ADA STANDARDS FOR ACCESSIBLE DESIGN 142–46, *available at* http://www.ada.gov/regs2010/RIA_2010regs/DOJ%20ADA%20Final%20RIA.pdf.

11. JON ELSTER, SOUR GRAPES (1983), provides relevant discussion.

12. *See* MARTHA NUSSBAUM, WOMEN AND HUMAN DEVELOPMENT: THE CAPABILITIES APPROACH (1999).

13. Cass R. Sunstein, *Cost-Benefit Analysis Without Analyzing Costs or Benefits: Reasonable Accommodation, Balancing, and Stigmatic Harms*, 74 U. CHI. L. REV. 1895 (2007). Note also the risk that if disabled people are given protection or accommodation that exceeds their willingness to pay, they might end up worse off on balance, just as in cases in which people are given any good (cars, car safety, air quality) that exceeds their willingness to pay. To come to terms with this risk, we would need to ask about whether there is a problem of bounded rationality (perhaps the good is worth a great deal, notwithstanding a relatively low willingness to pay) and also the incidence of benefits and costs (perhaps disabled workers would not have to pay much of the cost of the relevant good).

14. *See* JOHN STUART MILL, *Bentham*, in UTILITARIANISM AND OTHER ESSAYS 132 (Alan Ryan ed., 1987).

15. *See* Elizabeth Anderson, Value in Ethics and Economics (1993).
16. There is, however, a literature on "sacred values," for which many people seem inclined to reject trade-offs. *See* Martin Hanselmann & Carmen Tanner, *Taboos and Conflicts in Decision Making: Sacred Values, Decision Difficulty, and Emotions*, 3 Judgment & Decision Making 51 (2008).
17. *See* Exec. Order No. 13,563, 76 Fed. Reg. 3821 (Jan. 18, 2011).
18. *Id.*
19. *See* Cass R. Sunstein, Simpler: The Future of Government (2013). For an interesting and relevant discussion of intuitions in the domain of risk, *see* Thorsten Pachur & Ralph Hertwig, *How Do People Judge Risks: Availability Heuristic, Affect Heuristic, or Both?*, 18 J. Experimental Psychol.: Applied 314 (2012).
20. For valuable discussion, *see* Charles Manski, Public Policy in an Uncertain World (2013).
21. *See* Friedrich Hayek, *The Uses of Knowledge in Society*, 35 Am. Econ. Rev. 519 (1945).
22. *See* The Precautionary Principle in the 20th Century: Late Lessons from Early Warnings (Paul Herremoes et al. eds., 2002).
23. *See* Frank Knight, Uncertainty, Risk, and Profit (1921).
24. On this topic, *see* Eric Posner & E. Glen Weyl, *Benefit-Cost Analysis for Financial Regulation*, Am. Econ. Rev. (2013).
25. *See* the many illustrations of ranges in Office of Mgmt. & Budget, 2012 Report to Congress on the Benefits and Costs of Federal Regulations and Unfunded Mandates on State, Local, and Tribal Entities, *available at* http://www.whitehouse.gov/sites/default/files/omb/inforeg/2012_cb/2012_cost_benefit_report.pdf.
26. Interagency Working Grp. on Soc. Cost of Carbon, U.S. Govt., Technical Support Document: Updated Social Cost of Carbon for Regulatory Impact Analysis under Executive Order 12866 (2013), *available at* http://www.whitehouse.gov/sites/default/files/omb/inforeg/social_cost_of_carbon_for_ria_2013_update.pdf. *See also* Michael Greenstone et al., *Estimating the Social Cost of Carbon for Use in U.S. Federal Rulemakings* (Mass. Inst. Tech. Dep't of Econ., Working Paper No. 11-04, 2011), *available at* http://papers.ssrn.com/s013/papers.cfm?abstract_id=1793366. For assessments, *see* William Nordhaus, *Estimates of the Social Cost of Carbon* (Cowles Found., Discussion Paper No. 1826, 2011), *available at* http://dido.econ.yale.edu/P/cd/d18a/d1826.pdf; Jonathan Masur & Eric Posner, *Climate Change and the Limits of Cost-Benefit Analysis*, 99 Cal. L. Rev. 1557 (2011).
27. *See, e.g.,* Peter Diamond & Jerry Hausman, *Contingent Valuation: Is Some Number Better than No Number?*, 8 J. Econ. Persp. 45 (1994).
28. Note, however, that some rules under the Affordable Care Act are essentially transfer rules, imposing costs on some for the benefit of others. It is difficult to specify the social costs and social benefits of such rules, and agencies generally do not do so.

29. *Cf.* Revisions and Additions to Motor Vehicle Fuel Economy Label, 76 Fed. Reg. 39,478, 39,480 fig.I-1 (2011) (to be codified at 40 C.F.R. pts. 85, 86, and 600).

30. *Cf.* National Standards to Prevent, Detect, and Respond to Prison Rape, 77 Fed. Reg. 37,105, 37,111 (June 20, 2012) (to be codified at 28 C.F.R. pt. 115).

31. *Cf.* Nondiscrimination on the Basis of Disability in State and Local Government Services; Final Rules, 75 Fed. Reg. 56,163, 56,170 (Sept. 15, 2010) (to be codified at 28 C.F.R. pts. 35, 36).

32. In an analogous rule, the Department stated as follows:

> [T]he additional benefits that persons with disabilities will derive from greater safety, enhanced independence, and the avoidance of stigma and humiliation—benefits that the Department's economic model could not put in monetary terms—are, in the Department's experience and considered judgment, likely to be quite high. Wheelchair users, including veterans returning from our Nation's wars with disabilities, are taught to transfer onto toilets from the side. Side transfers are the safest, most efficient, and most independence-promoting way for wheelchair users to get onto the toilet. The opportunity to effect a side transfer will often obviate the need for a wheelchair user or individual with another type of mobility impairment to obtain the assistance of another person to engage in what is, for most people, among the most private of activities. . . . [I]t is important to recognize that the ADA is intended to provide important benefits that are distributional and equitable in character. These water closet clearance provisions will have non-monetized benefits that promote equal access and equal opportunity for individuals with disabilities.

Id. Note that the Department also spoke explicitly of breakeven analysis, in a passage that is worth quoting at length:

> The requirements relating the water closet clearances are among the most costly (in monetary terms) of the new provisions. Although the *monetized* costs of these requirements substantially exceed the *monetized* benefits, the benefits that have not been monetized (avoiding stigma and humiliation, protecting safety, and enhancing independence) are expected to be quite high. . . .
>
> We estimate that the costs of the requirement as applied to out-swinging doors will exceed the monetized benefits by $454 million, which when annualized over 54 years equals a net cost of approximately $32.6 million a year.
>
> We estimate that people with the relevant disabilities will use a newly accessible single-user toilet room with an out-swinging door approximately 677 million times per year. Dividing the $32.6 million annual cost by the 677 million annual uses, we conclude that for the costs and benefits to break even in this context, people with the relevant disabilities will have to value

safety, independence, and the avoidance of stigma and humiliation at just under 5 cents per use.

There are substantially fewer single-user toilet rooms with in-swinging doors, and substantially fewer people with disabilities will benefit from making those rooms accessible. And the alterations costs to make a single-user toilet room with an in-swinging door accessible are substantially higher (because of the space taken up by the door) than the equivalent costs of making a room with an out-swinging door accessible. Thus, we calculate that the costs of applying the toilet room accessibility standard to rooms with in-swinging doors will exceed the monetized benefits of doing so by $266.3 million over the life of the regulation, or approximately $19.14 million per year when annualized over 54 years.

We estimate that people with the relevant disabilities will use a newly accessible single-user toilet room with an in-swinging door approximately 8.7 million times per year. Dividing the $19.14 million annual cost by the 8.7 million annual uses, *we conclude that for the costs and benefits to break even in this context, people with the relevant disabilities will have to value safety, independence, and the avoidance of stigma and humiliation at approximately $2.20 per use.*

DEPARTMENT OF JUSTICE: DISABILITY RIGHTS SECTION OF THE CIVIL RIGHTS DIVISION, FINAL REGULATORY IMPACT ANALYSIS OF THE FINAL REVISED REGULATIONS IMPLEMENTING TITLES II AND III OF THE ADA, INCLUDING REVISED ADA STANDARDS FOR ACCESSIBLE DESIGN 142–43, *available at* http://www.ada.gov/regs2010/RIA_2010regs/DOJ%20ADA%20 Final%20RIA.pdf (emphasis added). Relevant additional discussion, including estimates of the value people with disabilities place on avoiding stigma (based on revealed-preference studies), can also be found in the Regulatory Impact Analysis.

33. OMB Circular A-4 states:

Whenever possible, you should use appropriate statistical techniques to determine a probability distribution of the relevant outcomes. For rules that exceed the $1 billion annual threshold, a formal quantitative analysis of uncertainty is required. For rules with annual benefits and/or costs in the range from $100 million to $1 billion, you should seek to use more rigorous approaches with higher consequence rules. This is especially the case where net benefits are close to zero. More rigorous uncertainty analysis may not be necessary for rules in this category if simpler techniques are sufficient to show robustness. You may consider the following analytical approaches that entail increasing levels of complexity:

· Disclose qualitatively the main uncertainties in each important input to the calculation of benefits and costs. These disclosures should address the uncertainties in the data as well as in the analytical results. However, major rules above the $1 billion annual threshold require a formal treatment.

- Use a numerical sensitivity analysis to examine how the results of your analysis vary with plausible changes in assumptions, choices of input data, and alternative analytical approaches. Sensitivity analysis is especially valuable when the information is lacking to carry out a formal probabilistic simulation. Sensitivity analysis can be used to find "switch points"—critical parameter values at which estimated net benefits change sign or the low cost alternative switches. Sensitivity analysis usually proceeds by changing one variable or assumption at a time, but it can also be done by varying a combination of variables simultaneously to learn more about the robustness of your results to widespread changes. Again, however, major rules above the $1 billion annual threshold require a formal treatment.

- Apply a formal probabilistic analysis of the relevant uncertainties, possibly using simulation models and/or expert judgment as revealed, for example, through Delphi methods. Such a formal analytical approach is appropriate for complex rules where there are large, multiple uncertainties whose analysis raises technical challenges, or where the effects cascade; it is required for rules that exceed the $1 billion annual threshold. For example, in the analysis of regulations addressing air pollution, there is uncertainty about the effects of the rule on future emissions, uncertainty about how the change in emissions will affect air quality, uncertainty about how changes in air quality will affect health, and finally uncertainty about the economic and social value of the change in health outcomes. In formal probabilistic assessments, expert solicitation is a useful way to fill key gaps in your ability to assess uncertainty. In general, experts can be used to quantify the probability distributions of key parameters and relationships. These solicitations, combined with other sources of data, can be combined in Monte Carlo simulations to derive a probability distribution of benefits and costs. You should pay attention to correlated inputs. Often times, the standard defaults in Monte Carlo and other similar simulation packages assume independence across distributions. Failing to correctly account for correlated distributions of inputs can cause the resultant output uncertainty intervals to be too large, although in many cases the overall effect is ambiguous. You should make a special effort to portray the probabilistic results—in graphs and/or tables—clearly and meaningfully.

34. *See* Table 5–9 of the Final Regulatory Impact Analysis for Particulate Matter, *available at* http://www.epa.gov/ttn/ecas/regdata/RIAs/finalria.pdf (2013).
35. Though I am bracketing them for purposes of this discussion, questions of

reversibility are also highly relevant here. *See generally* Kenneth J. Arrow & Anthony C. Fisher, *Environmental Preservation, Uncertainty, and Irreversibility*, 88 Q.J. ECON. 312 (1974); Anthony Fisher, UNCERTAINTY, IRREVERSIBILITY, AND THE TIMING OF CLIMATE POLICY 9 (2001). An agency might decide to act or not to act while it obtains more information; whether and in what sense the decision is reversible bears on that decision. *See* Cass R. Sunstein, *Irreversibility*, 9 LAW, PROBABILITY & RISK 227 (2010).

36. Valuable discussion can be found in Edna Ullmann-Margalit, *Big Decisions: Opting, Converting, Drifting*, 58 ROYAL INST. PHIL. SUPPL. 157 (2006).

37. Note the close connection between this point and the "regulatory lookback" required by Executive Order 13563. Retrospective analysis might well be able to shed light on whether the regulation with nonquantifiable benefits is in fact delivering sufficient benefits. *See* SUNSTEIN, *supra* note 19; Michael Greenstone, *Toward a Culture of Persistent Regulatory Experimentation and Evaluation, in* NEW PERSPECTIVES ON REGULATION 113, 113 (David Moss & John Cisterno eds., 2009).

CHAPTER FOUR

1. A comprehensive discussion, exploring many issues that I bracket here, is MATTHEW D. ADLER, WELL-BEING AND FAIR DISTRIBUTION: BEYOND COST-BENEFIT ANALYSIS (2011).

2. *See* James K. Hammitt & Jin-Tan Liu, *Effects of Disease Type and Latency on the Value of Mortality Risk*, 28 J. RISK & UNCERTAINTY 73, 80 (2004) ("The value of preventing a fatal cancer is often considered to be greater than the value of preventing a fatal trauma in a workplace or transportation accident.").

3. For evidence of a higher VSL for airline risks than for automotive risks, *see* Fredrik Carlsson et al., *Is Transport Safety More Valuable in the Air?*, 28 J. RISK & UNCERTAINTY 147, 148 (2004) ("There are several reasons why individuals would be willing to pay more for the same risk reduction when traveling by air compared to by other transport modes, such as car or train.").

4. *See* W. Kip Viscusi & Joseph Aldy, *The Value of a Statistical Life*, 27 J. RISK & UNCERTAINTY 5, 18 (2003) ("[T]ransferring the estimates of a value of a statistical life to non-labor market contexts, as is the case in benefit-cost analyses of environmental health policies for example, should recognize that different populations have different preferences over risks and different values on life-saving.").

5. *See* JOSEPH E. ALDY & W. KIP VISCUSI, AGE VARIATIONS IN WORKERS' VALUE OF STATISTICAL LIFE 1 (Nat'l Bureau of Econ. Research, Working Paper No. 10199, 2003) ("[O]ne might expect that older individuals may value reducing risks to their lives less because they have shorter remaining life expectancy.").

6. Such differences are found in W. Kip Viscusi, *Racial Differences in Labor Market Values of a Statistical Life*, 27 J. RISK & UNCERTAINTY 239, 252 tbl. 1.5 (2003). To get a bit ahead of the story: I am not arguing that government should assign a higher VSL to white lives than to African American lives.

I am speaking here of demographic differences that would emerge from a fully individuated approach to VSL, in which each person's WTP was calculated on an individual basis. Once these values are aggregated, the white VSL would likely be higher than the African American VSL, simply because of disparities in wealth and income. Richer people pay more for safe cars and smoke alarms than poor people do.

7. *See* John D. Leeth & John Ruser, *Compensating Wage Differentials for Fatal and Nonfatal Injury Risk by Gender and Race*, 27 J. RISK & UNCERTAINTY 257, 270 (2003) (finding that the implied VSL for Hispanic males is $5.0 million overall and $4.2 million for blue-collar workers, whereas the implied VSL for white males is $3.4 million overall and $4.2 million for blue-collar workers); Viscusi, *supra* note 6, at 252 (finding VSLs of $15 million for whites and $7.2 million for African Americans, $18.8 million for white males and $9.4 million for white females, and $6.9 million for African American females and $5.9 million for African American males).

8. Discrimination might well lay in the background, of course; it almost certainly accounts for the unequal opportunities that produce lower VSLs for African Americans than for whites. *See* Viscusi, *supra* note 6, at 255. Professor Viscusi goes on to suggest that "it is inappropriate to attribute the observed differences to a greater willingness by black workers to bear risk." *Id.* In a sense Professor Viscusi is correct; there is no reason to think that African American workers have an intrinsically greater predisposition to take risks. But in the market, one's willingness to bear risks is a product of "market opportunities," and hence those with fewer opportunities will show a greater willingness to bear risk.

9. *See* Fredrik Carlsson et al., *Is Transport Safety More Valuable in the Air?*, 28 J. RISK & UNCERTAINTY 147, 148 (2004) (finding that individuals' WTP to reduce the risk of airline deaths is more than double their WTP to reduce the risk of taxi deaths).

10. If the tax laws ensured the right level of redistribution, there would be little reason to use regulatory policy to promote redistributive goals. Regulation would be based on WTP, and tax laws would ensure such redistribution. Hence the analysis of VSL and WTP would be different with an optimal tax policy from what it must be without such a policy. If tax policy were optimal, a highly variable WTP would be appropriate and there would be no need to take account of distributional concerns. As discussed below, the argument for taking account of distributional considerations is based on the assumption that more redistribution is desirable and that regulatory policy can sometimes help to promote that goal, though less effectively than an optimal tax.

11. For different perspectives, *see* Arnold C. Harberger, *On the Use of Distributional Weights in Social Cost-Benefit Analysis*, 86 J. POLIT. ECON. S87 (1978); Robert Brent, *Use of Distributional Weights in Cost-Benefit Analysis: A Survey of Schools*, 12 PUB. FIN. REV. 213 (1984).

12. *See* ADLER, *supra* note 1.

13. *See id.*

14. ENVTL. PROT. AGENCY, GUIDELINES FOR PREPARING ECONOMIC ANALYSES 89 (2000).

15. *See generally* Russell Korobkin, *The Endowment Effect and Legal Analysis*, 97 NW. U. L. REV. 1227 (2003) (explaining the so-called endowment effect, by which individuals often demand more to relinquish an item [WTA] than they would pay to obtain that same item [WTP]).

16. *See id.* at 1228 ("[P]eople will often demand a higher price to sell a good that they possess than they would pay for the same good if they did not possess it at present." [footnote omitted]); Cass R. Sunstein, *Endogenous Preferences, Environmental Law*, 22 J. LEGAL STUD. 217, 226–27 (1993) ("The range of the disparity appears to vary from slight amounts to a ratio of more than four to one, with WTA usually doubling WTP.").

17. Thomas Kniesner et al., *Willingness to Accept Equals Willingness to Pay for Labor Market Estimates of the Value of Statistical Life* (2012), *available at* http://papers.ssrn.com/s013/papers.cfm?abstract_id=2221038.

18. On preferences, welfare, and cost-benefit analysis, *see* Matthew D. Adler & Eric A. Posner, *Implementing Cost-Benefit Analysis When Preferences Are Distorted*, 29 J. LEGAL STUD. 1105 (2000).

19. *See* FRIEDRICH HAYEK, THE ROAD TO SERFDOM (1944).

20. *See* http://aubreyherbert.blogspot.it/2004/10/amartya-sen-on-hayeks-road-to-serfdom.html (originally published in *The Financial Times*, 2004).

21. *See* Peter Dorman & Paul Hagstrom, *Wage Compensation for Dangerous Work Revisited*, 52 INDUS. & LAB. REL. REV. 116, 133 (1998) (finding "statistically significant positive compensation" for only a few categories of workers).

22. Viscusi & Aldy, *supra* note 4, at 44.

23. Leeth & Ruser, *supra* note 7, at 270.

24. Viscusi & Aldy, *supra* note 4, at 23.

25. *Id.* at 18.

26. The availability heuristic suggests that people will overestimate risks when an event is readily "available" to people's minds, and underestimate risks when no such event is available. Timur Kuran & Cass R. Sunstein, *Availability Cascades and Risk Regulation*, 51 STAN. L. REV. 683, 685 (1999). Optimistic bias suggests that people will be excessively optimistic about risks that they themselves face. Cass R. Sunstein, *Hazardous Heuristics*, 70 U. CHI. L. REV. 751, 772 (2003). On optimism in general, *see* TALI SHAROT, THE OPTIMISM BIAS (2010).

27. W. Kip Viscusi, *The Value of Life: Estimates with Risks by Occupation and Industry*, 42 ECON. INQUIRY 29, 39–41 (2004) (showing fatality risks ranging from about 1/100,000 to 45/100,000).

28. *Id.*

29. *See id.* at 33 (containing data clearly indicating that separate numbers for different occupation groups would emerge).

30. Richard L. Revesz, *Environmental Regulation, Cost-Benefit Analysis, and the Discounting of Human Lives*, 99 COLUM. L. REV. 941, 972–74 (1999); Hammitt & Liu, *supra* note 2, at 74.

31. Hammitt & Liu, *supra* note 2, at 84.

32. *Id*. at 81.

33. *See* George Tolley et al., *State-of-the-Art Health Values, in* VALUING HEALTH FOR POLICY 323, 339–40 (George Tolley et al. eds., 1994) (arguing that the value of avoiding a mortality risk preceded by morbidity includes the value of avoiding an instantaneous death plus the value of avoiding the preceding years afflicted with the particular condition).

34. *See* Revesz, *supra* note 30, at 972–74 (discussing "the dread aspects of carcinogenic deaths" and their impact on WTP studies). *See generally* PAUL SLOVIC, THE PERCEPTION OF RISK (2000) (exploring how risk perception affects individual behavior).

35. *See* Viscusi & Aldy, *supra* note 4, at 57 (finding that estimates of values for cancer mortality and accidental death were similar); *see also* Wesley A. Magat et al., *A Reference Lottery Metric for Valuing Health*, 42 MGMT. SCI. 1118, 1129 (1996) (finding no difference between valuations of cancer deaths and auto accident deaths).

36. *See* Viscusi & Aldy, *supra* note 4, at 57 (contrasting the United Kingdom Health and Safety Executive's use of a higher VSL for cancer deaths with the recommendation of the EPA's SAB not to make any "dread" modification to VSL for certain risks).

37. *See, e.g.*, FRANK ACKERMAN & LISA HEINZERLING, PRICELESS 147 (2004) (arguing that environmental risks are involuntary because they are "not allocated, even in theory, according to market transactions"); Cass R. Sunstein, *The Arithmetic of Arsenic*, 90 GEO. L.J. 2255, 2285 (2002).

38. Of course it is possible to question the idea that workplace risks are assumed voluntarily and in return for compensation. For example, many workers probably do not know the risks that they face. The distinction that I am drawing here is one of kind rather than degree. *See* Cass R. Sunstein, *Bad Deaths*, 14 J. RISK & UNCERTAINTY 259, 272 (1997) (proposing that low-wage workers involuntarily assume risks because they lack information).

39. *See, e.g.*, Paul Slovic, *Perception of Risk*, 236 SCIENCE 280, 282–83 (1987).

40. *See, e.g.*, Sunstein, *supra* note 37, at 2285 ("As compared to workplace risks, there can be little doubt that the risk of arsenic from drinking water is worse along the relevant dimensions. For this reason, it makes sense to think that people would be willing to pay a premium to avoid the risks associated with arsenic."). *See generally* ACKERMAN & HEINZERLING, *supra* note 37.

41. *See* Carlsson et al., *supra* note 9, at 159 (finding that people's WTP to reduce the risk of flying is double their WTP to reduce the risk of traveling by taxi, because the fear of flying produces particular mental suffering).

42. Viscusi & Aldy, *supra* note 4, at 25.

43. Revesz, *supra* note 30, at 982.

44. For VSL calculations based on types of diseases and disease latency periods, *see* Hammitt & Liu, *supra* note 2, at 88. For a metanalysis, *see generally* Viscusi & Aldy, *supra* note 4.

45. *See* Louis R. Eeckhoudt & James K. Hammitt, *Background Risks and the Value of a Statistical Life*, 23 J. RISK & UNCERTAINTY 261, 264–65 (2001) (illustrating that VSL decreases as the aggregate risk of a population increases).

46. *See* Viscusi & Aldy, *supra* note 4, at 50–51.

47. *See* ALDY & VISCUSI, *supra* note 5, at 42 (calculating a VSL of $5.76 million for people between twenty-eight and thirty-two years of age, $4.83 million for people between thirty-eight and forty-two years of age, and $2.51 million for people between fifty-eight and sixty-two years of age).

48. For an overview that turns out to be highly tentative and indeterminate, *see generally* ENVTL. PROT. AGENCY, CHILDREN'S HEALTH VALUATION HANDBOOK (2003).

49. Sean Hannon Williams, *Statistical Children*, 30 YALE J. ON REG. 63 (2013). *See also* Eric Posner & Cass R. Sunstein, *Dollars and Death*, U. CHI. L. REV. (2005).

50. *See, e.g.,* Richard Zeckhauser & Donald Shepard, *Where Now for Saving Lives?*, 40 LAW & CONTEMP. PROBS. 5, 11–15 (Autumn 1976) (measuring utility in terms of "quality-adjusted life years").

51. *See* Cass R. Sunstein, *Lives, Life-Years, and Willingness to Pay*, 104 COLUM. L. REV. 205, 206–08 (2004) (discussing the EPA's proposal to vary VSL based on age by setting the VSL for those under seventy at $3.7 million and the VSL for those seventy and older at $2.3 million).

52. Compare this with the EPA's explicit and unexplained refusal to consider differences "in age, health status, socioeconomic status, gender or other characteristic of the adult population." National Emission Standards for Hazardous Air Pollutants for Industrial/Commercial/Institutional Boilers and Process Heaters, 68 Fed. Reg. 1660, 1695 (proposed Jan. 13, 2003) (to be codified at 40 C.F.R. pt. 63).

53. Viscusi & Aldy, *supra* note 4, at 45.

54. *Id.* at 27–28.

55. *See id.*

56. Leeth & Ruser, *supra* note 7, at 266.

57. *Id.* at 270.

58. *See id.* at 275 (concluding that fatal injury risk compensation for black males is negative but insignificant).

59. *See* Viscusi, *supra* note 6, at 252 (calculating fatality risk estimates and implicit VSL by race, sex, and income category).

60. *Id.*

61. *Id.*

62. W. Kip Viscusi, *The Value of Life: Estimates with Risks by Occupation and Industry*, 42 ECON. INQUIRY 29, 39 (2004).

63. *See* Viscusi & Aldy, *supra* note 4, at 36–43 (using a metanalysis of U.S. and international VSLs to determine the relationship between income and WTP).

64. The leading case is Corrosion Proof Fittings v. EPA, 947 F.2d 1201 (5th Cir. 1991). There, the Fifth Circuit explained: "[T]he proper course . . . is to consider each regulatory option, beginning with the least burdensome, and the costs and benefits of regulation under each option. . . . Without doing this it is impossible . . . to know that none of these alternatives was less burdensome than the ban . . . chosen by the agency." *Id.* at 1217 (citation omitted); *see also* Am. Dental Ass'n v. Martin, 984 F.2d 823, 831 (7th Cir. 1993) (holding that the court's role is not to evaluate the quality, necessity, or cost-benefit rationale of an agency regulation, but "merely to patrol the boundary of reasonableness").

65. *See, e.g.,* 15 U.S.C. § 2605(c) (2000) (requiring cost-benefit analysis of regulations of chemical substances or mixtures under the Toxic Substances Control Act).

66. *See* ENVTL. PROT. AGENCY, A SAB REPORT ON EPA'S WHITE PAPER VALUING THE BENEFITS OF FATAL CANCER RISK REDUCTION 5–6 (2000) (finding that "existing studies provide little reliable information as to the magnitude of [the dread premium associated with cancer]" and that, "until better information becomes available, it is best not to assign such a premium"), *available at* http://www.epa.gov/science1/pdf/eeacf013.pdf.

67. *See* Viscusi & Aldy, *supra* note 4, at 57 (noting that the SAB's rejection of the "dread effect" of cancer is supported by the finding that contingent valuation estimates of cancer mortality risks are similar to estimates for accidental deaths).

CHAPTER FIVE

1. On definitional questions, *see* MATTHEW D. ADLER, WELL-BEING AND FAIR DISTRIBUTION: BEYOND COST-BENEFIT ANALYSIS (2011); Matthew D. Adler, *Happiness Surveys and Public Policy: What's the Use?*, 62 DUKE L.J. 1509 (2013); Carol Graham, *An Economist's Perspective on Well-Being Analysis and Cost-Benefit Analysis*, 62 DUKE L.J. 1691 (2013).

2. JOHN STUART MILL, ON LIBERTY 8 (Kathy Casey ed., 2002) (1859).

3. For evidence, *see* W. Kip Viscusi, *The Heterogeneity of the Value of a Statistical Life*, 40 J. RISK & UNCERTAINTY 1 (2010).

4. For different perspectives, *see* Sean Hannon Williams, *Statistical Children*, 30 YALE J. ON REG. 63 (2013); Joanne Leung & Jagadish Guna, *Value of Statistical Life: Adults Versus Children*, 38 ACCIDENT ILLNESS & PREVENTION 1208 (2006).

5. Joseph Aldy & W. Kip Viscusi, *Age Differences in the Value of Statistical Life*, 1 REV. EVNTL. ECON. & POL'Y 241 (2007).

6. *See, e.g.,* Ted R. Miller, *Variations Between Countries in Value of a Statistical Life*, 34 J. TRANSP. ECON. & POL'Y 169 (2000).

7. For an illuminating and different view (but not incompatible) view, *see* Matthew D. Adler, *Risk Equity: A New Proposal*, 32 HARV. ENVTL. L. REV. 1 (2008).

8. Of course it may be desirable for government to create "safety floors," for

automobiles and other consumer goods, perhaps as a response to an absence of adequate information in the market. But such floors should not be seen as a redistributive tool, because they are not likely to produce good redistribution. *Cf.* Susan Rose-Ackerman, Comment, *Progressive Law and Economics—And the New Administrative Law*, 98 YALE L.J. 341, 354 (1988) (arguing that occupational health and safety regulations are not an effective method of redistribution).

9. Matthew E. Kahn, *The Beneficiaries of Clean Air Act Regulation*, REGULATION, Spring 2001, at 34, 35–38.

10. PRICE V. FISHBACK & SHAWN EVERETT KANTOR, A PRELUDE TO THE WELFARE STATE 69, app. D at 231–38 (2000).

11. *See* CASS R. SUNSTEIN, RISK AND REASON (2002) (noting that a particular proposal to increase drinking water quality would have resulted in an annual increase of $30 in the water bills for most households).

12. For an analysis and explanation of the idea of "miswanting," *see* Daniel T. Gilbert & Timothy D. Wilson, *Miswanting, in* FEELING AND THINKING: THE ROLE OF AFFECT IN SOCIAL COGNITION 178, 179 (Joseph P. Forgas ed., 2000), who explain that

> Although we tend to think of unhappiness as something that happens to us when we do not get what we want, much unhappiness . . . has less to do with not getting what we want, and more to do with not wanting what we like. When wanting and liking are uncoordinated in this way we may say that person has *miswanted.*

Id. See generally Timothy D. Wilson & Daniel T. Gilbert, *Affective Forecasting, in* 35 ADVANCES IN EXPERIMENTAL SOC. PSYCHOL. 345 (Mark P. Zanna ed., 2003) (analyzing people's ability to accurately predict their own feelings).

13. *See* ELIZABETH DUNN & MICHAEL NORTON, HAPPY MONEY (2013).

14. *See* Daniel Kahneman & Carol Varey, *Notes on the Psychology of Utility, in* INTERPERSONAL COMPARISONS OF UTILITY (Jon Elster & John Roemer eds., 1991) (distinguishing between experience utility and predicted utility).

15. *See id.*; Cass R. Sunstein, *The Storrs Lectures: Behavioral Economics and Paternalism*, 122 YALE L.J. 1826 (2013). For a discussion on how preferences influence judgments, *see generally* Daniel Kahneman, *Maps of Bounded Rationality: Psychology for Behavioral Economics*, 93 AM. ECON. REV. 1449 (2003). *Cf.* Daniel Kahneman et al., *Back to Bentham? Explorations of Experienced Utility*, 112 Q.J. ECON. 375, 379–88 (1997) (arguing that utility's impact on human behavior can be understood better and researched more effectively by analyzing the normative idea of "total utility" as the discrete concepts of "experienced utility" and "decisional utility").

16. *See* JON ELSTER, SOUR GRAPES 109–10 (1983) (defining "adaptive preferences" as what happens when "people tend to adjust their aspirations to their possibilities"); Matthew D. Adler & Eric A. Posner, *Implementing Cost-Benefit Analysis*

When Preferences Are Distorted, 29 J. LEGAL STUD. 1105–47 (2000) (hypothesizing, for example, that "people are not willing to pay for parks because they have adapted to a world without parks").

17. ALEXIS DE TOCQUEVILLE, DEMOCRACY IN AMERICA 317 (1969).

18. *See generally* GEORGE A. AKERLOF & WILLIAM T. DICKENS, *The Economic Consequences of Cognitive Dissonance, in* AN ECONOMIC THEORIST'S BOOK OF TALES 123 (1984) (analyzing the incorporation of the psychological theory of cognitive dissonance into economic models).

19. *See* TALI SHAROT, THE OPTIMISM BIAS (2010).

20. *See* SARAH CONLY, AGAINST AUTONOMY (2012).

21. Kahneman & Varey, *supra* note 14, at 128–29.

22. Daniel J. Benjamin et al., *What Do You Think Would Make You Happier? What Do You Think You Would Choose?*, 102 AM. ECON. REV. 2083, 2085–86 (2012).

23. *See* Niklas Karlsson, George Loewenstein & Jane McCafferty, *The Economics of Meaning*, 30 NORDIC J. POL. ECON. 61, 62 (2004); Peter A. Ubel & George Loewenstein, *Pain and Suffering Awards: They Shouldn't Be (Just) About Pain and Suffering*, 37 J. LEGAL STUD. S195, S206–07 (2008).

24. Benjamin et al., *supra* note 22, at 2085.

25. *See* ELSTER, *supra* note 16.

26. *See* SERENE KHADER, ADAPTIVE PREFERENCES AND WOMEN'S EMPOWERMENT (2011).

27. For catalogs, *see* CASS R. SUNSTEIN, SIMPLER (2013); DANIEL KAHNEMAN, THINKING FAST AND SLOW (2011); RICHARD THALER & CASS R. SUNSTEIN, NUDGE (2008).

28. *See* THALER & SUNSTEIN, *supra* note 27.

29. *See* ADLER, *supra* note 1, at 155–236.

30. *See* discussion, *see* RICHARD THALER, QUASI-RATIONAL ECONOMICS (1993).

31. *See* Cass R. Sunstein, *Probability Neglect*, 112 YALE L.J. 61 (2002).

32. *See* SUNSTEIN, *supra* note 27; CASS R. SUNSTEIN, NANNY STATECRAFT (forthcoming 2014).

33. *See* ADLER, *supra* note 1, at 422–30, and *see also* the discussion of "lifetime prioritarianism" in *id.* at 430–42.

34. *See* ADLER, *supra* note 1.

35. There are of course complex questions about the relationships among rights, wealth, and risks. On one view, these variables cannot be separated from one another, and whether people have a "right" to freedom from certain statistical risks depends on an assessment of the level of resources in the relevant society. In that respect, some analysis of social welfare may be a precondition for any judgment about rights.

36. *See* AMARTYA SEN, RATIONALITY AND FREEDOM 546–47, 577 (2002).

37. *See* Richard H. Pildes & Elizabeth S. Anderson, *Slinging Arrows at Democracy: Social Choice Theory, Value Pluralism, and Democratic Politics*, 90 COLUM. L. REV. 2121, 2176 (1990) ("In the highly differentiated world of the modern liberal state, the same person may have distinct interests in her role as consumer from

those in her role as worker, or as citizen, or as a parent, or as member of a religious community."); *see generally* ELIZABETH ANDERSON, VALUE IN ETHICS AND ECONOMICS (1993).

38. *See generally* JOSEPH M. BESSETTE, THE MILD VOICE OF REASON: DELIBERATIVE DEMOCRACY AND AMERICAN NATIONAL GOVERNMENT (1994).

39. SEN, *supra* note 36, at 287.

40. *Id.* at 289 (emphasis omitted).

41. *See id.* at 196–98.

42. Relevant discussion can be found in M. W. Jones-Lee, *Paternalistic Altruism and the Value of a Statistical Life*, 102 ECON. J. 80 (1992); M. W. Jones-Lee, *Altruism and the Value of Other People's Safety*, 4 J. RISK & UNCERTAINTY 213 (1991).

43. For one effort, *see* Eric A. Posner & Cass R. Sunstein, *Dollars and Death*, 72 U. CHI. L. REV. 537 (2005).

44. Compare ADLER, *supra* note 1, at 92, for the suggestion that "CBA is not an attractive welfarist procedure for morally evaluating governmental policies and other large-scale choices—except in the case of distributively weighted CBA, which adjusts WTP/WTA amounts using weighting factors. . . ."

45. *See id.* at 92–114.

46. *See* Richard Arneson, *Luck Egalitarianism and Prioritarianism*, 110 ETHICS 339, 343 (2000): "Prioritarianism holds that institutions and practices should be set and actions chosen to maximize moral value, with the stipulation that the moral value of obtaining a benefit (avoiding a loss) for a person is greater, the greater the well-being gain that the person would get from it (the smaller the loss in well-being), and greater, the lower the person's lifetime expectation of well-being prior to receipt of the benefit (loss)." *See also* Matthew Adler, *Future Generations: A Prioritarian View*, 77 G.W. L. REV. 1478 (2009); ADLER, *supra* note 1.

47. A helpful discussion is MATTHEW ADLER & ERIC POSNER, NEW FOUNDATIONS OF COST-BENEFIT ANALYSIS (2006) (defending cost-benefit analysis as a decision procedure that operates as a proxy for welfare).

48. W. Kip Viscusi, *The Benefits of Mortality Risk Reduction*, 62 DUKE L.J. 1735 (2013).

49. For valuable discussion, *see* ADLER & POSNER, *supra* note 47.

50. *See id.*; ADLER, *supra* note 1.

51. *See* J. R. Hicks, *The Rehabilitation of Consumer Surplus*, 8 REV. ECON. STUD. 108, 111 (1941).

52. *See* ADLER, *supra* note 1.

53. *See, e.g.*, Louis Kaplow & Steven Shavell, *Why the Legal System Is Less Efficient than the Income Tax in Redistributing Income*, 23 J. LEGAL STUD. 667, 667 (1994) ("[R]edistribution through legal rules offers no advantage over redistribution through the income tax system and typically is less efficient."); Steven Shavell, *A Note on Efficiency vs. Distributional Equity in Legal Rulemaking: Should Distributional Equity Matter Given Optimal Income Taxation?*, 71 AM. ECON. REV.

PAPERS & PROC. 414, 414 (1981) (describing how an income tax can compensate for inefficient liability rules and redistribute income); David A. Weisbach, *Should Legal Rules Be Used to Redistribute Income?*, 70 U. CHI. L. REV. 439, 439 (2003).

54. *See* ADLER, *supra* note 1, at 185–201; INTERPERSONAL COMPARISONS OF WELL-BEING (Jon Elster & John Roemer eds., 1993).

55. Helpful discussion can be found in ADLER, *supra* note 1, at 567–71.

56. Consider, for example, the well-being approach in John Bronsteen et al., *Well-Being Analysis vs. Cost-Benefit Analysis*, 62 DUKE L.J. 1603 (2013), criticized in part on this ground in W. Kip Viscusi, *The Benefits of Mortality Risk Reduction*, 63 DUKE L.J. 1735 (2013).

57. A valuable collection is THE GLOBALIZATION OF COST-BENEFIT ANALYSIS IN ENVIRONMENTAL POLICY (Michael Livermore & Richard Revesz eds., 2013).

58. *Cf.* INTERGOVERNMENTAL PANEL ON CLIMATE CHANGE, THIRD ASSESSMENT REPORT: CLIMATE CHANGE 2001: MITIGATION 483 (finding that "[t]he VSL is generally lower in poor countries than in rich countries"), *available at* http://grida.no/climate/ipcc_tar/wg3.

59. INTERGOVERNMENTAL PANEL ON CLIMATE CHANGE, SECOND ASSESSMENT REPORT: CLIMATE CHANGE 1995.

60. *See* John Broome, *Cost-Benefit Analysis and Population*, 29 J. LEGAL STUD. 953, 957 (2000) (noting that this conclusion is a product of "a money-metric utility function to represent a person's preferences," an approach that Professor Broome rejects). In the Easy Cases, I suggest that a money-metric utility function is not absurd, and it is not quite absurd in the hard cases either. *See* INTERGOVERNMENTAL PANEL ON CLIMATE CHANGE, *supra* note 58, at 483:

> The VSL is generally lower in poor countries than in rich countries, but it is considered unacceptable by many analysts to impose different values for a policy that has to be international in scope and decided by the international community. In these circumstances, analysts use average VSL and apply it to all countries. Of course, such a value is not what individuals would pay for the reduction in risk, but it is an "equity adjusted" value, in which greater weight is given to the WTP of lower income groups. On the basis of EU and US VSLs and a weighting system that has some broad appeal in terms of government policies towards income distribution, Eyre *et al.* (1998) estimate the average world VSL at around 1 million Euros (approximately US$1 million at 1999 exchange rates).

CHAPTER SIX

1. Amos Tversky & Daniel Kahneman, *Judgment Under Uncertainty: Heuristics and Biases*, 185 SCIENCE 1124, 1124 (1974).

2. *See* HEURISTICS: THE FOUNDATIONS OF ADAPTIVE BEHAVIOR (Gerd Gigerenzer et al. eds., 2011).

3. Tversky & Kahneman, *supra* note 1.

4. *See* Daniel Kahneman & Shane Frederick, *Representativeness Revisited: Attribute Substitution in Intuitive Judgment, in* HEURISTICS AND BIASES: THE PSYCHOLOGY OF INTUITIVE JUDGMENT 49 (Thomas Gilovich et al. eds. 2002).

5. STEPHEN JAY GOULD, BULLY FOR BRONTOSAURUS: REFLECTIONS IN NATURAL HISTORY 469 (1991).

6. *See* DANIEL KAHNEMAN, THINKING, FAST AND SLOW (2011).

7. *See* Joshua Greene & Jonathan Haidt, *How (and Where) Does Moral Judgment Work?*, 6 TRENDS IN COGNITIVE SCI. 517 (2002); Jonathan Haidt, *The Emotional Dog and Its Rational Tail: A Social Intuitionist Approach to Moral Judgment*, 108 PSYCHOL. REV. 814 (2001).

8. Jonathan Haidt et al., Moral Dumbfounding: When Intuition Finds No Reason (2004) (unpublished manuscript).

9. *See* JOHN STUART MILL, UTILITARIANISM 28–29 (Bobbs-Merrill Co. 1971) (1863); HENRY SIDGWICK, THE METHODS OF ETHICS 199–216 (Hackett Publishing Co. 1981) (1907).

10. MILL, *supra* note 9, at 29.

11. I am of course bracketing many complexities here. For discussion, *see* 1 Derek Parfit, ON WHAT MATTERS (2011).

12. Amos Tversky & Daniel Kahneman, *The Framing of Decisions and the Psychology of Choice*, 211 SCIENCE 453 (1981).

13. Amos Tversky & Daniel Kahneman, *Loss Aversion in Riskless Choice: A Reference Dependent Model*, 106 Q. J. ECON. 1039 (1991).

14. *See* Shane Frederick, *Measuring Intergenerational Time Preference: Are Future Lives Valued Less?*, 26 J. RISK & UNCERTAINTY 39 (2003).

15. Maureen Cropper et al., *Preferences for Life-Saving Programs: How the Public Discounts Time and Age*, 8 J. RISK & UNCERTAINTY 243 (1994).

16. Frederick, *supra* note 14.

17. W. Kip Viscusi, *Corporate Risk Analysis: A Reckless Act?*, 52 STAN. L. REV. 547, 547, 558 (2000).

18. *See id.*; Philip Tetlock, *Coping with Tradeoffs: Psychological Constraints and Political Implications, in* ELEMENTS OF REASON: COGNITION, CHOICE, AND THE BOUNDS OF RATIONALITY 239 (Arthur Lupia et al. eds., 2000).

19. Viscusi, *supra* note 17.

20. *See* Tetlock, *supra* note 18.

21. I am grateful to Jonathan Haidt for this suggestion.

22. FRANK ACKERMAN & LISA HEINZERLING, PRICELESS: ON KNOWING THE PRICE OF EVERYTHING AND THE VALUE OF NOTHING (2004).

23. *See* Jonathan J. Koehler & Andrew D. Gershoff, *Betrayal Aversion: When Agents of Protection Become Agents of Harm*, 90 ORGANIZATIONAL BEHAV. & HUM. DECISION PROCESSES 244 (2003).

24. *Id.*

25. *Id.* at 244.

26. Ilana Ritov & Jonathan Baron, *Reluctance to Vaccinate: Omission Bias and*

Ambiguity, in BEHAVIORAL LAW AND ECONOMICS at 168 (Cass R. Sunstein ed., 2002).

27. Michael Sandel, *It's Immoral to Buy the Right to Pollute*, N.Y. TIMES, Dec. 15, 1997, at A23. Sandel makes a series of related arguments in MICHAEL SANDEL, WHAT MONEY CAN'T BUY (2012). I cannot demonstrate the point here, but I believe that many of Sandel's arguments against the use of markets actually depend on the use of moral heuristics, which misfire in a large number of cases.

28. CASS R. SUNSTEIN, LAWS OF FEAR (2005).

29. *See* RALPH HERTWIG ET AL., SIMPLE HEURISTICS IN A SOCIAL WORLD (2012).

CHAPTER SEVEN

1. Amos Tversky & Daniel Kahneman, *Judgment Under Uncertainty: Heuristics and Biases, in* JUDGMENT UNDER UNCERTAINTY: HEURISTICS AND BIASES 3, 11–14 (Daniel Kahneman et al. eds., 1982).

2. PAUL SLOVIC, THE PERCEPTION OF RISK 37–48 (2000).

3. Peter Huber, *The Old-New Division in Risk Regulation*, 69 VA. L. REV. 1025 (1983).

4. Timur Kuran & Cass R. Sunstein, *Availability Cascades and Risk Regulation*, 51 STAN. L. REV. 683, 703–05 (1999).

5. Howard Kunreuther et al., *Making Low Probabilities Useful*, 23 J. RISK & UNCERTAINTY 103, 107 (2001).

6. Daniel Kahneman & Amos Tversky, *Prospect Theory: An Analysis of Decision Under Risk, in* CHOICES, VALUES, AND FRAMES 17, 28–38 (Daniel Kahneman & Amos Tversky eds., 2001); Amos Tversky & Daniel Kahneman, *Advances in Prospect Theory: Cumulative Representations of Uncertainty, in* CHOICES, VALUES, AND FRAMES, *supra*, at 44, 64–65.

7. Roger G. Noll & James E. Krier, *Some Implications of Cognitive Psychology for Risk Regulation*, 19 J. LEGAL STUD. 747, 769–71 (1990).

8. Yuval Rottenstreich & Christopher K. Hsee, *Money, Kisses, and Electric Shocks: On the Affective Psychology of Risk*, 12 PSYCHOL. SCI. 185, 188 (2001)

9. An important discussion, showing the difference between valuation of money and valuation of things without reference to emotions, is A. Peter McGraw et al., *Valuing Money and Things: Why a $20 Item Can Be Worth More and Less than $20*, 56 MGMT. SCI. 810 (2010).

10. This section draws on Cass R. Sunstein & Richard Zeckhauser, *Overreaction to Fearsome Risks*, 48 ENVTL. & RESOURCE ECON. 435 (2011).

11. George F. Loewenstein et al., *Risk as Feelings*, 127 PSYCHOL. BULL. 267 (2001)

12. *Id.*

13. *Id.*

14. Peter Sandman et al., *Agency Communication, Community Outrage, and Perception of Risk: Three Simulation Experiments*, 13 RISK ANALYSIS 35 (1994); Peter Sandman et al., *Communications to Reduce Risk Underestimation and Overestimation*, 3 RISK DECISION & POL'Y 93 (1998).

15. *Id.*

16. *Id.*

17. Paul Slovic et al., *Violence, Risk Assessment and Risk Communication*, 24 LAW & HUM. BEHAV. 271 (2000).

18. Loewenstein et al., *supra* note 11, at 275–76.

19. E. J. Johnson et al., *Framing, Probability Distortions, and Insurance Decisions*, 7 J. RISK & UNCERTAINTY 35 (1993).

20. Ali Siddiq Alhakami & Paul Slovic, *A Psychological Study of the Inverse Relationship Between Perceived Risk and Perceived Benefit*, 14 RISK ANALYSIS 1085, 1094–95 (1994).

21. *See* Paul Slovic et al., *The Affect Heuristic, in* INTUITIVE JUDGMENT: HEURISTICS AND BIASES (Tom Gilovich et al. eds., 2002).

22. DANIEL KAHNEMAN, THINKING, FAST AND SLOW (2012).

23. *See* Robertson v. Methow Valley Citizens Council, 490 U.S. 332, 354–56 (1989); ROBERT PERCIVAL ET AL., ENVIRONMENTAL REGULATION 903–04 (3d ed. 2000).

24. 40 C.F.R. § 1502.22 (2001).

25. *See* JON ELSTER, EXPLAINING TECHNICAL CHANGE 185–207(1983).

26. Kuran & Sunstein, *supra* note 4.

27. LOIS MARIE GIBBS, LOVE CANAL: THE STORY CONTINUES 25 (1998) (discussing the rising level of fear as a result of the contamination of Love Canal).

28. *Id.*

29. JAMES T. HAMILTON & W. KIP VISCUSI, CALCULATING RISKS: THE SPATIAL AND POLITICAL DIMENSIONS OF HAZARDOUS WASTE POLICY 91–108 (1999)

30. Kuran & Sunstein, *supra* note 4.

31. One journalist described the recent hue and cry over shark attacks in the following terms:

> A maritime expert said on last night's "NBC Nightly News" that more people die from bees, wasps, snakes or alligators than from shark attacks. But there's no ratings in bees. Unpleasant little critters, but not scary-looking enough. With "Jaws" music practically playing in the background, the media have turned this into the Summer of the Shark. Never mind that the number of attacks has actually dropped since last year. They're here, they're nasty and they could be coming to a beach near you.

Howard Kurtz, *Shark Attacks Spark Increased Coverage*, WASH. POST, Sept. 5, 2001, *available at* http://www.washingtonpost.com/wp-dyn/articles/A44720 -2001Sep5.html.

32. PHANTOM RISK: SCIENTIFIC INFERENCE AND THE LAW 427–28 (Kenneth R. Foster et al. eds., 1993).

33. W. Kip Viscusi, *Corporate Risk Analysis: A Reckless Act?*, 52 STAN. L. REV. 547, 556–58 (2000).

34. Boaz Keysar et al., *The Foreign Language Effect: Thinking in a Foreign Tongue Reduces Decision Biases*, 23 PSYCHOL. SCI. 661 (2012).

EPILOGUE

1. Other and better methods might emerge. For discussion of foundational issues, *see* MATTHEW D. ADLER, WELL-BEING AND FAIR DISTRIBUTION: BEYOND COST-BENEFIT ANALYSIS (2011).
2. http://aubreyherbert.blogspot.it/2004/10/amartya-sen-on-hayeks-road-to -serfdom.html.

APPENDIX B

1. Interagency Working Grp. on Soc. Cost of Carbon, U.S. Govt., Technical Support Document: Updated Social Cost of Carbon for Regulatory Impact Analysis Under Executive Order 12866 (2013), *available at* http://www.whitehouse .gov/sites/default/files/omb/inforeg/social_cost_of_carbon_for_ria_2013 _update.pdf.
2. Interagency Working Grp. on Soc. Cost of Carbon, U.S. Govt., Technical Support Document: Social Cost of Carbon for Regulatory Impact Analysis, tbl. A1 (2010), *available at* http://www.epa.gov/oms/climate/regulations/scc -tsd.pdf.

APPENDIX C

1. OFFICE OF MGMT. & BUDGET, DRAFT 2012 REPORT TO CONGRESS ON THE BENEFITS AND COSTS OF FEDERAL REGULATIONS 23 tbl. 1-5(a) (2012), *available at* http://www.whitehouse.gov/sites/default/files/omb/oira/draft_2012 _cost_benefit_report.pdf. Note that the two footnotes in this appendix are taken directly from the relevant reports.
2. OFFICE OF MGMT. & BUDGET, 2011 REPORT TO CONGRESS ON THE BENEFITS AND COSTS OF FEDERAL REGULATIONS 25 tbl. 1-5(a) (2011), *available at* http://www.whitehouse.gov/sites/default/files/omb/inforeg/2011_cb/2011 _cba_report.pdf.
3. The agency provided benefit and cost estimates for 2020. In order to annualize, as with previous NAAQS rulemakings, OMB assumed that the benefits and costs would be zero in the first year after the rule was finalized, the benefits and costs would increase linearly until year 2020, and the benefit and cost estimates would equal the 2020 estimates thereafter. [This note is taken directly from 2011 REPORT TO CONGRESS, *supra* note 2.]
4. DOT and EPA estimates differ somewhat due to programmatic differences between the two rules and differences in estimation modeling. The range of cost and benefit are based on the total cost and benefits estimates for model years 2012–16 in DOT's RIA, annualized over the life of those vehicles. The primary

estimates are based on the total cost and benefits estimates for model years 2012–16 in EPA's RIA annualized at 7% over the life of those vehicles. [This note is taken directly from 2011 REPORT TO CONGRESS, *supra* note 2.]

5. OFFICE OF MGMT. & BUDGET, 2010 REPORT TO CONGRESS ON THE BENEFITS AND COSTS OF FEDERAL REGULATIONS 22 tbl. 1-4 (2010), *available at* http://www.whitehouse.gov/sites/default/files/omb/inforeg/2011_cb/2011_cba_report.pdf.

APPENDIX D

1. Transportation Worker Identification Credential (TWIC)—Reader Requirements, 78 Fed. Reg. 17,782 (2013).
2. "If implementing this regulation would lower the likelihood of a successful terrorist attack by more than 1 percent each year, then this would be a socially efficient use of resources. This proposed rule is estimated to cost approximately $26.5 million annually. This proposed rule would be cost effective if it prevented one terrorist attack with consequence equal to the average every 130.9 years ($3,468.7/$26.5)." (p. 17,822).
3. Introduction to the Unified Agenda of Federal Regulatory and Deregulatory Actions, 78 Fed. Reg. 1317 (2013).
4. "TSA has not quantified benefits. TSA, however, expects that the primary benefit of the Security Training NPRM will be the enhancement of the United States surface transportation security by reducing the vulnerability of freight railroad systems, public transportation agencies, passenger railroads, and over-the-road bus entities to terrorist activity through the training of security-sensitive employees." (p. 1400).
5. Introduction to the Unified Agenda of Federal Regulatory and Deregulatory Actions, 78 Fed. Reg. 1317 (2013).
6. "TSA has not quantified benefits. However, a major line of defense against an aviation-related terrorist act is the prevention of explosives, weapons, and/or incendiary devices from getting on board a plane . . . With this rule, attention is given to aircraft that are located at repair stations and to aircraft parts that are at repair stations to reduce the likelihood of an attack against aviation and the country." (p. 1403).
7. Standards to Prevent, Detect, and Respond to Sexual Abuse and Assault in Confinement Facilities, 77 Fed. Reg. 75,300 (2012).
8. "DOJ estimates extrapolate from the existing economic and criminological literature regarding rape in the community. The RIA concludes that when all facilities and costs are phased into the rulemaking, the breakeven point would be reached if the standards reduced the annual number of incidents of sexual abuse by 55 from the estimated benchmark levels." (p. 75,302).
9. National Highway-Rail Crossing Inventory Reporting Requirements, 77 Fed. Reg. 64,077 (2012).
10. "The main benefit derived from the rule would be improved crossing inven-

tory data. This more precise information would better enable FRA, railroads, and any other entity to accurately analyze pertinent data, detect trends, and if needed, initiate crossing-related safety initiatives. In this break-even analysis, FRA determined that if there were a decrease of 0.015 percent of crossing accidents over the twenty-year period the costs associated with the rule would break-even." (p. 64,086).

11. Passenger Train Emergency Preparedness, 77 Fed. Reg. 38,248 (2012).

12. "The proposed regulation would generate safety benefits by preventing injuries in passenger rail accidents from becoming more severe . . . A break-even analysis quantifies what minimum safety benefits are necessary for the proposed rule to be cost-effective, considering the estimated quantified costs. For this proposed rule, this analysis estimates that the break-even point is met when 3.84 injuries are prevented from increasing in severity from AIS 1 to AIS 2." (p. 38,258).

13. National Standards to Prevent, Detect, and Respond to Prison Rape, 77 Fed. Reg. 37,106 (2012).

14. "Executive Order 13563 states that agencies 'may consider (and discuss qualitatively) values that are difficult or impossible to quantify, including equity, human dignity, fairness, and distributive impacts.' Each of these values is relevant here, including human dignity, which is offended by acts of sexual violence. While recognizing the limits of monetary measures and the difficulty of translation into dollar equivalents, the RIA extrapolates from the existing economic and criminological literature regarding rape in the community. On the basis of such extrapolations, it finds that the monetizable benefit to an adult of avoiding the highest category of prison sexual misconduct (nonconsensual sexual acts involving injury or force, or no injury or force but high incidence) is worth $310,000 to $480,000 per victim; for juveniles, who typically experience significantly greater injury from sexual abuse than do adults, the corresponding category is assessed as worth $675,000 per victim . . . The RIA concludes that the break-even point would be reached if the standards reduced the annual number of victims of prison rape by 1,671 from the baseline levels, which is less than 1 percent of the total number of victims in prisons, jails, and juvenile facilities." (p. 37,111).

15. Carbon Dioxide Fire Suppression Systems on Commercial Vessels, 77 Fed. Reg. 33,860 (2012).

16. "The breakeven analysis of the NPRM (which included all new and existing fire suppression systems on certain classes of commercial vessels) found that the rule would need to prevent 0.22 fatalities per year to break even, or about one fatality every 4–5 years . . . This analysis did not include the value of potential non-fatal injuries and secondary impacts. As this rulemaking seeks to reduce risk to the crew on vessels with CO_2 fire suppression systems, the potential value of the avoided damages at risk is quite large in comparison to the relatively minor costs of the proposed safety measures in the NPRM." (p. 33,865).

17. Training, Qualification, and Oversight for Safety-Related Railroad Employees, 77 Fed. Reg. 6412 (2012).

18. "FRA has performed a breakeven analysis of the proposed rule, estimating the reduction in human factors–caused accidents that would be required in order for the benefits of the proposed rule to at least offset the costs . . . Reductions in human factors–caused accidents will result in fatalities avoided, injuries avoided, and property damage avoided." (p. 6413).

19. Passenger Train Emergency Systems II, 77 Fed. Reg. 154 (2012).

20. "The proposed rulemaking is expected to improve railroad safety by promoting the safe evacuation of passengers and crewmembers in the event of an emergency. The primary benefits include a heightened safety environment in egress from a passenger train after an accident. This corresponds to a reduction of casualties and fatalities in the aftermath of an accident or other emergency situations. FRA believes the value of the anticipated safety benefits would justify the cost of implementing the proposed rule." (p. 172).

21. Drivers of CMVs: Restricting the Use of Cellular Phones, 76 Fed. Reg. 75,470 (2011).

22. "Threshold analysis for this rule shows that restricting hand-held mobile telephones would lead to an estimated one-year cost of $12.1 million. Current guidance from DOT's Office of the Secretary places the value of a statistical life at $6.0 million. Consequently, this rule will need to eliminate any combination of crash types equivalent to two fatalities per year in order for the benefits of this rule to equal the costs. . . . Because FMCSA and PHMSA are addressing two of the risky activities—reaching for and dialing on a hand-held mobile telephone—cited in the Olson, et al. (2009) study, restricting the use (including holding) of hand-held mobile telephones is expected to prevent more than two fatalities and the benefits to justify the cost." (p. 75,483).

23. Air Cargo Screening, 76 Fed. Reg. 51,848 (2011).

24. "The CCSP allows for more standardized governance in cargo screening and provides fourfold benefits in terms of increased security of commercial passenger aviation . . . The estimate of the economic impacts of the [terrorist] attack scenarios used in these break-even analyses is limited to direct costs only (value of casualties and loss of aircraft). This analysis does not consider any indirect or macroeconomic consequences these terrorist attacks might cause." (p. 51,865).

25. Ammonium Nitrate Security Program, 76 Fed. Reg. 46,908 (2011).

26. "In this break-even analysis, DHS compared the annualized costs of the proposed rule to the expected benefits of preventing an ammonium nitrate based terrorist attack, such as the attack on the Murrah federal building. In order to estimate the impact of this attack in dollar terms, DHS must assume a value per statistical life (VSL) . . . The Department is assuming a VSL of $6 million, which is equivalent to saying someone is willing to pay $6 to receive a one-in-a-million reduction in the risk of death or $60 to receive a one-in-a-one-

hundred-thousand reduction in the risk of death. Applying the $6 million VSL to the 168 deaths from the Murrah attack plus the cost of other expenditures that are directly related to the attack (such as the cost of replacing the Murrah Building), DHS estimates the cost to society of the Murrah attack to be approximately of $1.35 billion (2010 dollars). As this proposed rule is expected to cost society approximately $95.5 million annually, this proposed rule would be cost effective if it prevented one terrorist attack similar to the Murrah building attack every 14.1 years." (p. 46,936).

27. Food Labeling; Nutrition Labeling of Standard Menu Items in Restaurants and Similar Retail Food Establishments, 76 Fed. Reg. 19,192 (2011).

28. "FDA has not estimated the actual benefits associated with proposed requirements. Food choice and consumption decisions are complex, and FDA is unaware of any comprehensive data allowing accurate predictions of the effect of the proposed requirements on consumer choice and establishment menus. Therefore, FDA has constructed a plausible individual effect of the proposed rule, and has conducted a break-even analysis in order to determine the proportion of the U.S. obese adult population that would need to attain this minimal response in order for the proposed requirement to yield a positive net benefit. Using a 100 calorie per week reduction in intake as the benchmark effect, FDA estimates that at least 0.06 percent of the adult obese population would need to reach at least this benchmark in order for the rule to break even on the primary, or mean annualized cost." (p. 19,221).

29. Food Labeling; Calorie Labeling of Articles of Food in Vending Machines, 76 Fed. Reg. 19,238 (2011).

30. "FDA has not estimated the actual benefits associated with proposed requirements. Food choice and consumption decisions are complex and FDA is unaware of any comprehensive data allowing accurate predictions of the effect of the proposed requirements on consumer choice and vended foods. Therefore, FDA has constructed a plausible individual effect of the proposed rule, and has conducted a break-even analysis in order to determine the proportion of the U.S. obese adult population that would need to attain this minimal response in order for the proposed requirement to yield a positive net benefit. Using a 100 calorie per week reduction in intake as the benchmark effect, FDA estimates that at least 0.02 percent of the adult obese population would need to reach this benchmark in order for the rule to break even on the initial total cost." (p. 19,246).

31. Hazardous Materials: Cargo Tank Motor Vehicle Loading and Unloading Operations, 76 Fed. Reg. 13,313.

32. "Based on the assumptions and estimates described above, the breakeven point for this rule—that is, the point at which benefits and costs are approximately equal—occurs at an incident-reduction effectiveness level of approximately 40 percent for affected firms. For this analysis, based on available literature and expert judgment, we believe that an effectiveness level of 40 percent is a

reasonable assumption for this group of safety interventions, particularly since
the subject incidents have been defined narrowly as those in which (largely
preventable) human error occurs during the loading or unloading phase, such
as overfilling, over-pressurizing, or loading incompatible materials." (p. 13,323).

33. Mandatory Inspection of Catfish and Catfish Products, 76 Fed. Reg. 10,434
(2011).

34. "Epidemiological evidence suggests that salmonellosis leads to both acute and
chronic illnesses. The acute illness that accompanies salmonellosis generally
causes gastrointestinal symptoms that can lead to lost productivity and medical expenses. In rare instances, salmonellosis may result in acute or chronic
arthritis. Arthritis is characterized by limited mobility, pain and suffering,
productivity losses, and medical expenditures. Finally, salmonellosis can result
in death. The risk of death appears to be higher in the elderly, children, and
people with compromised immune systems. FSIS has estimated the costs for
each of these severity levels. If roughly 790 illnesses were averted, the benefits
of the proposed rule would equal the additional costs." (p. 10,456).

35. Introduction to the Unified Agenda of Federal Regulatory and Deregulatory
Actions, 75 Fed. Reg. 79,459 (2010).

36. "The benefit of this rule is the improvement of CBP's risk assessment and
targeting capabilities, while at the same time, enabling CBP to facilitate the
prompt release of legitimate cargo following its arrival in the United States.
The information will assist CBP in increasing the security of the global trading
system, and thereby reducing the threat to the United States and the world
economy." (no page).

37. Federal Motor Vehicle Safety Standard, Rearview Mirrors; Federal Motor Vehicle Safety Standard, Low-Speed Vehicles Phase-In Reporting Requirements,
75 Fed. Reg. 76,186 (2010).

38. "The proposed solution is the most comprehensive and effective, currently
available solution to mitigate backover crashes, fatalities, and injuries. As we
discussed above, the quantitative analysis does not offer a complete accounting. We have noted that well over 40 percent of the victims of backover crashes
are very young children (under the age of five), with nearly their entire life
ahead of them. Executive Order 12866 also refers explicitly to considerations
of equity. ("(I)n choosing among alternative regulatory approaches, agencies
should select those approaches that maximize net benefits (including equity),
and there are strong reasons, grounded in those considerations, to prevent the
deaths at issue here. In addition, this regulation will, in many cases, reduce a
qualitatively distinct risk, which is that of directly causing the death or injury
of one's own child. Drivers will also benefit from increased rear visibility in
a variety of ways, including increased ease and convenience with respect to
parking. While these benefits cannot be monetized, they could be significant.
A breakeven analysis suggests that if the nonquantified benefits amount $65 to
$79 per vehicle, the benefits would justify the costs." (p. 76,238).

39. Limiting the Use of Wireless Communication Devices, 75 Fed. Reg. 59,118 (2010).

40. "Current guidance from the Office of the Secretary of Transportation (OST) places the value of a statistical life at $6.0 million. Consequently, the texting restriction would have to eliminate at most one fatality every year in order for the benefits of this rule to at least equal the costs. Given the unchecked expansion of texting, FMCSA believes the rule will save lives and prevent a substantial number of crashes. Therefore, the rule is justified based on the safety benefits." (p. 59,132).

41. Nutrition Labeling of Single-Ingredient Products and Ground or Chopped Meat and Poultry Products, 74 Fed. Reg. 67,736 (2009).

42. "The average reduction in risk for the benefits of POP nutrition information for major cuts of single ingredient, raw products to equal their cost is 0.53 lives saved annually ((2.88+2.93)/2)/5.5) assuming a value of life of $5.5 million (Table 25). The reduction in risk for the benefits of on-package nutrition labels for ground or chopped products to equal their cost is about ten times greater (5.34 lives saved annually).The estimated total reduction in risk in order for the benefits of these combined measures to exceed costs is 5.87 lives saved annually or about one-ninth (5.87/50.1) of the estimated 50.1 lives saved annually under the composite scenario, using a value of life saved of $5.5 million." (p. 67,785).

43. Aircraft Repair Station Security, 74 Fed. Reg. 59,874 (2009).

44. "A major line of defense against an aviation-related terrorist act is the prevention of explosives, weapons, and/or incendiary devices from getting on board a plane . . . With this rule, attention is given to aircraft that are located at repair stations, and to aircraft parts that are at repair stations, themselves to reduce the likelihood of an attack against aviation and the country. Since repair station personnel have direct access to all parts of an aircraft, the potential exists for a terrorist to seek to commandeer or compromise an aircraft when the aircraft is at one of these facilities." (p. 59,884).

45. Air Cargo Screening, 74 Fed. Reg. 47,672 (2009).

46. "TSA has assessed the benefits of this rule via a break-even analysis of the cost of the reduction in risk with the dollar amount of the benefit from the rule. The break-even analysis illustrates the tradeoff between program costs and program benefits. For purposes of the analysis, TSA evaluated four scenarios in which an explosive device was placed in the aircraft's cargo hold via air cargo and detonated, destroying the airplane and all passengers and crew on board. For each scenario, TSA derived a total monetary cost of consequence from an estimated value of the statistical human lives lost and the value of the plane (including cargo) destroyed. TSA obtained a value of the monetary cost of an attack under a certain probability (the value of which equals the total estimated monetary cost of the attack multiplied by the probability of an attack of that nature over a year-long time period) and compared it to the undiscounted, an-

nualized cost of the CCSP to estimate how often an attack of that nature would need to be averted for the expected benefits to equal costs." (p. 47,693).

47. Flightcrew Alerting, 74 Fed. Reg. 32,810 (2009).

48. "By examining the historical data, we have shown that over the past twenty years, there were both non-fatal events and fatal events, which might have been prevented with the requirements contained in this NPRM. The potential severity of an event is demonstrated in the DC 9-82 accident on August 16, 1987, that occurred shortly after takeoff from Detroit Metropolitan Airport, which resulted in 154 deaths. The National Transportation Safety Board (NTSB) determined that one contributing factor was the airplane takeoff warning system, which failed to warn the flightcrew that the airplane was improperly configured for takeoff. This finding led to the current proposed rulemaking." (p. 32,815).

49. Organ-Specific Warnings; Internal Analgesic, Antipyretic, and Antirheumatic Drug Products for Over-the-Counter Human Use; Final Monograph; Corrections, 74 Fed. Reg. 31,177 (2009).

50. "Because of the uncertainty in these estimates, we estimated an annual average number of adverse events that would need to be avoided over a 10 year period to reach a break-even point (i.e., the present value of the cost of compliance divided by the present value of the monetary value of avoiding an adverse event each year for 10 years). The following calculations are based on 2001 dollars, which will not affect the estimated break-even values to be calculated. For benefits to equal costs, this final rule would need to prevent about 2 deaths each year over 10 years [1.9 deaths ($71.0 million/$37.6 million at a 7 percent discount rate) and 1.7 deaths ($72.9 million/$43.9 million at a 3 percent discount rate)]. This estimate of deaths avoided is based on a value of $5 million per statistical life. Alternatively, if no deaths are avoided, the final rule would need to prevent about 1,058 hospitalizations each year over the 10-year period at the 7 percent discount rate ($71.0 million/$67,156), and 928 hospitalizations a year at the 3 percent discount rate ($72.9 million/$78,513). This estimate of hospitalizations avoided is based on the lowest monetized value of a poisoning episode requiring hospitalization: $8,936 per episode over 10 years at a 7 percent discount rate. Although we lack evidence to predict with certainty a specific level of reduction in adverse events, if we assume only a 2 percent reduction in the illnesses and deaths analyzed, the benefits of this final rule [*31,180] outweigh the costs. We find that this final rule will enhance public health and promote the safer use of OTC acetaminophen and NSAID drug products." (p. 31,178)

51. Organ-Specific Warnings; Internal Analgesic, Antipyretic, and Antirheumatic Drug Products for Over-the-Counter Human Use; Final Monograph, 74 Fed. Reg. 19,385 (2009).

52. "This final rule would need to prevent about 1 death each year over 10 years . . . Alternatively, if no deaths are avoided, the final rule would need to prevent

about 476 hospitalizations ($32 million/$67,000) each year over the 10-year period . . . Although we lack evidence to predict with certainty a specific level of reduction in adverse events, if we assume only a 1-percent reduction in the illnesses and deaths analyzed, the benefits of this final rule outweigh the costs." (p. 19,405).

APPENDIX E

1. See table 5–9 of the Final Regulatory Impact Analysis for Particulate Matter, *available at* http://www.epa.gov/ttn/ecas/regdata/RIAs/finalria.pdf (2013).

INDEX

The letter *t* following a page number denotes a table.